MW00603440

The Impossible Imperative

The Impossible Imperative

Navigating the Competing Principles of Child Protection

JILL DUERR BERRICK

With

ERIKA ALTOBELLI, ALYSSA BARKLEY, TRACI BERNAL, MARIA BURCH, VIVIANA COLOSIMO-BLAIR, FRENY DESSAI, TRUDI FRAZEL, LESLIE LAUGHLIN, SASHA McGOWAN, MONICA MONTURY, VERONICA PEREZ, HANNA RASHKOVSKY, SOCORRO REYNOSO, MARTHA ANGELICA RODRIGUEZ, WENDY WIEGMANN

OXFORD
UNIVERSITY PRESS

OXFORD
UNIVERSITY PRESS

Oxford University Press is a department of the University of Oxford. It furthers the University's objective of excellence in research, scholarship, and education by publishing worldwide. Oxford is a registered trade mark of Oxford University Press in the UK and certain other countries.

Published in the United States of America by Oxford University Press
198 Madison Avenue, New York, NY 10016, United States of America.

CIP data is on file at the Library of Congress
ISBN 978-0-19-067814-2

Printed by Sheridan Books, Inc., United States of America

To my mom and dad, with thanks for a truly wonderful childhood.

*To my husband, Ken, my love, my confidante,
my intellectual companion.*

To my children, Sierra and Elias, my inspiration.

Contents

Acknowledgments

I HAVE NEVER been a practicing child welfare worker, though I've dedicated my adult professional life to the field of child protection. My limitations are my alumni's strengths. I am deeply indebted to the Berkeley alums who participated in this project with me, and to the many alums who have taught me so much, first as students and then as professionals in this vital field. I am also grateful to several student assistants who helped to identify reference material and related tasks. They include Marta Galan, Juliana Nicolas, Laura Brignone, and Analia Valdavia. My recent doctoral student graduates have also had an important hand in my thinking about child protection, and I owe them my gratitude. They include Reiko Boyd, Colleen Henry, Bryn King, Jennifer Lawson, and Wendy Wiegmann.

I am especially indebted to the Zellerbach Family Foundation for their embrace of my work and their support for my academic development. All of the members of the Zellerbach family have treated me with tremendous generosity and kindness for which I am forever grateful. I am also appreciative of my Dean, Jeffrey Edleson, and to the University of California at Berkeley for its liberal sabbatical policy. Leave from my regular teaching duties and committee assignments made it possible to dedicate time to this project. My mentor of almost 30 years, Neil Gilbert, provided an invaluable platform to share ideas, and the Berkeley Family Book Group and Center for Child and Youth Policy offered a context for testing and shaping my ideas.

My recent involvement in an international comparative project with Professors Marit Skivenes, Tarja Pösö, and Jonathan Dickens has been instrumental in sharpening my understanding of US child welfare policy and practice. Sometimes we learn best about our own systems when we understand them in contrast to others. This important project has given me a perspective I would have otherwise missed, in addition to offering lifelong friendships with dear colleagues.

The five anonymous reviewers were essential to the development of my ideas. Their perspectives helped me clarify my thinking and my writing and the book is better for their engagement. My thanks is finally extended to my editor at Oxford University Press, Dana Bliss, for his confidence in the ideas articulated in this book. I hope the book can serve as an additional tool to shape the future of child welfare practice, policy, and the child welfare workforce.

About the Book

THE IMPOSSIBLE IMPERATIVE brings to life the daily efforts of child welfare professionals working on behalf of vulnerable children and families. Stories that highlight the work, written by child welfare staff on the front lines, speak to the competing principles that shape everyday decisions. The book evolved from my work over many years with MSW students at UC Berkeley who prepare for employment in the field of child welfare. The federally supported Title IV-E program is designed to support the professionalization of child welfare workers in public child welfare agencies. In California, 22 university-based Schools of Social Work participate in the specialized training program for MSW students. Students engage in a stipend-based training program for two years with a promise to work in public or tribal child welfare for at least two years following graduation. My work with child welfare staff in many public child welfare agencies has also inspired this work.

In both settings, I often hear discussions about the simple principles of *child safety, permanency,* and *family,* with little discussion about the conflicting nature of each principle and the tensions that arise when one principle is pitted against another. Similarly, I've witnessed at least two decades of child welfare policy and practice where a "new" principle is seemingly discovered (e.g., the importance of family or the value of permanency), and the field rushes to embrace that one principle without thoughtful consideration about how the wholesale adoption of one principle will, inevitably, involve a conflict with another central principle in this field. This book is therefore designed to inspire conversation about the fundamental nature of child welfare and about the principles that undergird the work. Further, the book is designed to encourage newcomers to the field to engage with this work and to do so with eyes open about the complexity of the task before them.

The "stories" in each chapter come from my former Title IV-E students in the MSW program at Berkeley. In 2015, I reached out to the alums of our program to determine their interest in participating with me in developing the book. Those who volunteered to participate were briefed about the overall purpose and organization of the book. They were asked to consider an actual case where their practice approach was not straightforward, where their views about how to handle the case were different from one or more respected colleagues in their agency, and where they experienced a "tension" of some kind between competing themes. In particular, I asked alums to only consider cases they experienced as "typical" rather than "extraordinary." I spoke with each interested alum, and we reviewed together one or more cases that might be appropriate for the book. Several of the competing principles outlined in the book were readily apparent in many of the cases; determining which principle to highlight in each chapter came later.

Alums were given some general parameters to follow in terms of case content and length. Following consultation with IRB staff at Berkeley, each student was given clear instructions about how to anonymize and protect the confidentiality of families described in their stories. All identifying information was removed from their stories, and details of events that might reveal the identities of individuals were removed or changed. The project was reviewed by IRB staff at UC Berkeley. I was informed that the project was "like a journalism project and (did) not . . . contribute to generalizable knowledge (research)." As such, "CPHS review and approval (would) not be needed for this project."[1]

I told alums in advance that I would edit their stories in order to smooth some of the differences between their writing styles and mine, but I ensured them that all edits would be approved by them before completing the book draft and final product. The editing process was extensive and iterative as the stories were shared back and forth over several months to clarify the practice approach, the questions of concern, the details of each case, and to maintain the authenticity of experience for the principal author.

Each story is written in the first person, because the story is an account of that author's experience in the field. My role in shaping or reshaping their story was instrumental, just as the reviewers who assessed this full manuscript were instrumental in the book's shape and development, but I take no credit for the individual stories in this book. These are the accounts of others who do this work every day and who live with the consequences of their decisions. My job, in comparison, is easy. I teach, I write, and I do research on child welfare, but I don't feel the daily press of these decisions. My co-authors do, and it is important to me that although I have played a role as an editor of their work, they are the authors of their stories; I honor their work and their voice.

Because this book relies upon the stories that emerge from California child welfare workers, the book privileges the California perspective. I recognize that California may be different from many other jurisdictions. In part because our Title IV-E program is so robust and longstanding (it was started in 1990), the child welfare workforce in many public agencies in California is populated by a large percentage of MSW-trained social workers. This is not the case in many other jurisdictions in the United States. Where possible, I try to point out practices or terms that may be California specific and have included a glossary for this purpose as well. California is also a diverse state where the racial/ethnic composition of the population is changing rapidly. Today, almost two fifths of the California population is composed of Latino/Hispanic families. As such, issues relating to work with Latino clients are featured in Chapter 8, though professionals working in other jurisdictions might regularly engage with families from different racial or ethnic backgrounds. Practice and policy also varies markedly across the 50 United States, so readers from other states or countries may need to make certain adjustments to consider the implications of the practice described here to their own context. I believe, however, that the general principles of practice outlined herein are relevant to a national and, possibly, to an international audience.

The alums who participated in this project are passionate about their work. All are deeply committed to the children and families touched by the child welfare system. At the core of their work is a sincere belief that social workers, in partnership with parents and children, can improve family life. This is a belief that I share. Of course, this is not to suggest that child welfare workers do not, sometimes, make grievous errors that can be harmful to children and families. This happens, too. But my view is that child welfare practice can improve and can be more responsive to families if child welfare staff are thoughtfully prepared for the work. I also believe that we need many more adults in the United States (and globally) to step up to do this work. As a result of these views, the reader may find my characterization of many child welfare workers as tilting toward the positive (though I also feature stories of social work decisions that did not support children or families). This positive tilt is intentional because I hope to inspire future child welfare workers to engage in this work with passion, but to do so grounded in the principles that shape the work and in an understanding of the conflicted space that occupies the center of all child welfare practice. Children and families need them.

The Impossible Imperative

1

Child Welfare

PERILOUS TERRITORY FOR THOSE WHO CARE

EACH YEAR, over 6.5 million children are reported to child welfare agencies in the United States with allegations of child abuse or neglect. We take child abuse seriously in this country in part because the consequences are significant. According to the Centers for Disease Control and Prevention (CDC), the average lifetime cost associated with child maltreatment for a single child is over $200,000. Given the prevalence of maltreatment in the United States, the total cost for all affected children exceeds $125 billion.[1]

Adults who suffered child abuse or neglect are at increased risk of an array of chronic diseases such as cancer, heart disease, lung disease, and obesity.[2] Young adults who have a history of maltreatment are very likely to show significant mental health problems such as anxiety, depression, or eating disorders.[3] And these childhood adversities correlate strongly with problematic behaviors such as smoking, drug use, criminal activity, and early parenting.[4] Adults who were maltreated in childhood are at least twice as likely to maltreat their own children when they become parents.[5] And for some children, the ultimate consequence of child maltreatment is an early and untimely death. Almost 1,600 children are killed in the United States each year for reasons relating to child abuse or neglect.[6] Infants and very young children are especially vulnerable. Almost three quarters of all child maltreatment-related fatalities occur to children ages 3 years or younger.[7]

Although death is a relatively rare event, child maltreatment is not. Some studies suggest that upward of one quarter of children may experience physical abuse, and almost 5% may experience sexual abuse.[8] But child maltreatment is hardly an equal opportunity phenomenon. Poverty puts children at a significant disadvantage in many ways, and research indicates that parenting under conditions of poverty is extremely challenging.[9] According to the National Incidence Study of Child Abuse and Neglect (NIS-4), children living in families with very low socioeconomic status[10] are five times more likely to be maltreated than other children.[11] And rates of maltreatment for children of color are especially troubling. Some estimates indicate that before kindergarten, about 5 per 100 White children are verified (substantiated) as victims of maltreatment. Among African American children, the likelihood of maltreatment prior to kindergarten (ages 0–5 years) is more than twice that (11.8 per 100).[12] Some of the factors correlated with child maltreatment such as poverty, single parent status, lower educational achievement, parenting stress, neighborhood stress, and other factors[13] are also correlated with race or ethnicity in the United States, suggesting a great deal about the constellation of socioeconomic risks that accrue to groups divided along racial or ethnic lines.

And just as maltreatment is divided by income and race, its prevalence and implications are far different depending on the age of the child. When infants or toddlers experience food scarcity because of their parents' omission or commission, or when they are the victims of violence, the consequences of these circumstances are amplified. Of all reports of maltreatment in the United States annually, over one quarter focused on a child age 3 years or younger.[14] Very young children in the United States are at significant risk of suffering maltreatment from their parents or other caregivers and these children, of course, are especially unlikely to be able to protect themselves from their fate.

The United States has an elaborate set of policies developed to signal public officials when children may be maltreated and to call for a response. Each state has procedures mandating that professionals who have contact with children report cases of suspected child abuse and neglect. These might include medical professionals, teachers, animal control officers, photographic film processors, or first responders.[15] If these professionals know of, or suspect child abuse, they are required to make a report to the local child abuse hotline. But what happens to the flood of calls that come to these government officials? Who takes the call at the other end of the line? What questions do they ask to determine how to proceed? And who is there to help children and families after the call is logged?

Child welfare workers[16] (or caseworkers) serve as the backbone of the child welfare system, responding to allegations of child abuse and neglect, assessing children's circumstances, planning for children's futures, and working with parents to improve family life. Their work is imperative; the safety of children is at stake. But their work is extremely challenging. Each child has any variety of special needs and circumstances, and many families present with multiple, complex issues. As they work to secure children's safety, caseworkers must earn children's and parents' faith that they share a common interest in the well-being of the child—this, against a backdrop of high emotional intensity, anger, and fear. They wield the enormous power of the state with the authority to recommend the ultimate devastation to a parent: the removal of a child from a parent's home. But child welfare workers rarely feel like powerful actors. Constrained by limited agency resources, sometimes overlooked by judges or attorneys whose professional titles wield greater status, and too often targeted in the media when mistakes are made, child welfare workers carry out difficult work.

Their job is made more difficult by the contexts in which they work. Child welfare agencies vary dramatically across the country. Many are challenged by high demand for services and constrained resources. They are sometimes chaotic and always complex, characterized by cumbersome processes and a bewildering array of local, state, and federal regulations. Some of the toughest settings are those that also suffer from high rates of staff turnover,[17] where even the most resolute champions of the family don't stay long.

Efforts to improve the child welfare workforce and the agencies in which child welfare work is conducted have been vigorous over the past couple of decades.[18] Much is now known about the factors associated with a satisfied workforce: staff who feel a sense of self-efficacy and who experience the support of their supervisor, for example;[19] and the factors in the agency culture and climate that promote positive staff experiences such as shared expectations, shared perceptions about agency priorities, and shared views about client interactions.[20] Important evidence suggests that the culture and climate of the child welfare agency not only affect child welfare staff but also the outcomes for children and families.[21] Healthier agencies bring about positive changes for families. There's so much at stake for these families, so having a stable, satisfied, effective workforce in a positive work environment means everything to the outcomes for the families who are at the center of this work.

Sometimes, of course, workers get it wrong. As public entities ultimately responsible to the community and to local, state, and federal legislators, the work of child welfare occurs under a constant microscope of scrutiny. Child welfare workers' errors in judgment can sometimes have devastating effects. Too many headlines have been written about mistakes that resulted in injury or even death for children. The landslide of public opprobrium upon reading the news about a child's tragedy is swift and decisive.[22] But these are the outliers. Many decisions caseworkers make every day are less momentous than death, but certainly impactful for children and families.

The importance of the work can't be exaggerated. Studies that consider why child welfare workers remain in the field indicate that the work is "exciting, challenging, and unpredictable." Furthermore, satisfied staff point to the importance of the work and the personal value they derive from engaging, every day, in work that is meaningful.[23]

But there is so much more to child welfare. If it were simply a question of the heart, then many passions would be stirred and countless college graduates would flock to the field. Instead, the work is emotionally satisfying at the same time that it is emotionally taxing. It can be deeply intellectually engaging, but the bureaucratic rules that govern the work sometimes stifle workers' most creative thinking. Child welfare workers help children and families daily, but in order to help, they must first determine how. Much of their work involves consequential decision making.[24] Is this child eligible for our services? Is this child safe? What will happen to this child tonight, if I walk away? What type of service can best help this family? Can we provide the services this family needs? Where should this child live, if not with parents? Can this child safely return home?

This book brings to life the daily efforts of child welfare professionals working on behalf of vulnerable children and families. Stories that highlight the work, written by child welfare staff on the front lines, speak to the challenges the families face, the complexity of the work, and the demands for decision making in the face of ambiguity, inadequate information, and limited resources. Finding the "right" solution for each unique family may be impossible, in part, because what is "right" probably requires insight into the long-term outcomes of children well beyond the service horizon of child welfare. Rather than claim that child welfare professionals can be educated always to make "correct" decisions, this book argues that child welfare workers can and should be supported always to make principled decisions.

What are the principles that guide this work? Surely there is more to this field than just protecting children from harm. Child welfare policy and practice are embedded in a common frame of ideas. Federal law outlines the service priorities of the child welfare system: to promote children's safety, permanency, and well-being.[25] But this triumvirate is limited. Notions of safety and permanency are too restrictive to capture the state's relationship and responsibility to vulnerable families. At the same time that the triumvirate is too narrow, it is also larger in philosophy than it is embodied in practice. Promoting children's well-being, for example, is more aspirational than real.[26]

In fact, in Chapters 2 and 3, I argue that the United States does *not* embrace a focus on child well-being, though a number of benefits might accrue to children if it did.[27]

Indeed, child welfare rests on a larger base of ideas than these three concepts suggest. This book offers eight fundamental principles that guide child welfare in the United States. Comparative work between Western industrialized countries gives reason to believe that many of the principles outlined here are, or could become, a framework for child welfare elsewhere.[28] Their importation, however, would certainly be reshaped to reflect the political, cultural, and historical context of a different nation.

Why eight principles? Reasonable people could argue that there are more than eight principles underlying child welfare.[29] Caseworkers, however, might find an excessively long list difficult to enact regularly. Examples from the field of child welfare training suggest that practitioners should be "competent" in dozens of practice skills.[30] These exhaustive lists quickly become background noise rather than a judicious frame to consider the metagoals that shape the work. Aiming for parsimony, therefore, but responsive to the arc of experiences children and families may have with the child welfare system, the following fundamental principles are offered as a guide to the field:

1. Parents who care for their children safely should be free from government intrusion in their family.
2. Children should be safe.
3. Children should be raised with their family of origin.
4. When children cannot live with family, they should live with extended relatives.
5. Children should be raised in families.
6. Children should have a sense of permanence—that the caregivers they live with will care for them permanently.
7. Families' cultural heritage should be respected.
8. Parents and children (of a certain age and maturity) should have a say in the decisions that affect their lives.

These principles form the basis for the conduct of child welfare workers, and they offer an essential guide to policy. Child welfare is not about swapping one arbitrary alternative for another. We prefer that children live with their parents rather than in foster care. We want children to live in families rather than in institutions. Child welfare is not about spinning a wheel and selecting a path forward at random. Child welfare workers should be guided by a foundational structure that clarifies how and why we privilege some choices over others.

At first blush, the sheer simplicity of each principle is alluring and suggests a field where decision making in individual cases is straightforward. But what if, upon closer examination, we discover that these foundational principles collide with one another—not in the rare, exceptional cases, but in the average cases that serve to typify child welfare? In fact, these are the tensions that live at the heart of child welfare, and they play out in policy and practice almost every day. Caseworkers, attempting to carry out principled practice, regularly encounter circumstances that test their intellect as they wrestle with prioritizing one value over another. Moreover, these situations often strain their moral compass as they wonder at the value of privileging one principle over another and thereby devaluing the alternative principle also at stake.

Children should have a say in decisions that affect their lives. But what if what they want hurts them? Children should be safe. But what if their safety is compromised when they live with their family? These are not merely philosophical debates; child welfare workers live out these conflicts on a daily basis and must regularly favor one principle at the expense of another. Indeed, the imperative of child protection is sometimes impossible to carry out when one principle is pitted against another equally worthy and principled imperative.

This book explores that liminal space—the place where reasonable people likely disagree. It reveals the intellectually competing circumstances that highlight the moral conundrums of child welfare. These disputed spaces expose the fault lines in child welfare policymaking where seemingly simple, principle-based policies[31] often obscure the unique challenges of families the policies are designed to help. And the street-level agents—caseworkers—embody the policies with a service response that is fundamentally principled, but that must also respond to the deep complexity families present.[32]

Some cases are less complicated. A child welfare worker, describing a case that is morally unambiguous yet emotionally taxing, focuses on a child who was not safe, parents unwilling to raise him, and relatives who were sought out but unavailable. In this case, the decisions the worker faced were hard but relatively clear: given the harms they exacted on their child, *these parents could not be free of government intervention in their lives*. Their boy was not *safe*. The work surrounding the case was difficult because the gravity of the situation was profound and the plight of the child severe. But the need for some state response to the child is evident; the tragedy is that the state was not aware of this child's conditions earlier.

"Xander"

"Watch your head!" screamed the principal. I turned and a large, black garbage can was reeling toward my face. Instinctively, I dropped to the ground. Luckily, it missed me. Another day and another challenge in child welfare.

I saw him, the young boy who threw the can. He was standing, defiant, on the playground. I could see the anger in his face. His eyes told me it was another bad day in the life of a boy who had not seen many good days. When would Xander have a so-called normal day? When would he be liberated from his emotional pain? Is the word "never" too close to the truth?

Xander entered foster care when he was 8 years old. Parents of children placed in care are usually offered services to help them reunify. Not so for Xander's family. His parents proclaimed often in those early months that they didn't want Xander to return. "We'll keep our other children, but we don't want Xander." His father was cruel beyond words and made it clear that his preference was for Xander to die.

How do you tell an 8-year-old boy, brutalized by his father, that his parents don't want him? You don't. Instead, you try your best to become one of the people in his life that shows him that he is wanted, and that he deserves something better in life. Sometimes, that's the best and the most you can do.

Xander had already been kicked out of two foster homes. On the day I met him, the foster parent told me she couldn't handle him anymore. This was foster home number three over a period of 3 months. I entered Xander's room. He was sitting on the ground and he was mad. Fortunately, I had in tow a social worker's[1] toolkit: A new set of colored pens, paper, play dough, and a small set of Legos. I pulled out the coloring set, with little success. I then offered the play dough. Xander smiled and immediately began to press and mold the material. I asked what he was making. "A knife for a knife fight," he replied. He then told me about an incident with his father when they had fought with knives. He pointed to the scar on his forehead.

1. All of the child welfare workers featured in this book have an MSW degree and are referred to as "social workers" by their employers and by one another. These titles are retained in their stories.

The next time I saw Xander was at his school. His teacher was genuinely worried about me. "If you take him for an appointment, you must take a police officer with you!" I ignored the warning and instead began a relationship with a young boy built on trust, warmth, and compassion. I'll never regret that choice.

After consulting my supervisor, I moved Xander from his foster home into a group home outside of the city where he could be surrounded by animals and nature. His behaviors were challenging, but the staff worked tirelessly to keep him safe and in school. After several months my supervisor and I agreed that he needed a second chance in a foster home; we thought he was ready to move to a less restrictive environment.[33] I asked the placement unit to identify an appropriate foster home and only asked that they not place him with any other children; I wanted to heed the warnings I'd been given about his propensity to inflict violence on other children.

Ms. Thomas offered her home to Xander, and it was there that I came to understand him and his history much more clearly. Xander's estranged parents had very different relationships with their son. Xander's father had brutally physically, sexually, and emotionally abused him for years. Xander's mother loved him, but she gravely feared her former husband. She refused offers of visits to Xander, and her calls to her son were infrequent, short, and furtive; she insisted he promise not to reveal their conversations to his father. I tried to contact her regularly so that I could keep her apprised of Xander's well-being and activities, but it was difficult. She'd rarely return phone calls and when she did, she too anxiously expressed her fears that her former husband might learn about her contact with our agency.

Ms. Thomas became very attached to Xander, and we began to discuss options for his permanency. I spoke with Xander about where he wanted to live, and he told me how he longed for his mother. As he came to understand how unlikely a return to her home might be, he shared with me his growing affection for Ms. Thomas and his comfort in her home. I realized, however, that a search for Xander's relatives had never been conducted by his previous social worker, so I began that legally mandated process to determine if he might find a new, permanent home with extended family. My efforts quickly exposed more details about Xander's dreadful childhood. Although concerned about this young boy, no family member was willing to accept him into their home. All of them feared Xander's father. They knew that he intended to kill his son, and he had ready access to weapons to complete the deed.

Ms. Thomas grew to love Xander, and she tried diligently to be the caregiver he needed. In addition to her efforts to show him a world he was unfamiliar with, including trips to the beach or to a local farm, she tried to maintain Xander's connection to his mother. Regardless of a permanency outcome for this boy, Ms. Thomas knew that Xander and his mother would always be family; Xander's family also connected him to his cultural heritage and to his developing identity as a young, Black man. But in spite of her efforts, Ms. Thomas was unprepared to manage his extremely challenging behavior. The **foster family agency**[2] she worked with offered a great deal of support and assistance, but Xander's behaviors continued to escalate. Ms. Thomas called me frequently, day and night, as his behaviors became more extreme, and both suicidal and homicidal tendencies were discerned. I tried to offer concrete advice about what to do during his more explosive moments; sometimes it meant intervening with Xander directly, and other times I simply advised that she separate herself to keep safe.

My work with Ms. Thomas taught me so much about how to support foster parents. I created charts and behavior boards to help her manage Xander's behaviors, and we role-played what to do if a situation got out of control. I tried everything possible. I enrolled Xander in a nonpublic school, registered him for various extracurricular therapeutic activities, and brought additional therapeutic services into the home. But Xander's behaviors were becoming more extreme—he was jumping off of roofs and taking a knife to the throat. After one particularly serious incident, Xander was placed on a psychiatric hold by the police. It was the first of many.

2. Words highlighted in **bold** can be found in the glossary for more detailed information.

Xander's circumstances never improved appreciably. In and out of psychiatric facilities, then juvenile hall, he was a sad, angry boy turning into a man.

I learned so much about childhood trauma through my work with Xander. I learned about its unspeakable damage—harms that bear few visible marks, but scars that are cut deep into the soul. Xander fortified my belief that children have human rights that must be respected. Because of Xander, I redoubled my commitment to the field of child welfare.

Freny Dessai

Although Xander's case reminds us of the trauma associated with some forms of maltreatment, all child welfare cases are not as extreme, nor the path forward as clear cut. In Xander's case, the need to "do something" was clear. Absent a child welfare response, Xander probably would have been killed by his father. But the child welfare response that was ultimately offered to Xander was also likely insufficient to address the deep emotional scars inflicted by his family.

Many of the principles of child welfare are evident in this caseworker's efforts with Xander. Xander could not live safely with his parents, and thus government involvement in his family was inevitable (principle 1). Xander was not safe (principle 3). He could not be raised by his dangerous father, nor could he be kept safe if left in the home of his mother (principle 2); even his relatives feared for his safety if he lived with them (principle 4). Perhaps his safety would have been better assured if he had remained in the group home where he lived for awhile, but the principle of family-based care prevailed (principle 5), and even when circumstances in his foster home began to deteriorate, the goals of permanency that were expressed by his foster mother (principle 6), suggested that he should remain in her care. Xander's own views about where he should live were also honored in this case (principle 8), and the foster mother's commitment to Xander's continued ties with his birth mother was, in part, her understanding of Xander's need for family, and for his need for cultural continuity (principle 7).

Xander's case was hard. The abuse Xander sustained was not only appalling for this child, but the revelations about the severity and duration of the maltreatment left many of the professionals who worked with him deeply upset and, for some, also traumatized.[34] Other cases are difficult for different reasons. Not because of the obvious danger to a child, but because of the ambiguity of the situation. In some cases, the path forward is opaque, and reasonable people might judge the available facts differently. Another colleague, describing a challenging case, highlights the significant limitations of a parent but that parent's tenacious fight for her right to raise her children free from government intrusion. In this case, the principle that *children should be safe* was pitted against the equally important principle that *children should be raised with their family of origin.*

"Parker and Winona"

The first time I met Jewel, it was just hours after I'd placed her 3-year-old son, Parker, into protective custody. I was still a relatively new social worker, only working in the field for about a year. Although the facts I had already gathered that morning looked pretty serious, I was willing to approach the situation with an open mind. After all, the reason for Parker's removal was not *directly* attributable to Jewel's actions.

Parker had been staying with his cousin, Yolanda, in a home that earlier that day had been found in violation of about a dozen housing codes. The power to the house had been shut off, so Yolanda and her boyfriend had run extension cords from the neighbor's house to provide electricity. The floorboards in the kitchen were so rotted that the whole room shook when anyone walked through it. The police officers that accompanied me were worried that the whole thing would give way at any moment.

We found Parker in an unpermitted converted garage; Parker was sleeping on a raised platform made of two-by-fours and plywood. Nearby was a power strip with thick extension cords running in every direction with various appliances—a fan, a portable heater, a flat iron—plugged into it. The room had no entrance or exit other than the doorway we were all standing in, not even a window, and the officers who accompanied me were worried about the possibility of an electrical fire. In the event of such a catastrophe, Parker would have been trapped. Then there was the rest of the house: the rooms with so much stuff I couldn't manage to get through; the backyard that was serving as trash service for the home; the complete absence of food, aside from a pan of biscuits sitting on the stove. Parker's situation was further complicated by the fact that Yolanda couldn't produce Jewel's phone number when it became clear that neither Parker nor anyone else in the home would be able to stay there. In the absence of a parent to interview and assess, my supervisor recommended that we detain Parker and place him in temporary foster care.

When Jewel arrived at the office, I was curious to hear what she had to say, but I was also familiar enough with her referral history that I wasn't completely naïve. She had multiple prior referrals to child welfare over the years alleging neglect of her four older children due to methamphetamine abuse and possible untreated mental illness. Poor supervision on Jewel's part had resulted, years earlier, in the drowning death of one of her young children. I knew all of Jewel's older children were being cared for by various relatives, through formal and informal guardianship arrangements.

I've always been reluctant to remove children from their parents unless I have exhausted every option to keep them safe. Some people might view this as a "pro-parent" stance, but I have always thought of this philosophy as being both realistic and compassionate. Removal of children creates trauma: for kids, for parents, for the entire family system, and even for the community. Removal of children should never be taken lightly, and I take very seriously my responsibility to do everything within my power to develop **safety plans** that will allow children to remain at home. However, it is often the case that the amount of time and effort involved in building a strong safety network to keep kids at home is daunting and sometimes impossible: social workers lack resources, timelines are tight, and caseloads are high. Not removing children means social workers have to think creatively about who should be involved in a safety plan, how we will measure whether a child is safe, and how long to monitor the situation before walking away. All of this requires what is so often the hardest resource to come by: time.

By the time I met with Jewel to figure out what would happen with Parker, I was already feeling the press of time. Once a child is placed in protective custody, a legal clock starts ticking. I had only 48 hours from the time Parker was placed in protective custody by the police to file my petition and detention report with the juvenile court. In that time I had to interview the family members, find a foster placement, write the report, and complete several bureaucratic forms that accompany the legal process. Four hours had already slipped away. Even though I was under pressure to get everything done, meeting with Jewel was a critical piece of the puzzle I had to solve.

Short, wiry, pierced, and tattooed, Jewel met with me in an interview room in the agency. Jewel made her case: she had nothing to do with Parker's situation in Yolanda's home, and he should be returned to her immediately. I began to ask questions: How long had Parker been staying in Yolanda's house? How often was Jewel visiting? Was she aware of the conditions of the home? Where was Jewel living? And so on. As we talked, a picture emerged: one of housing instability, food scarcity, and volatile relationships with romantic partners. Jewel told me that her children were living with relatives in voluntary arrangements largely because she felt she was not stable enough to care for them. We talked about the drowning death of her baby years ago, and how that led to her serious addiction to methamphetamines, which she simultaneously acknowledged and minimized. She told me she was a cutter and pulled up her sleeves to show me the dozens of angry red slashes and scars up and down her forearms. She grew angry with herself for disclosing these problems and began to shut down.

While we talked, I tried to ascertain if the safety threat that had brought Parker into protective custody—hazardous housing conditions immediately threatening to his safety—could be resolved if returned to Jewel's care. Jewel told me that Parker had been staying with Yolanda because her own housing situation was tenuous: She was staying in a trailer parked behind a local shop with at least three other adults. Jewel told me that she had asked Yolanda if Parker could stay with her for a while because she knew this situation was not the best for Parker, and she believed that staying temporarily with his cousin would be better. I gave Jewel credit for choosing the better option, even though there were some serious flaws with her plan. Jewel would not agree to let me come out to assess the trailer she was staying in, as she did not want to involve her friends in "the system," and she also didn't want her friends to know what was going on. All of this was further complicated by the evidence that led me to suspect she was actively using or abusing methamphetamines, which makes planning for safety much more difficult. Based on the information available to me, I determined that we would be unable to make a safety plan to return Parker to her care, especially since I could not assess the safety of the housing I would be returning him to, and that I would recommend detention during the court hearing the day after tomorrow. I told her and she blew up. She stormed out of the room, cursing me on the way out.

I left the interview shaken and drained. Even though I knew I was doing the right thing, I felt such compassion for Jewel. She had experienced so much trauma and loss in her life, and she was continuing to experience further trauma and loss. I understood completely why she sought an escape by abusing substances and carving up her own flesh. I felt horrible.

I saw Jewel again a few more times during this period, most notably at her contested **jurisdiction hearing**—contested because Jewel never thought she should be held responsible for the condition of her cousin's home, because she knew (and I made sure she knew) it was her right to contest, and because she was a fighter and I admired her fight for her son. As the petitioner, I was called to testify. As I sat on the witness stand, and objectively answered questions, it became clear that Parker would not yet be returning to Jewel's care. I felt a complicated mix of emotions: empathy for Jewel, sadness that a family was torn apart, and hope that Jewel could accept responsibility and make changes so she could resume parenting her child.

Fast-forward 5 years: I was a relatively new supervisor in **Emergency Response**, and the hotline received a fresh referral relating to Jewel and her newborn, still in the hospital following delivery. In the intervening years, Parker had remained in foster care, and Jewel's reunification services had long since been terminated. Parker had experienced a rocky path in foster care, moving in and out of relatives' and nonrelatives' foster homes, reunified with Jewel, and later returned to care. He'd been abused in one of his foster homes, and finding permanency for him had been elusive. None of this made Jewel's opinion of our agency any more favorable. Jewel's most recent contact with our agency related to her 17-year-old son, also in trouble with criminal activity and methamphetamine use. Despite Jewel's intermittent contacts with our agency, when Jewel and her baby were assigned to a worker in my unit for an investigation, I had not seen her since that contested jurisdictional hearing.

The concerns reported to the hotline were pretty minimal. At the time of the birth, neither Jewel nor the baby, Winona, tested positive for any substances, and Jewel was providing Winona with attentive, nurturing care. But based on her previous contact with child welfare and past substance use, hospital personnel felt obligated to call in the referral. Due to Jewel's inability to reunify with Parker, having a newborn in her care was sufficient basis for our agency to investigate in order to assess Winona's safety.

The worker assigned to investigate was even less experienced than I was the first time I met Jewel. Stacy was objective and cool-headed, with good instincts and great assessment skills, but she was very green, and Jewel was well known to our agency for being incredibly intimidating. Rumors had circulated that the social worker who had been assigned to Jewel and Parker's reunification case ended up quitting after a **family team meeting** in which Jewel had screamed at her, blocked her exit from the room, and made her feel threatened. Stacy reviewed a synopsis of Jewel's prior child welfare history so that she could consider it a factor when assessing Winona's safety, and then she headed into the field, alerted to be cautious of possible volatility.

Stacy and I were aware of the range of opinions that existed in our agency about Jewel and her new baby. Jewel was well known; many of the social workers and supervisors had worked with her at some point and had strong feelings about the next steps. They argued that Winona should be removed, based on the high level of risk posed by Jewel's history of mental illness, substance abuse, criminal history, childhood abuse, and prior child welfare services involvement, including failed reunification, and the high level of vulnerability of the infant. They had seen the damage done to Parker during returns to Jewel's care under a brief period of **Family Maintenance** services and unsupervised visits, and they knew how destructive Jewel's parenting could be. These staff voiced the research, evidence, and wisdom behind actuarial risk assessment models, which correlate the likelihood of future maltreatment with what is known about past behavior.

Others, however, thought we had no authority to place Winona in protective custody. They argued that there were no concerns regarding the circumstances of Winona's birth; Jewel and Winona had both tested clean, Jewel claimed to have stayed off methamphetamine throughout the pregnancy, and social workers who had interacted with Jewel in the community in the recent months prior to Winona's birth provided accounts that she seemed to be doing well. Further, some workers argued, there was a nonoffending father with no prior child welfare history. He was present, involved, and living in the home with Jewel and the baby, along with the paternal grandparents. They asserted there was no legal basis to remove Winona or even to file a petition recommending court oversight of the child within the home, as there were no active or imminent safety threats. Their position embodied the **Core Practice Model**'s mantra, "We believe families can grow and change."

There was no real tension between workers espousing these distinctive perspectives, but the tension in philosophy was palpable. I felt the tension within myself. How comfortable was I "living with" risk and how much risk was too much? What was the ethical course of action?

Stacy's investigation revealed nothing to indicate that Jewel was actively abusing methamphetamine; she was living with Winona's father and the paternal grandparents, all of whom stated they did not condone nor support methamphetamine use, and all of whom indicated they would take action to protect Winona if Jewel appeared to be using or was triggered. Stacy organized a family meeting to develop a safety plan so that Winona could remain at home. Jewel agreed to seek help for her mental health, although it also did not appear that she was acutely suffering from debilitating symptoms. At the family meeting, Jewel remembered me and did not appear happy to see me, but when I gave her the opportunity to allow another supervisor to sit in on the meeting instead, Jewel declined. During the meeting, it was clear to me that Jewel had changed quite a bit: The anxious person was still there, and the potential for volatility shimmered just below the surface, but Jewel was able to recover when she felt her anger rise, request a break when she needed one, and participate productively despite her bitterness toward the agency and her belief that we were trying to take her daughter away from her.

The safety plan included the continued involvement of Stacy for a period of 30 days to monitor the situation. The paternal grandmother, Anne, and the father, Sean, agreed to call the agency right away if Jewel used methamphetamine, and they agreed to keep the baby in their care in the event of any concerning behavior on Jewel's part. Jewel acknowledged that her housing was not stable in the event of a disagreement with Sean, but she agreed with the plan to provide stability for Winona by leaving her with Sean and Anne should such an argument ensue.

Less than a week later, Anne called Stacy. Jewel and Sean had fought, Jewel had left the home with Winona, and now, Anne did not know where they were. Stacy spent the morning on the phone, tracking down people and information, and by the afternoon, Jewel, Sean, and Winona were back in our office meeting with Stacy and me. We learned that following the argument, Anne drove Jewel and Winona to a friend's house; Sean joined Jewel and the baby shortly thereafter. Jewel and Sean both swore that there had been no physical fighting, just a lot of yelling, and that they had made up right away. They had also taken Winona for her well-baby check-up just prior to our meeting. We reviewed and refined the safety plan, and after the meeting, Stacy called Anne to clarify Anne's role in ensuring Winona's safety.

Shortly before the end of the **30-day services plan**, Jewel called Stacy from her Probation Officer's (PO) office, asking Stacy for a letter proving that she had not tested positive for substances at Winona's birth. Jewel's PO advised Stacy that Jewel had not been submitting to drug testing, which was a condition of her probation, and a hearing would be held within a week or two to review Jewel's compliance with her probation terms. The PO said the result of the hearing could land Jewel in a residential treatment program or jail. This information led to a new decision point: Was Jewel's lack of compliance with probation sufficient evidence that Winona was at risk of harm? Although no one within the agency felt comfortable with missed drug tests—a very good indicator that Jewel was almost certainly continuing to use methamphetamine—there was general agreement that the baby was in the care of a father who had done nothing wrong, a safety network was in place, and the safety plan had been tested for 30 days. Ultimately, we decided that the baby's home was sufficiently safe to end our involvement with the family despite our knowledge that the baby's risk continued to be very high.

Within a month, Jewel and Sean got into a physical fight, police responded to the home, both parents were arrested, and Winona was detained and placed in foster care with her grandmother, Anne. Winona was not injured in the fight, but now the agency had evidence that the parents' behavior constituted a direct threat to child safety, and a petition was filed.

Had we erred? Had we left an infant in harm's way, ignoring the red flags of risk? Had we viewed the circumstances through rose-colored glasses, believing too fervently in Jewel's ability to grow and change? I believe the answer to all of these questions is "no." During the course of the investigation and the 30-day services plan, Stacy and I met regularly, discussing the risk factors, why we were worried, and the specific, necessary ingredients in a viable safety plan. After these meetings, I met regularly with my manager, getting input and feedback about the decisions we were making. No one involved in the situation was naïve about the level of risk to Winona. But in our agency, the assessment tools that we use to help guide our decisions have separate assessments for risk and safety, and at no point during the investigation was there an identified safety threat. Even when we were worried that Jewel was using methamphetamine again, Stacy conducted unannounced home visits and was unable to find concerns regarding Jewel and Sean's care of Winona. At the end of the day, all we had was risk. And we had a lot of risk.

Over the years, I've had the opportunity to examine my professional values—my view that we should keep children in their family of origin whenever it's safe to do so. I believe individuals can grow and change, and I believe it's our obligation to support parents to identify needed changes and help them find the resources within themselves to change. But it would be wrong to say that my beliefs blind me to the risks inherent in the families that frequently come to our attention.

Jewel had a lengthy history to overcome, and probably insufficient support to overcome it. Stacy had laws and regulations to which she had to adhere, including a requirement to conduct an assessment and reach a conclusion about child maltreatment within 30 days of making contact with the family. Stacy and I were realistic about the lack of evidence we had—evidence we needed in order to pursue court action to monitor the family—and the high level of risk to Winona. Although we could have offered voluntary services, Jewel's history with the agency guaranteed that these would be spurned. In the end, I think we followed the best course of action available to us at the time. And I'm grateful Winona never suffered serious harm at the hands of her parents.

Trudi Frazel

Readers might look at Jewel's story and come to very different conclusions about whether these child welfare workers' actions were right and just. Some might argue that the ultimate decisions to separate Parker and later, Winona, from their parents were appropriate, that they secured greater safety for these young children, and that they reflected a just response to the children's needs. Others might argue that the child welfare workers' actions were wrong, and that this family was hurt by the government's intervention and that safeguarding the family's ties should have been privileged over family separation. Indeed, Parker was eventually abused in foster care, and he never secured permanency—a travesty by any measure.

But we often don't know what is right or just in child welfare. No one has a crystal ball that can predict children's outcomes over time; no one knows whether parents will or will not change with time. Instead, we use principles to help guide the work and to craft a child welfare response that pulls us closer to justice.

When the child welfare worker initially interviewed Jewel about the caregiving conditions for Parker, she was attempting to enact the third principle: *Children should be raised with their family of origin.* But again, the second principle of child *safety* collided squarely. When Parker was placed in care, the child welfare worker also attempted to enact the fourth principle: *When children cannot live with family, they should live with extended relatives.* Absent appropriate relatives available to care for this child, however, he was ultimately placed in foster care with an alternative family (enacting the fifth principle: *Children should be raised in families*), but with caregivers whom he didn't know.

In the case of Winona, the child welfare worker and her supervisor attempted to enact the first principle: *Parents who care for their children safely should be free from government intrusion in their family.* The safety plan they developed in collaboration with Jewel, Sean, and Anne not only offered this family another opportunity to raise their child outside of government involvement, but it honored their voice in decision making (*parents and children should have a say in the decisions that affect their lives*). Later, when the baby was involved in a domestic violence dispute, the second principle, *children should be safe*, came into play. And when Winona was eventually placed in care, Anne was enlisted as her caregiver, ensuring that the fourth principle relating to *extended family* was upheld.

In these examples, the principles serve as a guide to practice to help align decisions more closely with a just response. The principles, however, are hardly a road map to select a straightforward path. As is evident, the principles frequently collide with one another depending on the context of the case. The decisions child welfare workers are required to make in many cases are involved, typically perplexing, and they too often lead to an outcome where there are no guarantees of success.

The stories in this book come from child welfare workers who make these difficult decisions every day. Their stories embody hope—a relentless optimism in the strengths of parents and parents' capacities to raise their children well. These workers are fierce advocates for children and families, sometimes telling tales of determination against slow-moving bureaucracies or other actors who do not prioritize children or families' needs. They are thoughtful, critical analysts, assessing limited available information. And they are cheerleaders and mentors, encouraging the small (and sometimes very large) changes that they and the courts ask of parents.

Children can tell us a great deal about child welfare workers and the roles that they play. In one study, children in foster care were asked how they view their caseworker. Some of their comments are revealing and speak to the vital role these professionals play in children's lives:

They help families where children are getting abused or neglected.
Someone who comes over, watches out for you. If there's anything bad, they'll help you.
A person who helps with family problems.[35]

The more concerning studies, of course, reveal the divide that can occur between child welfare workers and children or parents, when family members are not listened to or are misunderstood.[36] Child welfare workers who help and those who hurt are both part of the story. The goal of all child welfare agencies should be to grow a workforce that helps and to create an agency frame where positive work thrives.

This book examines that helping through an honest portrayal of the conflicting space that characterizes much child welfare practice. Helping is hardly a simple task when the choices are not usually win-win. The book follows child welfare practice from the entry point of the system to the endpoint. The purpose is to reveal some of the tensions that are embodied in the principles we take for granted and that typify this field. And although each chapter highlights one point of contention between conflicting values, several of the stories actually capture more than one principle colliding with another.

The entry point to the system, the child abuse hotline, is where it all starts in Chapter 2. Staff who manage the hotline take calls 24 hours a day in response to community and mandated reporters' concerns about children. Because child welfare in the United States is very narrowly defined as a service for children who have been maltreated by their caregivers and who—as a result—are harmed or are at significant risk of harm, these child welfare workers try to determine eligibility. Who do we serve? Who do we not serve? And how quickly should we respond? Loyal to our first principle, *parents who care for their children safely should be free from government intrusion in their family,* the hotline screener determines when or if the government will become involved. At issue is a fundamental tension about whether we are underinvolved or overinvolved in the lives of families.

Chapter 3 features the principle: *Children should be safe.* The emphasis on "safety organized practice" means that when children have needs beyond safety, these are relegated to agencies that may or may not have an obligation to help or to family choice where some may exercise their right to decline voluntary services. One child welfare worker illustrates how she assesses risk and safety and how she manages the tension between offering voluntary services versus requiring involuntary services. Another caseworker shows the limits of only securing children's safety and the opportunities lost when this frame is narrowly applied.

One of the oldest debates in the field of child welfare is the tension between family preservation and child protection. In its starkest contrast, an orientation toward family preservation privileges the family's interests over the child's; an orientation toward child protection privileges the child's interests over the family's. The difference may seem semantic, but in child welfare, it is not. The competing ideas are not really about two sides of a coin, but about a continuum, where issues of children's rights sometimes conflict with parents' rights, all of whom live in a family very much in the middle. The principle, that *children should be raised with their family of origin*, tilts the field toward a family preservation orientation, but honoring family is not always as straightforward as it seems. Chapter 4 examines the historical roots of this divide and its modern incarnation played out in social work practice.

Chapter 5 scrutinizes the fundamental value of family and our principle that *when children cannot live with family, they should live with extended relatives.* Recent changes in policy and practice have emphasized child welfare workers' efforts to search diligently for and engage extended family members as children's caregivers. But sometimes the value of family clashes with other fundamental principles of safety or permanence. Social work is much easier when all of these principles align in a single case; how to proceed when some principles can be optimized at the expense of others is much more challenging and is explored in one worker's narrative in Chapter 5.

Along a continuum of care, family care can be characterized at one end of the spectrum, and congregate or group care might be seen at the other. Although congregate care played a large role in child welfare historically, professional sensibilities and legal mandates have changed. Today, most child welfare professionals would argue that *children should be raised in families*. But some children, victims of profound maltreatment, have been deeply traumatized by their experiences in families and struggle with extreme mental health issues that challenge their capacities to live peaceably in any environment. In these circumstances, the aspirations of foundational rights sometimes conflict with the pragmatism of limited resources or the organizational constraints of unbending bureaucracies. Chapter 6 reveals child welfare workers' advocacy efforts as they fight for children's needs for family connections and sometimes for—and sometimes against—the services that group care can provide.

In Chapter 7, we examine the fundamental principle of *permanence—that the caregivers children live with will care for them permanently.* All children deserve a family, and they should know that their family is always there for them. In the United States, we place a great deal of emphasis on securing children's legal permanency either through reunification with a birth parent, adoption, or guardianship. But permanency has many dimensions and families are complex. The child welfare workers portrayed in this chapter reveal the challenges they face securing children's legal rights to permanency at the same time that children experience the essential meaning of a forever family.

These decisions about permanency, safety, and family are complicated and consequential. When issues of race, ethnicity, or immigration status are overlaid onto already complex circumstances, the opportunity for misunderstanding and for misuse of state power is amplified. As described in each chapter, race and ethnicity have played a dominant role in child welfare for generations, sometimes resulting in state underinvolvement, and other times in state overinvolvement in families' lives. The child welfare workers featured in this chapter illustrate the challenges that result when they attempt to *respect a family's cultural heritage* at the same time that a child's safety is in question. If caseworkers make recommendations to separate children and parents, they are exercising an extreme form of state power. When the subjects of these separations are immigrants unfamiliar with US customs or laws, who do not understand or who cannot be understood by agents of the state, their involvement with child welfare agencies may be terrifying. Chapter 8 focuses on the "difference" dimensions of race, ethnicity, or immigration, but all differences in child welfare are important, whether they be related to disabling condition, religion, national origin, sexual orientation, or gender identification. How child welfare workers understand and navigate "difference" with respect and thoughtful consideration is tricky territory.

Finally, the decisions involved in child welfare are weighty. Where will this child live? Can this child live safely with her family? Is this the appropriate permanency decision for this child? These fundamental decisions about the family should be guided by the views of parents and children. As such, the principle that *parents and children (of a certain age and maturity) should have a say in the decisions that affect their lives* is central in this field. But engaging parents in decision making can be hard. Who is the parent? What if two parents disagree? And the degree to which children are engaged agents is in part related to how much information they have about the facts of the case and whether children have the capacity to handle the somber details of their circumstances. Thoughtful child welfare workers are appropriately protective of children who have already experienced trauma. But the dilemmas are more complicated still. Children and parents do not always make decisions in their best interest, and they do not necessarily agree. And separating a parent's or child's wishes from their best interests is another layer of difficulty. Chapter 9 illustrates one worker's efforts to navigate this mine field thoughtfully and the hazards of privileging some interests and views over others.

Child welfare workers are engaged with complicated families. Many of the families served by child welfare agencies are simultaneously assisted by other, complex systems. Nothing about the work is simple. Everything about the work is emotionally charged, much of it is intellectually demanding, and some of it can be morally compromised. Impossible? Perhaps impossible to always get it "right" since the right path—the principled path—means that an equally valued principle will probably be rejected along the way. But imperative because the families at the center of child welfare are fragile, their needs are often significant, and children's protection hangs in the balance. Too often, child welfare is presented to students and the public at large as a straightforward matter of "simply" protecting children. These pages suggest it is anything but that. Chapter 10 shows that the field will be strengthened if that complexity is embraced by practitioners, policymakers, and educators. All professions use principles or a code of ethics to guide their work, and child welfare should be no different. The principles laid out in these pages can be adopted as an articulated guide to practice, but the utility of the principles will only be realized if staff recognize the inherent tensions in child welfare and their role in balancing the competing principles in their everyday work. Child welfare requires deeply thoughtful professionals who want to make a difference in the lives of children and families, and who are ready to tackle the conflicted intellectual spaces that typify the work. The child welfare professionals highlighted in these pages are our exemplars. But we need more of them. Navigating the principles of child protection requires a cadre of professionals ready to take on the challenge, prepared to embrace complexity, and poised to serve thoughtfully.

2

Screening and Assessment

WHOM DO WE SERVE?

IN THE UNITED STATES, child welfare is fairly narrowly defined as a state response to child abuse or neglect. Although many of our European counterparts might have an approach to child welfare that is more broadly conceived, serving children's well-being needs, or responding when children's development or well-being is compromised, the United States has for several decades focused its services on the children and families struggling with maltreatment. These definitional boundaries were established in 1974 when the federal government passed the Child Abuse Prevention and Treatment Act (P.L. 93-247) indicating that—along with many other provisions—funding would be available to those states that established mechanisms for accepting and responding to reports of child abuse.[1]

Today, all states and/or counties have child abuse "hotlines" that community members and mandated reporters can access to log their suspicions about potential maltreatment. The child welfare workers who accept these referrals make challenging decisions, often in the face of insufficient evidence. They collect as much information as they can from the reporting party and based on limited information make a determination about whether the call should be "screened in" or "screened out." In some counties, workers have the benefit of using screening tools that can aid in decision making. These tools have become much more sophisticated with time, helping staff determine whether the call fits within the legal mandate of their state, and whether an in-person response should be immediate.[2] Although the tools are not designed to override staff judgment, they ensure greater equity in decision making between staff, and they provide a helpful aid in decision making, particularly in the imperfect world of child welfare.

Screened-in reports include those where it appears that the situation falls within the mandated authority of the child welfare agency. The collected information is passed along to another child welfare worker who makes contact with the family directly. Screened-out cases include those calls where there is insufficient evidence to respond (e.g., perhaps there is no known name or address where the child may be located); where the child is over the age of 18; where the issue falls more appropriately under the jurisdiction of another agency (e.g., an educational concern referred to a school); or if the matter does not relate to child maltreatment. The caller might be referred to another agency or a community provider, but staff in most child welfare agencies do not provide services to families whose cases have been "screened out." Across the United States, child welfare agencies receive almost 10,000 child maltreatment referrals each day (a rate of 48.8 per 1,000 children). About 6,000 of those calls are screened in, and the remaining 4,000 are screened out.[3]

Hotline screeners are listening for information to help them categorize the type of maltreatment the child may or may not be experiencing and the severity of the concern so that they can better determine whether the agency has authority to become involved, whether the child is safe, and whether the safety threat is imminent. Maltreatment may be in the form of physical abuse, sexual abuse, or emotional abuse or neglect, and within each of these categories, staff are usually provided with definitions that help them determine the nature and the extent of the concern. For example, in California, the Structured Decision Making (SDM) screening tool includes nonaccidental or suspicious injuries under the definitional framework of "physical abuse"; if the child is age 1 year or younger, the hotline screener is instructed to pass the case along for an immediate—meaning 2- to 24-hour (rather than 10-day)—response.[4] Nationally, and in most states, general neglect accounts for the large majority of referrals.[5]

Maltreatment definitions vary across the states. The federal government offers general guidelines for defining the parameters of different types of maltreatment, but state legislatures are free to expand on these or limit their definition. For example, only about two dozen states have laws defining the parameters of child emotional abuse, though all include child physical and sexual abuse in their scope.[6] And states demonstrate variability in the individuals they recognize as mandated reporters. In some states, mandated reporters might include any individual who works with children in a professional capacity. In 18 states, however, all citizens are required to file a report if they suspect child maltreatment.[7] Guidelines for making a report typically suggest a standard of "reasonable suspicion" though studies suggest that interpretations of these recommendations vary dramatically.[8] Even when professionals recognize maltreatment and understand their professional duty, variability in reporting practices is widespread.[9]

In addition to the inconsistencies between states regarding maltreatment definitions and reporters, screening practices vary considerably between and within states. Depending on the jurisdiction, some counties may screen in the large majority of cases, whereas in others, a small proportion of cases are screened in.[10] Organizational [11]and community context[12] appear to exert an influence on the likelihood of a "screen-in" decision, but case factors such as the child's age, the source of the report, a referral history, or whether there are observable injuries, are especially important in determining whether a referral will be screened in by the agency.[13] Although the evidence is mixed, some studies also point to racial disparities between the rates of African American children screened in for investigation compared to White children.[14] These disquieting findings raise ongoing concerns about the role of race in child welfare decision making and should herald a point of caution for screeners.

Some have argued that the system of mandated reporting calls attention to too many children in the United States who will never be served by the child protection system.[15] The argument is persuasive because of the resource expense associated with fielding calls that will never be acted on. Moreover, given the differential reporting rates for low-income children and children of color, widespread mandatory reporting laws may inequitably bring to the state's attention families who might otherwise enjoy greater family privacy. According to one study, almost two fifths of African American children are subjects of a child maltreatment referral by age 7;[16] this is compared to about one fifth of White children, 17% of Hispanic children, and about 7% of Asian children.[17] And some evidence suggests that reporting practices may, in part, reflect racial biases.[18] One study showed that low-income families experiencing common events related to family life such as moving, having a baby, or less common events such as having a child suspended from school are associated with an increased likelihood of being investigated for maltreatment.[19] Other studies have shown that doctors, presented with the same case characteristics, are more likely to assume maltreatment among low-income families and accidental injury among higher income families.[20] Because of the differential reporting practices of mandated and nonmandated reporters based on income and race, our current reporting policies may unfairly target children and families who are not maltreated.

But other evidence indicates that we should be cautious before changing our reporting policies too much. Although mandated reporters could benefit from standardized training to align their practices with a common framework of understanding,[21] the research evidence still shows that many children who are indeed maltreated go unreported. According to the National Incidence Study of Child Abuse and Neglect (NIS-4), the gap between the number of children reported for maltreatment and the number actually maltreated may be substantial.[22]

And the 40% of children who are screened out may, in fact, be experiencing considerable risk. What happens to the child who is not maltreated but whose well-being is seriously compromised? Or the child who is not maltreated but has serious needs that should be addressed? Some evidence suggests that about two fifths of children whose maltreatment referrals are screened out at the hotline are rereferred to CPS within 2 years—surely an indicator of some community member's concern.[23] More troubling still, one study of fatalities among young children found that a report of maltreatment—whether screened in or screened out—was the single most important predictor of death. The author concludes that a referral for maltreatment—at least among young children—"is an independent signal of child risk."[24] Given this somber backdrop, the child welfare worker responsible for screening in or screening out is not only intellectually challenged to make firm recommendations based upon limited information, but she lives in a world of moral ambiguity,[25] where her decision to assess a child out of services often weighs heavily with the knowledge that there is no other government agency obliged to respond.

The debate about overinvolvement versus underinvolvement in family life puts into sharp relief exactly what our child protection system is not: It is not a child welfare system. It does not attend principally to the welfare or developmental needs of children at risk. For young professionals who care about children's well-being and who come to the field of child welfare to make a difference, the realization that the scope of their task is strictly proscribed can be disheartening.

There is no "children's well-being" system in the United States to which child welfare workers can refer children in need. Instead, we have a siloed set of service systems that may or may not be child focused. Children with educational needs are referred to schools; children with health or reproductive concerns are referred to health professionals; homeless children are referred to shelters; children living in bitter or violent marriages or relationships are referred to private therapists; but few of these providers are compelled to serve, many require a fee, and wait times to access services may be days or years.

The US welfare state is referred to as a "residual state," meaning that it attends to individual problems at the margins, or as Duncan Lindsay has indicated: "the residual approach demands that aid should be invoked only after the family is in crisis and other immediate support groups (kin, neighborhood) fail to meet a child's minimal needs."[26] For parents, a residual child welfare state responds to the first principle noted in Chapter 1: *Parents who care for their children safely should be free from government intrusion in their family.* For children, however, the residual state translates into a system designed singularly for youngsters who are identified as maltreated and whose abuse or neglect is severe. For the staff who are the gatekeepers at the front door to this system, their job is complex and nuanced. Closing the door at entry means that children may or may not gain access to any services that might help them with their suffering. Opening the door to let children in could mean any number of things—from an offer of voluntary support to an involuntary placement into foster care. A look at a day in the life of one child welfare worker speaks to the volume of calls; the importance of supervisors who can be a sounding board for talking through the knowns and the unknowns; the ambiguity preceding so many decisions; and the variability of response depending on the worker or the county in which the call is logged.

The "hotline screener" serves as the doorman/woman at the front door of the "house of child protection."[27] She may open the door or shut the door. Some of those choices may be clear and unambiguous. But very likely, at the end of most days, she'll go home wondering whether some of the decisions she made were sound and sufficiently protective of children.

"Children in Need"

I work on the frontlines of child welfare. I'm a **hotline screener** and every day I answer phone calls from mandated reporters and concerned community members. My role is to determine if and how staff in our agency can respond. Each day brings different challenges and issues. Basically, my job entails listening to the information presented and collecting as many specific facts and pieces of identifying information as I can. I utilize the **Structured Decision Making (SDM)** tool to determine if the case includes risk or safety threats to the child and, if it does, the tool helps me determine if our agency needs to respond and how quickly a social worker needs to investigate. Next, I run a child protective services history check on our computer system and then a computerized check to determine if there is any criminal background associated with the caregiver(s) or child. If there is, that helps determine if the case will be assigned as an "**immediate**." In those cases, an **Emergency Response social worker** will be assigned the case and asked to conduct an investigation within 2 hours. Cases that require an investigation but that are not immediate can be assessed at any point within the next 10 days. I write a brief report that I submit to my supervisor and she has the discretion to make changes in the response time I've noted if she believes the SDM was unable to capture all the information presented. On average, I answer 10 to 15 calls a day, though on busier days I might respond to up to 20. Some calls are consultations and others require immediate intervention by child protective services.

It was a pretty typical day. I had calls relating to physical abuse and general neglect. In one case the caller reported that a 6-year-old boy arrived at school with a bruise on the side of his face and what appeared to be finger marks. The boy reported that his mother had slapped him the night before. The boy said that his mother had asked him to clean his room and the boy didn't listen. The case was assigned as an immediate, given that there were marks, bruises, and a clear disclosure.

Later in the morning I received another call from a mother who was in desperate need of housing for herself and her two children. The mother reported that she had been in an abusive relationship, that the man was now incarcerated, and as a result, she and her children were living in a car. She needed services for her family and hoped that our agency could help. But in this situation there was no abuse or neglect being reported, so I had no cause to open a case. Instead, I offered her referrals to shelters, food banks, and agencies that would likely provide the services she needed.

But there were three calls that stayed with me long after I'd left work. They raised questions about how I should or could respond, and they made me wonder how far our obligation extends to care for vulnerable families, or if we sometimes overextend, imposing ourselves on families who can cope without our involvement.

Early in the morning I received a call from a concerned family member who reported that her 17-year-old niece had given birth a few weeks earlier and was now homeless. The 17-year-old would be turning 18 in only 2 weeks, and the caller—who had spent some time in foster care herself—knew that her niece would no longer qualify for child welfare services once she became an adult. The caller explained that her niece had stayed at a shelter for a few nights but was mostly sleeping on park benches. The caller tried to help her niece, but her own living situation was unstable and she was moving out of town herself later that day. She explained that the mother had chosen not to nurse and the baby had an allergy that required a special formula.

The caller had tried to get help from various county agencies. She had also called a different county's child abuse hotline but was told that they couldn't help due to the mother's age.

I found this last comment especially puzzling. Just because the mother's legal status was going to change from child to adult didn't change her circumstances or the vulnerability of the baby. Who was the "client" at the center of our concern? Was it the infant sleeping on park benches at night or the mother? And did homelessness constitute a threat to either child's safety?

I consulted with my supervisor and read over the case notes thoroughly. The computer system confirmed that the caller had contacted another county's child welfare agency and was turned away. The notes read that the mother would be an adult in 2 weeks and it seemed that she could get some help from family members. The previous report had been closed with no investigation and a comment: "Someone is there to help."

In my view, and based on the evidence, family members were no longer available to this mother. Based on the SDM screening, including the vulnerability of the infant and the lack of supportive resources, I was concerned that the risk to the infant was high. I spoke with my supervisor at length and persuaded her to assign an investigator to the case. Later that day, I learned that a fellow social worker had assessed the case and placed the mother and baby in foster care together.

I wonder what would have happened had another screener picked up the phone. It was a call full of complexities. The caller told me that this young, homeless woman was abandoned by her own mother years ago and had largely taken care of herself for much of her life. Were we going to do the same? At 2 weeks from her 18th birthday a screener in another county thought "Let's have that be someone else's problem." In my view, the risk to both of these children was high and required our full attention.

As soon as I'd moved that referral off my desk, a new call came in concerning a 6-year-old boy who was having "accidents" at school, soiling his pants. This time, the caller was a mandated reporter who was somewhat familiar with the family's circumstances. She knew that the boy's sister had been sexually abused about a year earlier when she lived in her mother's home. The caller was unclear about the details, but she knew that Child Protective Services was involved and that the sister had been removed from the home. The caller explained that the boy's behaviors started last year, around the time the allegations of sexual abuse had emerged.

The caller told me that so far this year, the boy had about six accidents. Each time, the school called the boy's mother and she came to the school to pick him up. I asked the caller if the boy's mother had been given any guidance to take him to his pediatrician, and she admitted that the issue had not been raised with the mother. I advised that the mandated reporter might want to speak to the mother about this and rule out a medical condition; it was clear the boy needed further assessment by a medical specialist.

After the call, I felt uneasy. I reviewed what I knew about the case. In the prior year, we'd substantiated allegations of sexual abuse toward the boy's sister. The perpetrator was the mother's cousin, who, at that time, lived in the home. When we got involved, the cousin moved out of the home.

Could the boy's behavior signal that he, too, had been sexually abused? If the cousin had returned to the home, could he now be perpetrating sexual abuse with the boy? I met with my supervisor and we discussed the case at length. The facts presented were not enough to meet the standards of child abuse or neglect. Although there was an important history with this family, none of the information provided by the caller warranted a CPS response. Ultimately, we decided not to assign the case for investigation. The case left me wondering if the response from the child protective agency was adequate. Was this call a signal of concern? Shouldn't there be a response from someone to determine if this family needed help? But under the narrow definition of what constitutes maltreatment, and CPS's jurisdiction to only respond to child abuse or neglect (rather than a range of other childhood concerns), this was a stretch. There were no disclosures, medical conditions had not been ruled out, and assumptions about sexual abuse based on previous circumstances with a different family member pushed us to close the case.

I took other calls throughout the day where my decisions were less ambiguous. Late in the afternoon, however, another call came in that made me question again whether our agency sometimes erred on the side of underinvolvement in families' lives. The caller was a family member who was concerned about a 1-year-old baby girl. The girl's mother lived with her boyfriend (not the father of the child) and the boyfriend's mother. According to the caller, the mother used marijuana and possibly cocaine and left the baby in the care of the boyfriend's mother who was a regular cocaine user. The caller had witnessed the mother using drugs and knew that the mother's boyfriend both used and sold cocaine from their home. The caller told me that she'd seen the baby the previous day and that the baby was not wearing shoes or a jacket, in spite of the cold weather. Finally, the caller said that the mother and her siblings had spent some of their childhood in foster care and the caller knew that—in better moments—the mother did not want to see her baby experience the same fate.

I knew that this was a case that merited an investigation, but I wasn't sure about the best course of action. Should I assign it as an "immediate response"? Or could we wait? Could I assign it as a "10-day referral," giving the assigned social worker a bit of breathing room, but potentially raising the risk to the child? Given the age of the baby, I was concerned that she could be in danger. After reviewing the case with my supervisor, however, we determined that a 10-day response would be sufficient. The caller had not witnessed the caregiver under the influence while caring for the baby, so her immediate risk was not necessarily at stake.

It isn't always clear how I should make decisions in this work. Even risk assessment tools, which I rely on a lot in my work, are a guide, not a crystal ball. If we'd assigned this case to an immediate response, we might have been encroaching on the privacy of this family and over-intruding, given the facts available. On the other hand, if the social worker assigned to the case waited a week or ten days, something could have happened to the baby—surely an indicator that we were underinvolved in protecting the child.

My day reminded me that even if we want to think of ourselves as a child welfare agency, we're really a child protection agency. Sometimes families have significant needs for help, but if their concerns aren't about child maltreatment, we have to send them elsewhere. **Differential response**, a service designed for families with more moderate rather than severe concerns, is a very limited resource in my county and the wait list to get services is long. And when it *is* maltreatment, or I *think*

> what I hear on the phone is maltreatment, there's so much I don't know. Callers usually have only partial information to provide to me, regardless of how many questions I ask. I can only hope that the next worker who takes the case can determine the family's needs and activate services to keep the child safe.
>
> *Maria Burch*

Is the state overinvolved in the lives of families? Is it underinvolved? In which of these circumstances were the children safe enough that their families could have or should have been free from government involvement? A mother who slaps her 6-year-old during a family dispute probably needs assistance learning new strategies to discipline her child. In such a situation, the system probably didn't "underrespond" by screening in the call. However, the screener who passed this referral on to an investigating worker never found out what actually happened—whether the response was appropriate to the need. Did the mother receive an offer of support to participate in voluntary services? Did she accept or spurn such an offer? Or was she pulled into the court-mandated side of the child welfare system? And did her child remain at home with her? What additional issues or concerns were or were not revealed during the course of the investigation? Did the next worker determine that the slap was a rare impulse or a signal of ongoing physical abuse? What was determined about the safety of this child? These are the questions the child welfare worker ponders every day, unaware—except in a few cases—of what actually happens to all of the families who have been made eligible for a system response.

The child welfare worker's next caller—a mother who is desperate for housing for her family—tugs at her conscience. The child was probably safe. As such, there was no need for the government's intrusion. But the family's need was nonetheless great and the mother *asked* for the government's help. The child welfare worker's response—offers of phone numbers and referrals to other agencies (with no obligation to respond)—may reflect underinvolvement in the life of that family, but it reflected actions consonant with the first principle of child welfare. It also reflects the limits of a child protection system that is not responsible for ensuring children's well-being and not obligated to respond to family poverty. Again, the uncertainty is pressing. This worker never learns the fate of the family she is mandated to turn away.

A 17-year-old homeless girl with a neonate surely has a need for help, but the hotline screener in the first county assessed her need as outside the scope of child welfare (i.e., the state should not intrude), whereas the screener highlighted here stretched the definition of maltreatment in order to make her eligible for further assessment (i.e., the state should be involved). Again, the role of poverty loomed large in shaping this young family's vulnerability, but in order to open the door to a child welfare response, the child welfare worker had to label the teenager's actions maltreatment. In fact, even if this teenager was attempting to raise her baby safely, this worker interpreted her living situation as putting the infant at risk.

What about the 6-year-old boy with a family history relating to maltreatment and worrisome accidents in school? In our siloed system of response and services, his needs were passed over to medical professionals. Again, there are no assurances that the boy received any help at all. The teacher, confident that she had extended herself to the limits of the law by making a child maltreatment referral, may not have done anything further, in spite of this worker's advice. And even if the teacher encouraged the boy's mother to contact his medical doctor, we have no assurance that such a contact was ever made. When a child welfare agency does not accept responsibility for a child's well-being, referrals to other individuals or other agencies guarantee nothing.

Finally, the 1-year-old was screened in for further evaluation (i.e., the safety of the child required government intrusion), but if something serious happened to the baby before a child welfare worker could show up at her door, the hotline screener's judgement would have been called into question and the state would have been vilified for underinvolvement.

Setting the threshold for involvement high (i.e., severe) and narrow (i.e., child maltreatment) means that some families with important needs will not be served by the child welfare system. Whether this system is "right" or "good" are different questions. The child welfare worker in this instance was assiduously trying to simply determine eligibility based upon the principles and the laws that shape this field. For the children who were turned away, family, friends, and other systems may have stepped in to respond to their needs. But maybe not. And for the children who were made eligible for child welfare, this worker hopes that in partnership with parents, they were also made safe.

3

Are They Safe (Enough)?

CHILDREN IN the United States do not fare well compared to children in many other Western industrialized nations. UNICEF has conducted three assessments over the past decade to examine the world's children residing in "rich nations." Their index of child well-being targets five dimensions, including children's material well-being, health and safety, education, behavior and risk, and housing and environment.[1] Among the 29 countries studied, the United States ranks 26th; only children in Lithuania, Latvia, and Romania are worse off.

How do we make sense of our nation as the "greatest country on Earth"[2] juxtaposed with these findings? What are the ingredients of success that our European and other neighbors employ that set us apart? In Finland, children are assessed to determine their need, and a range of services are offered to help parents meet children's needs.[3] In Belgium, maltreatment is not separated out from the other domains of children's well-being, and an array of comprehensive policies and programs are designed to support children's welfare and parents' capacities.[4] If a child's well-being needs are compromised, these and other European countries' child welfare systems offer an array of services, from day care to homemaker services, transportation to income support, therapeutic services to job training. The framework for state involvement in these and many other countries rests on child well-being or a "best interests of the child" standard.[5] Eligibility to receive services is deep and wide—children can be referred for a child welfare service based on a large range of needs or concerns. These family-service-oriented systems[6] aim to promote a healthy childhood in general. In addition to protecting children from harm, they seek to prevent harm altogether, with the expectation that a framework of prevention will reduce the likelihood that family difficulties will escalate.[7]

The United States, in contrast, does not seek to make children eligible for inclusion in the child protection system based upon their needs or upon their welfare but instead focuses resources on assessing children's eligibility based upon each state's definition of child maltreatment. Eligibility for services tapers further as child welfare workers assess whether the child is safe or at risk of harm. As detailed in Chapter 2, the circumstances of the report may suggest an urgent response—an in-home assessment within 24 hours in most states—or a response within several days. Child welfare workers interview the child (depending on age), the caregiver, and others who may be knowledgeable about the family's circumstances in order to determine whether the report can be substantiated, meaning that there is sufficient harm (or risk of harm) to the child to constitute child maltreatment; and that there is sufficient evidence to support the claim of maltreatment.[8] Depending on the state, staff then have several days to a month to make these determinations. Nationwide, an astonishing 37% of children are investigated for child maltreatment before their 18th birthday. We see racial differences persist, and by age 18, over half of African American children (53%) are investigated for child abuse or neglect.[9]

Child welfare workers employed to investigate allegations of maltreatment are laser focused on the safety of the child. Safety, of course, is a very slim interpretation of child welfare. Think about what it means to be safe from harm versus well or thriving. Under a safety principle, any number of untoward events might happen to a child, possibly seriously compromising the child's well-being, but unless posing a threat to a child's safety, these would not warrant a state response.

When did safety become the guiding principle in child welfare? And is that principle broad enough to capture children's needs? The Adoption and Safe Families Act of 1997 made clear that the child's health and safety are "paramount" concerns in child welfare.[10] The policy was enacted, in part, as a correction to a perceived practice that favored keeping children with parents at any cost. Whether these concerns were grounded in reality will never be known; there are no systematic data describing staff who compromised children's safety in order to promote the preservation of an intact family. But news headlines at the time told a story of staff who sometimes erred by privileging the interests of family stability over the safety interests of the child.[11] This narrative helped to propel Congressional leaders to reexamine the system as a whole.

Today, "safety-organized practice" serves as the framework that characterizes public child welfare workers' responses to needy families.[12] The model encourages staff to create a "safety plan," developed in partnership with parents, their extended family members, the youth, and other supportive adults in the context of a team meeting. The safety plan serves as a kind of informal contract between the agency and the family. The purpose is to identify the family and friends who will rally to help parents and who will offer a protective circle around the child, in addition to identifying the behaviors parents engage in that result in risks to the child that need to be avoided. Child welfare workers and family members can monitor the safety plan for compliance, but caseworkers also serve to coach, support, and encourage parents to draw on their strengths in an effort to fulfill the plan's goals and to parent their child safely. Team decision making represents positive social work values such as consumer participation and community inclusion; it is also favorably evaluated by parent participants who generally feel as though they were authentically engaged in decision making regarding their families' needs.[13]

Safety planning rests on the notion that parents can care for their children with support from family and friends, referrals to services for which they're responsible for accessing, and minimal government intrusion. Safety planning represents the ultimate manifestation of the residual state. In a residual welfare state that has few services to offer, better to give families the tools to recognize unsafe behaviors and to rely on themselves. Safety planning expresses the principle that *children should be safe*, but it does so as a minimal standard of childhood. The unanswered question remains: Is safety enough?

Should our framework be different? Would children's well-being be better secured if we relied upon a "best interests" standard instead of a safety standard? Perhaps, but it depends on the "service" offered after the signal for eligibility has been lit. When state intervention is viewed as helpful and supportive, opening the door to include many children with different types of problems may be warranted—indeed, beneficial. In the Nordic countries, it appears that public confidence in the services offered by the child welfare system is indeed higher than it is in the United States.[14]

However, the US safety net is, by many measures, rather more porous than what is found in the Nordic countries. Here, parental leave, day care, income support, and other services are more restricted in availability, time limited, conditionally provided, or costly. The services we have available to help families are mixed and highly dependent upon the communities in which families live. If the United States were to use a "best interests" standard rather than a "safety" standard, many more children would come to the attention of child welfare agencies. But would we have services available to help them? And would the state be perceived as a helpful and supportive entity or as intrusive and punitive? In other words, depending upon what the state has to offer families and whether that offer is perceived as supportive or punitive drives, in part, how narrowly or broadly we define who we should serve.

All this is to say that we could do so much more to help children and families do better than "safety," but we've made public policy choices that limit the government's involvement to only the extreme ends of risk. As a result, the children who typically are served by child welfare agencies come from families who have struggled to raise their children largely on their own; they have made grievous errors, used extremely poor judgement, made priorities other than their children, or been caught up in powerful forces beyond their control (namely substance abuse) that have clouded their decision making. These are the families who remain clients of the child welfare system, and their plight deserves considerable attention from staff whose compassion and intelligence helps them navigate relationships where they may not be wanted, where parents may feel wary of their intentions, and where feelings of vulnerability and hostility may be high.

The children's circumstances that come to the attention of child welfare workers might lead some to feel blame or anger toward parents for their actions. But parents in the United States largely raise their children on their own in this complex world, absent a framework of government support. Child welfare workers who interact with these parents do best when they approach families with humility and grace.

"Josiah and Jaden"

It was a typical foggy morning in the Bay Area. My work cell phone rang just as I was dropping off my son at day care. With my toddler in my arms, I answered. It was my supervisor on the line informing me that we had an emergency call. There was a **tox-positive** baby at the local hospital. Although this was an **immediate referral**—meaning I needed to see the baby within the next 2 hours—the frequency of scenarios such as this no longer spiked my adrenaline. I drove the rest of the way to work, grumbling about getting a call before I was even "on the clock," and thinking about the information I would need to collect in order to keep this newborn safe.

Over the past several years, I've seen child welfare agencies change their approach to **pos-tox** babies. I remember one county agency that used to remove every newborn exposed to illegal substances and ask questions later. The state legislature also developed a bypass law where the court can "bypass" the offer of reunification services to the parent if he or she has had previous failed attempts to reunite after giving birth to a pos-tox newborn. Today, the state policy is more clear about **prenatal substance abuse**; removal is only warranted under certain specified conditions—in particular, if it's expected the parent will continue to use after taking the baby home, and if the parent is unwilling or unable to care for the infant after discharge. It's difficult to determine risk while the mom and baby are still at the hospital; these are questions I need to address through a close examination of the environment the child will be dependent on. In essence, the safety threat is gone after the baby is born; the baby is no longer ingesting substances that can harm him or her. So my role is to assess risk.

I arrived at the office, and my supervisor handed me the **screener narrative** while she explained the situation: The family included a father and mother, a 1-year-old baby, and a newborn. According to the hotline document, the mother claimed she didn't know she was pregnant until a few weeks ago. She did not have prenatal care and reported that she smoked some marijuana when her stomach hurt and didn't know there was "meth" in it. A few hours after smoking, she was in labor and gave birth after 38 weeks' gestation. Both the newborn and the mother tested positive for methamphetamine. There was no prior CPS involvement.

My supervisor reminded me of the usual list of assessment tasks as I collected keys to a county car: Determine the vulnerability of the infant, assess the 1-year-old, get a report from the father, assess the protective and supportive factors of extended family, and so on. As I gathered myself for the job ahead, I called the hospital to get more details and scribble down the baby's weight, health, and delivery details. The hospital social worker told me that the mother was very good with the newborn, responding to the baby's needs, was affectionate, wanted to breast feed; she had been "**pumping and dumping**" until she could pass a drug test. She added that the father had been coming in with their older child and the child appeared well cared for, content, and not at all fearful of either parent. She said that members of the extended family had also been around, and the mother had not yet told them about the positive drug test. I called the local Police Department to discuss the plan of response with one of the detectives. He told me they had not yet placed the baby on a **hold**, but that if I needed him to do so, he would. He said he had confidence in me and would wait to hear from me with my report. This, of course, was good news. It meant that he wouldn't accompany me to the hospital. No woman wants a police officer staring down at her just after having a baby.

In my county, every baby born tox positive with an illegal substance becomes an immediate response. We're encouraged to open a voluntary case, at minimum, to solidify the family's chances of increasing safety and reducing or even eliminating risk to the child. But sometimes the risk to the child may be too great and mandatory services may be required. In order to get the court involved, the social worker's investigation—my investigation—is the key evidence outside the positive drug test.

At the hospital, I talked with the medical social worker first. She said that the mother knew a child maltreatment report had been filed and she was expecting me. She said that the infant was holding his original birth weight and although he did not suckle during the first few hours, he now seemed interested and had no other signs of withdrawal. The mother, Ruby, told her that she had been using off and on for the last few years, that she only used with friends on the weekends, and that she'd stopped using a month ago when she found out she was pregnant. Ruby also said that her boyfriend, Ray—the baby's father—didn't use drugs. Her first baby, Jaden, she said, was not born with drugs in his system.

I've worked with the medical social worker for a long time, and I trust her. She has years of experience, deep relationships with the community, and her skill at building rapport and assessing family members is strong. I asked for her views about the family. She thought Ruby was minimizing the extent of her use out of fear that CPS might take the baby. Instead, she believed the mother and the father were probably using regularly. She said Ruby slept for many hours after the birth—much more than is typical—and she thought she was probably detoxing off of meth. In spite of their drug use, she thought the parents were young and seemed reasonably concerned. She thought they would probably work with me and wouldn't resist my efforts to help.

The medical social worker invited me in to see the baby and the mother. Ruby had in her arms a perfect baby boy whom she introduced as Josiah. I introduced myself and asked if she knew why I was there. She said it was because of the drugs. I asked all about her pregnancy and birth, and she was open and talkative, telling me about the previous night's labor and delivery. She told me she'd been using since before she had her first child and that she only used irregularly with friends. I tried to impress on her the importance of telling me the truth so that I could arrange for the most appropriate help for her family. She continued smiling and confirmed everything she'd said.

Ray joined us shortly thereafter, and I asked that he meet with me in an empty room next door. I introduced myself and told him why I was there. When I asked him to tell me more about their situation, he told me everything. Frankly, I was surprised by his candor. He told me that he and Ruby were using regularly. He'd tried to make Ruby stop after they found out about the baby—they both did for a few days—but she begged him to find more drugs.

In my career as a social worker, I've heard so many excuses for positive test results. Common among these are the following: I was in a car when others were smoking; I smoked a joint and didn't know something was in it; I only used this one time. Often the parents have already made a plan about what they'll say to me. And usually, they deny or minimize their addiction. In this case, I was so grateful that the family's real story came so quickly.

Ray and I joined Ruby in her room again and we talked together. Ruby let me hold Josiah, and I was touched by how cute and healthy he appeared. I reminded them that they had a perfect baby who was vulnerable and completely dependent on them. I reassured them that my goal was to keep their family together, as long as they could raise their children safely. I then thanked Ray for his honesty about their drug use, and I complimented Ruby on her attentiveness to her infant's needs. I wanted them to know that I saw many strengths in their family. But I also expressed my concerns and impressed on them the seriousness of their circumstances. I asked whether they wanted to get clean, and they both told me enthusiastically that they would do whatever it takes.

I called my supervisor as I was leaving the hospital. Summarizing what I knew, so far, I told her that the parents were young, that they'd been using methamphetamines for about 2 years, and that more recently they'd used almost daily. I explained that the infant had not shown signs of withdrawal, appeared healthy according to the medical professionals, and was showing typical infant behaviors. Although the mother initially minimized her drug use, the father seemed to be very honest about the extent of their addiction. They both expressed their willingness to seek out treatment in the next 24 hours and to submit to drug testing. I'd given them the phone number to the substance abuse agency, where they would go to get tested, and gave them other substance abuse referrals with contact phone numbers so that they could enroll in a treatment program. My supervisor asked that I visit the parents' home and develop a safety plan with the maternal grandparents. She told me that based on what she'd heard so far, she was going to suggest that I recommend court-ordered **Family Maintenance**, due to the parents' continued use during the mother's pregnancy.

I arrived at Ruby and Ray's home, a one-bedroom apartment adjoining the main house where the maternal grandparents lived. I introduced myself and gently explained the reason for my visit. The tears started to flow. The grandmother, full of worry and feeling helpless, told me that she suspected that her daughter was using. We talked at length about the need to secure the children's safety and for a plan that involved family members always caring for, or co-caring for the infant, until Ruby and Ray could verify their sobriety. They agreed to take shifts so that someone would always be with both children. They also offered the names of other extended relatives and the paternal grandparents, who were involved with Jaden's care.

Jaden, previously sleeping, woke from his nap, and the grandmother brought him in to join us. He fell into his father's arms, and I watched the sweet tenderness of their relationship. Ray told me all about his son's development—how he was almost walking, how he cruised around the couch for hours, and how he was drinking formula but had graduated to a sippy cup. He was clearly attentive to his son's needs and showed me that he knew his son well. He told me that when he and his girlfriend used, they always left Jaden with others. They had tried to stop previously but had failed. This time, he assured me, he was committed to succeed and had already made an appointment for the following day for assessment and treatment. Ray told me, several times, that he loved his boys and would do anything to keep them.

Our safety plan drew on the strengths of this family; the grandparents were attentive and engaged. The father clearly loved and was attached to his young son and infant, and he showed a strong commitment to engage in treatment. The safety plan included drug assessment, treatment, and testing. The parents would bring another family member with them when attending doctor appointments, shopping, or other activities outside the home with the children. I told them that I would recommend mandatory in-home services at the initial court hearing. I was concerned about the power of the parents' addiction, the fragile age of the children, and the high risk of relapse and continued substance abuse that reduced their parenting capacities. I considered a recommendation of voluntary services, but given the age of the two children, I thought it prudent to err on the side of caution.

Before leaving their home, we made arrangements for a **team decision meeting** (TDM) to take place at the hospital the next day. The meeting accomplished exactly what I'd hoped for. Ruby and Ray said how sincerely they loved their children. They showed tremendous remorse for their mistakes and never made excuses for their behaviors. The extended relatives made their commitments, too. The extended family made it clear to the parents that they loved them, but they would ultimately protect the children if their safety were at stake. All members of the TDM agreed with the plan.

My role in the case was over and it was time to pass the family along to the next social worker who would follow their circumstances through the initial court hearings. After that, another social worker would likely take the case while the family was served in court-ordered Family Maintenance.

I felt pretty good about my work with Ruby and her family. I believe that my approach, from the very beginning, helped Ruby and Ray remain calm, and my honesty was a vehicle for them to envision hope. If I had come into the hospital room threatening or admonishing ("I can take your children if you don't get clean" or " If you can't stop using, you will lose your baby"), then I believe I would have extinguished their motivation to try. Instead, they fought for their children, addressed their drug problem, and moved on with their lives.

Ruby, Ray, and their children taught me so much about risk and safety; how they're not the same thing and that my work is all about balancing both. The main safety threat—that Josiah was ingesting illegal substances—was eliminated once he was born. So I was never really concerned about the safety of the infant or little Jaden. But their risk made me apprehensive. On the one hand, the risk factors in this family were low: the parents were willing to access treatment and to test; they had a large extended family willing to help and supervise the children; they were assertive about seeking support for their addiction early on; and their older child was obviously well cared for. But low risk does not equate with no risk, and this family was risky nonetheless. The parents' recent acceleration in drug use, Ruby's initial dishonesty, her lack of prenatal care, and her inability to stop using despite trying during the pregnancy all raised important concerns.

Without our agency's support and supervision, I don't know if Ruby and Ray would have made it. I don't know if they would have been able to parent their young children safely. I don't know if their extended family members would have felt sufficiently emboldened to get involved and to help raise the little boys. And I don't know if the considerable risk to the boys would have turned into serious safety threats. It's that uncertainty that's a big part of this job. It helped when, about a year later, Ruby called me. She called to say that she and Ray were clean and their case had been dismissed. But most of all, she called to offer her thanks.

Leslie Laughlin

Josiah and Jaden were safe, yet as this child welfare worker recounts, their risk of harm, coupled with their age and vulnerability, required a service response. Some states, acting on the principle that the government has an interest in protecting the safety of the unborn child, have developed policies that mandate a child welfare response at the birth of a substance exposed newborn.[15] In California, substance exposure usually elicits a call to the hotline, but as this child welfare worker shows, a full assessment of the child's circumstances is required to determine the child's safety and risk of harm in order to substantiate a report and recommend involuntary services.

The child welfare worker handling Ruby and Ray's case had to consider her service options in light of the fundamental principles we have recounted previously. Should these parents be free of government intrusion if their children were safe? And were these children safe? Should she offer voluntary services, given the parents' compliance and their supportive family network? Or were involuntary services warranted?

In the end, she recommended mandatory drug treatment, given the strength of the parents' addiction, the age of the children, and the significant risk of harm associated with their continued drug use. Josiah and Jaden remained in their home while the parents made substantial changes to their lifestyle and behaviors, surrounded by a supportive, extended family. The children were not placed in foster care.

For some years, the main "service" that child welfare agencies had to offer families was foster care—an intervention that is intrusive, sometimes coercive, and often perceived as punitive. Child welfare agencies were long criticized for too often using foster care as their primary "tool" to respond to children's safety needs. In fact, when foster care—which requires separating a child from his or her parent—is used as the main strategy for helping families, it might seem appropriate to keep eligibility for services rather narrow so that fewer families are subject to such a contested intervention.

But agencies are increasingly relying on a range of service responses to families, sometimes using foster care as the intervention tool, sometimes using mandatory in-home services, and sometimes referring families to voluntary in-home services with community agency providers. The latter, variously referred to as Differential or Alternative Response, has the potential to offer families a wider selection of supportive services customized to their individual concerns.

The theory behind Differential Response (DR), that families have differentiated needs and that lower risk families can benefit from voluntary services provided by local, nonprofit agencies,[16] is highly attractive and speaks to a child welfare system redesign that aspires to the family-service systems of Europe, described previously. Differential Response, however, is highly uneven across the United States and is therefore difficult to describe as a model. Critiques of DR have been especially pronounced when it appears that the approach withdraws resources from the few families who would otherwise be triaged into conventional child welfare services, and where risk of harm to children is too high. When especially challenged families are sorted into differentiated systems, questions arise about whether child welfare analytics are sufficiently sophisticated to differentiate family need and, thus, whether children's concerns are sufficiently addressed.[17] As resources expand so that families who would have otherwise been turned away from child welfare are offered supports, DR finds favor with many in the child welfare community.[18]

The signature problem with voluntary DR services, of course, is that they're voluntary. Parents who would prefer to decline the services are not compelled to do otherwise. Although DR is attractive for its "softer" approach with families (for example, several authors who write about DR characterize the approach to families as "engaging the parents" rather than "determining findings" or that the approach "assesses families' needs" rather than "investigating the allegation"),[19] this ostensibly gentler approach does not appear to change parents' enthusiasm for engaging in services. In one study, only about one third of families who were offered DR said "yes" to accepting services.[20]

Shunning foster care as too intrusive, and recognizing the limitations of voluntary DR for families who are struggling to raise their kids, child welfare workers are often left with few options: They can recommend mandatory in-home services, such as those required of Ruby and Ray, or they can make a safety plan, close the case, and walk away. Significant evidence suggests that in-home child welfare services are limited in many jurisdictions, and that families often receive little from the child welfare agency.[21] This is the great conundrum in child welfare, as we see in this caseworker's experience:

"Bill and Jane's Family"

I work in a county near the "Emerald Triangle," comprised of three counties in Northern California that, together, constitute the largest cannabis-producing region in the United States, and possibly in the world. While in the past, agriculture in my county referred primarily to grape, vegetable, and wheat production, the climate, plentiful water supply, and relatively long growing season here have ushered in a creep of the Emerald Triangle. As cannabis production and distribution have sidled in, referrals alleging child neglect secondary to cannabis operations have steadily increased. By October of 2014, more than half of the referrals I was assigned to investigate each week included allegations related to parents using, growing, selling, or providing their (teenage) children with marijuana.

I was hired almost two decades ago as a social worker at about the same time that California legalized medical marijuana.[22] I came to my new job with no training or experience with respect to marijuana in a child protection context. I had no idea of the challenges, personally and professionally, that I would face in assessing risk to children in homes where marijuana was being used, cultivated, and sometimes sold and distributed by their parents.

It was against this backdrop that I sat in my county-issued car one afternoon. I was waiting for a law enforcement officer for civil standby to assist me in investigating a referral. Although the referral came in at 10:30 a.m., my supervisor handed it to me at 3:00 p.m., with instructions that I needed to respond immediately, just as darkness approached and my shift was scheduled to end. It was my second referral of the day, and it came at the end of a busy week in which I had worked late into the evening two of the three past days. I was tired, the agency was short staffed, and although **immediate response** referrals were often handled in pairs, I was alone because there were no other staff available.

I hoped that there would be a quick resolution, or that the referral had been made in an excess of caution, but the high canopy of lush marijuana plants I observed extending over the six-foot residential fence made an easy in-and-out seem unlikely. The reporting party had provided photos, printed from a public Facebook page, showing both the forest of marijuana I was now observing and the house number painted in black and white on the curb. To me, and to the supervisor assigning the referral for investigation, this indicated that the growers, identified in the referral as the mother of a young child and her boyfriend, were not being appropriately cautious about the safety of their family, as an easy search on Google Maps could pinpoint the exact location of this urban grow. What would happen next certainly reinforced this perspective.

Waiting for law enforcement officers is an unpleasant part of every **Emergency Response** social worker's day. Calls for civil standby are a low priority for law enforcement, and on this day, I knew I would be waiting, as I had called for assistance at 3:00 p.m., right at shift change. Waiting until after shift change to call would guarantee that I would be walking into a home in the dark. If the call did not go well and I could not engage the parents in cooperatively developing a safety plan for the night, that too would bring more complications. If I were to determine that there was an imminent risk to a child, I wouldn't be able to leave the home, and if the parents didn't agree with my assessment of risk, removal without their consent would be especially hard after hours. I've had to track down judges in fitness centers and restaurants to get their signature on a warrant to remove a child; nothing about it is simple.

That afternoon, I chose wrong; I should have waited to make the call. As I sat in my car one house down, waiting for law enforcement, the mother and her boyfriend rushed from the house, running at my car and yelling; the boyfriend had something in his hands that I could not clearly see. Mistakenly, they thought I was there to rob them. No university class teaches you what to do in this situation or how to override the adrenaline rush. Workers have to rely on their own life and work experiences, along with common sense, to guide their responses and to stay safe. I slowly opened the car door, keeping my hands visible, and loudly identified myself as "CPS!" I stood there, using the car door as a shield between me and the angry adults, and made visible my county badge. As they reached me, the boyfriend dropped the golf club to his side, and both slowed to a trot, appearing less agitated. Gesturing to the clearly visible plants, I explained to the mother, in my friendliest voice, that concern had been expressed about the large marijuana grow on her property and the possibility that its presence was compromising the welfare of her young child. Both the mother and her boyfriend resumed yelling and berating me, and I instantly regretted my approach, which had worked well in a similar situation earlier in the week.

The two homes I'd visited that week, both regarding allegations of neglect relating to marijuana, were almost identical: Both were on well-travelled suburban streets with a leafy green canopy visible over the fence and a smell that even from 10 yards clung to your clothing and hair. Inside, there were similarities as well: extra sleeping areas for a mobile workforce of trimmers and security; ammunition left out on the kitchen table, an open space for the child and friends to play situated among the many rows of healthy, fragrant plants.

But in every other way, the two situations differed. In the first home, I encountered the parent that every social worker hopes to meet—polite, open, and responsive to concerns about her child's welfare. She embodied the reasons that drew me to this field: I'd imagined a world in which parents and social workers came together, cooperatively addressing brief failings in discipline or neglect in the face of an absence of needed resources related to social inequalities. The mother in the previous incident listened to my list of concerns that posed a safety risk to her child: the largely unknown backgrounds of transient trimmers, accidents involving children and accessible firearms, the possibility of federal or local agents raiding the grow, and the very real danger of robberies when plants were at harvest capacity, as they soon would be. She responded with her intent to immediately move herself and her child out of their home temporarily. She thanked me for the conversation and engaged in a thoughtful and insightful reflection of how easy it could be to overlook risks to a child's emotional development and well-being while espousing the positive economic aspects of marijuana legalization.

It was clear that my current referral was not going to resolve so easily. The mother, Jane, and her boyfriend, Bill, were wedded to an interpretation that I was "harassing" them, when their business was "perfectly legal." The more I tried to elicit their cooperation, the more entrenched their position became. They asked if I had a warrant to come inside, and I let them know that I did not. I explained that I could get one, and carefully and calmly detailed the process to them. After hearing my explanation, they agreed to let me into the home to see the conditions and to verify the safety of their child. Law enforcement had not yet arrived, but as the parents were not behaving in a threatening manner, I decided to proceed without an officer. I explained to Jane, as we walked to the front door, that I had asked law enforcement to accompany me, and that an officer would likely be arriving shortly. She shrugged, and said, indifferently, "It won't be the first time they've been here." Jane did not elaborate, and I was momentarily distracted by a large Rottweiler throwing himself against the metal screen door. Behind the dog, a toddler was standing in the hallway. Bill assured me that the dog was "friendly," but I have a healthy fear of guard dogs and remained nervous as we went inside.

Inside the home, the marijuana smell, which had been pungent outside, was now overpowering. My eyes began to itch and redden, and I saw that the toddler also had red, running eyes. Through the living room sliding glass door, a forest of marijuana plants was visible. On a low patio table was an open black gun case, with a clearly visible shotgun inside. Jane volunteered that the gun belonged to her and that she had legally purchased it at the local sporting goods store. She noted that it was loaded, to prevent thefts from occurring in the "garden." When I inquired about a trigger lock, Bill commented that it would be "hard to get to it fast if the trigger was locked!"

In the house, a locked garage had plants hanging from the ceiling to dry, and the remnants of a winter indoor grow were evident, indicating year-round operation. Electrical extension cords dangled from the garage ceiling, and florescent lighting had been installed throughout. Bongs and pipes littered the surfaces, as did jars of bud (the resin-secreting flowers of the female plant) and open dishes of shake (loose leftover marijuana, mostly stems and seeds).

I was well acquainted with the indicia associated with marijuana cultivation and concentrated cannabis production, and I did not miss many details when responding to referrals involving marijuana. My family had deep ties to the marijuana growing industry. I dreaded the summers of my childhood when we would visit my aunt and all of us—siblings, cousins, parents, aunts, and uncles—worked on my aunt's grows, irrigating, trimming, and generally making ourselves useful. There was much to fear in that environment; I was scared of the helicopters that flew overhead, my aunt's volatile behavior, the adult men with lowered inhibitions and poor personal boundaries, the dogs that roamed free, the ready cash changing hands. I understood that our activities were "secret" and the adults in our lives required silence when in situations involving authority. I wondered if my family would be taken to jail if the police came, or shot and killed if robbers came. There was no one to ask and no safe adult with whom to confide my fears.

Some argue that the marijuana industry has no real casualties,[23] but we probably owe it to children to keep the question open. What we know is that sometimes things end badly. I lost a family member to death because of the industry, so perhaps I'm naturally wary. The loaded, accessible gun, the various electrical extension cords, and the "staff" coming and going from this house all made me pause to think about the risks to these young children.

A police officer knocking at the door interrupted my thoughts. Jane and Bill invited him in, and he took a cursory look around, stating that "it looked like everything was legal." He told Jane to lock the rifle case with a padlock, which she did. He instructed her to "keep kids out of the garage," and told Jane and Bill that having such a visible grow was risking robbery. He provided them with some anecdotal evidence of how common marijuana robberies were this time of year, viewed the medical marijuana licenses posted on the garage wall, wished me luck, and hastily left after having determined to his satisfaction that everyone in the home, including me, was safe.

Here is the place I pause. What should I have done? Was everything, in fact, "legal?" Assessing what constitutes a "legal" grow in my county is painstaking and complex, and falls far outside the purview of child welfare assessment. Determining whether or not a grow is legal, by state and local standards, is tasked solely to law enforcement, and the thoroughness of assessment varies from officer to officer. This officer's lackadaisical stance was not uncommon, a product of a tolerant local culture, combined with a history of frustration with unaligned decision making between law enforcement and the district attorney's office. Had Jane or Bill been cited or arrested, I would have had more leverage with which to involve Jane in cooperative safety planning to place her young child outside of the inherent risks present in the home. Instead, the officer's dismissive involvement served to bolster the parents' interpretation that my presence was an unwanted and intrusive exercise in government interference.

About half of the US states and the District of Columbia have approved the use of medical marijuana. In California, the medical marijuana program was legalized in 1996.[24] In California counties, the law allows for cultivation of six mature plants or twelve immature plants, and allows for local governments to exceed these limits if they see fit.

In my county, the local ordinance specifies that each adult may possess 3 pounds of dried marijuana and 30 plants per person, provided that the entire grow does not exceed 100 square feet of canopy. Generally, this allowance of space translates to about 100 plants, as growing a plant on less than a square foot is not feasible. The grow in which I stood that night had at least 100 plants. It is also difficult to assign a monetary value to a grow; for purposes of description, most law enforcement agencies estimate that one mature plant is valued at $1,000, but true market estimates are closer to $3,000–$5,000 per plant.

As medical and recreational marijuana laws loosen across the country, the gap between what is legal and what constitutes risk for vulnerable children is only widening. As I considered the situation, I thought about all of the information I wanted to know, yet didn't. What is the number of plants associated with increased probability of robberies and raids? What chemicals, byproducts, and marijuana products present a health risk to children? What is the threshold of marijuana use that causes a deficit in parenting capacity? Are children living in marijuana grows at increased risk of weapons accidents? What are the fire hazards related to butane processes and ad hoc electrical wiring? All caseworkers should receive training regarding the risks to children associated with marijuana use and cultivation, but such standardized training does not yet exist.

With limited information but concern nonetheless, I began my negotiations with Jane to determine a way forward that would keep her child safe, but without the intrusion of government that she so sharply felt. Hours later I was able to convince Jane that while the conditions in her home might be legal, it was less certain that they were free from risk. Jane agreed to take the children to a relative's home, leaving Bill at home to harvest the grow over the coming weeks. The children, temporarily living with their mother in their relative's home, were certainly safe, and their ongoing risk of harm dramatically reduced. This was a much better outcome, of course, than a late night, traumatic removal to foster care.

Parents and social workers share the same perspective about foster care: We want to avoid it, if at all possible. Children want to live with their parents, and parents want to raise their children. My role is to try to engage parents in developing an understanding of the risks inherent in their conduct on the road to providing a safe, secure environment for their children. Some days, that work is harder than others.

Erika Altobelli

The family at the center of this story speaks volumes to contemporary child welfare practice. The children were not taken into foster care—an important success in light of current philosophy to minimize the use of out-of-home care. And the children were safe at the time of her visit. But the children were nevertheless at risk. Recent evidence suggests that marijuana use is positively associated with increased rates of child physical abuse,[25] and research from one state indicates that poisoning among children (from ingesting marijuana either intentionally or unintentionally) has increased significantly following legalization.[26] The unlocked, loaded, and easily accessible firearm posed an additional danger. Indeed, the child welfare worker appropriately assessed the child's circumstances as risky. Balancing the child's right to safety against the parents' right to raise their child absent government intrusion, the child welfare worker had to negotiate two of the fundamental principles of this field.

The parents, in this case, did not experience their behaviors as a risk to their child. As such, they probably could have benefited from a service to help them see an alternative parenting approach. And other aspects of the child's needs might have been revealed if a more lengthy assessment had been conducted. Yet because the child's risk of harm was diminished with the promise of a temporary stay with relatives, this child welfare worker had nothing else to offer the family. She could have made a referral to a local nonprofit agency to encourage the parents to enroll in a parenting class, but given the parents' unwelcome response to her gestures, it's unlikely they would have followed through. Balancing the tension between offering voluntary services (that were unlikely to be heeded) and involuntary services (that would not be sustained in court once the child's safety was addressed), the result was no service at all. No offer of help. No additional supports. Nothing.

The parents had their right to freedom from government intrusion honored, and the child had her right to safety addressed, but it's questionable whether the child's needs were acknowledged. Indeed, in a child welfare system that emphasizes the principle of child safety, children with fewer needs and risks are unlikely to be served. Instead, we draw into the service system those families whose problems are acute, sometimes chronic, and typically severe, where parents often struggle with multiple, complex problems.[27] These are the adults who are most challenged by the demands of parenting in a complex world. And these are the families to whom child welfare workers dedicate their time, their intelligence, and their passion.

4

The Oldest Debate in Child Welfare

THERE'S A LEGEND surrounding the origins of the modern child welfare state.[1] It revolves around a little girl named Mary Ellen who lived in New York City in 1874 and who was savagely abused by her caregivers, a stepmother and putative father.[2] A Methodist missionary named Etta Wheeler became aware of her circumstances but was unable to offer services to help the girl, ostensibly because there were no laws upon which she could turn that allowed for the protection of children.[3] Mrs. Wheeler enlisted the support of the local Society for the Prevention of Cruelty to Animals and, in combination with the police, rescued Mary Ellen from her otherwise bleak fate. Mary Ellen was sent to live in an orphanage and thereafter with Ms. Wheeler's family. Her stepmother was condemned to a year of hard labor at the state penitentiary. Voluntary associations called Societies for the Prevention of Cruelty to Children (SPCC) were established in several major cities and a child-saving movement was birthed, a movement focused on rescuing children from perilous family circumstances.[4]

The Mary Ellen story is rife with exaggeration, but the societies that were birthed in the ensuing years were real; these focused on the "cruelties" children endured and were designed to respond to children's especially harsh treatment. The societies took on a unique flavor, depending on their leaders' philosophies. The most dramatic differences in approach could be seen in the New York Society and the SPCC established in Massachusetts. In New York, caseworkers were given broad police powers to intervene in the lives of families. Staff were allowed to carry firearms and could remove children at will. The majority of children separated from their parents were placed in institutions or orphanages. The Boston SPCC took a different approach. Rather than place children in institutions, they were more likely to use foster homes and, with social work services, made efforts to reunify children with their original parents if conditions changed.[5] The Boston Societies also signaled an interest in strengthening institutional supports to prevent family breakup. That model can be seen as one of the birthplaces of the modern family preservation movement, where efforts were developed to help families stay together, thus circumventing the need for out-of-home care entirely.[6]

The long debate between family preservation and child protection has centered largely on fundamental differences in philosophy about whether parents' rights to family integrity should prevail over children's rights to safety. Of course, there are significant risks associated with adopting a strictly pro-child protection stance or a strictly pro-family preservation stance. Child protection—taken to its extreme—results in children separated from their parents when other, less intrusive measures would have kept the family together safely. Family preservation—taken to its extreme—results in children being hurt by parents who are unable or unwilling to change their dangerous behaviors.[7]

Few professionals (if any) believe that large proportions of American children should be taken from their parents, and few professionals (if any) believe that children should be kept at home in dire circumstances. The debate at the margins is absurd, yet some commentators assert that foster care is broken and should therefore be abolished. Claiming that the trauma of separation from a caregiver overrides the trauma of serious abuse or neglect by a caregiver, the view that foster care should be dismantled entirely is not without its adherents.[8] But extreme pro-preservation perspectives do little to honor the voices of youth who express their gratitude to their child welfare worker or foster parent for offering them an opportunity for a safe childhood they would have otherwise missed; and extreme pro-protection perspectives insufficiently regard the voices of youth who experienced mistreatment or abuse in care. [9]

The debate is not, and should not, be at the ends of the continuum. The divisions typically are animated not in the cases that are black and white, but in the cases that occupy the center, gray area of child welfare. In that murky space where too much is unknown, a pro-protection stance might result in unwarranted removals—what Richard Gelles refers to as "false positives"—and a pro-family preservation stance might result in children being harmed by their parents, or "false negatives."[10] The shared view, that *children should be raised with their family of origin*—one of the central principles of child welfare described in Chapter 1—is commonly held and tilts the field to a family preservation stance.

Pro-preservation and pro-protection views are largely ideological. If the research evidence consistently showed positive outcomes associated with one perspective versus another, the scales might tip strongly in favor of the evidence. But the various studies designed to assess foster care outcomes are largely ambiguous. Research in this field is difficult to carry out. Studies that randomly assign equally needy children to care or to home will never (and should never) occur. Measuring the initial impact of maltreatment versus the foster care environment is difficult to tease out; the heterogeneity of maltreatment in terms of type, severity, and chronicity is difficult to control; the variety of out-of-home care contexts (including kin versus nonkin, and, for many children, placement changes across both types of care) is complex; the duration of exposure (i.e., length of time in care) can vary dramatically; and the selection of meaningful outcomes both short and long term create a high degree of complexity for social science researchers. As a result, various methodological devices have been employed to try to approximate similar samples of children under different conditions. The findings are equivocal. Some research shows somewhat positive effects of care; [11] other research concludes that hazards may be associated with care.[12] Research by Doyle shows that the borderline cases at the center should be assessed conservatively; long-term outcomes for children placed in foster care who were judged as having a marginal need for care did not do particularly well in adolescence.[13]

Given the limited definitive data on the topic, the child protection/family preservation argument has continued for years. In the 1990s, the debate played out vividly on the policy stage. A model program called Homebuilders was designed to provide very intensive, short-term, home-based services to families whose children were at imminent risk of being separated to foster care. Initial results from studies of the Homebuilders model were very positive.[14] Funded by the Edna McConnell Clark Foundation, the mounting evidence suggested that children could be raised safely in the homes of their parents if an array of intensive services were deployed. Although the child protection/family preservation debate had previously been expressed on the stage of dueling philosophies, family preservation devotees were armed with a more powerful arsenal of data to help sway the discussion.

But social science research methods were, at that time, also catching up with the field's developing appetite for data. Research experiments were growing more sophisticated and new studies employing random assignment to experimental and control conditions offered a more equivocal assessment of the benefits of an intensive family preservation model.[15] Nevertheless, the groundwork for shifting the federal conversation away from foster care and toward prevention services had been laid. Federal funding was added to state coffers in 1993 with the Family Preservation and Family Support bill (P.L.

103-66), allowing for the deployment of additional services to help struggling families and to provide "reasonable efforts" to prevent removal to out-of-home care.[16]

The debate was only temporarily quelled. Just four years later, the federal government's next foray into child welfare policy brought caseworkers' "unreasonable efforts" back into focus.[17] Congress passed the Adoption and Safe Families Act (ASFA) (P.L. 105-89), tipping the scales once again toward a pro-protection stance. Provisions of the new law promoted more assertive efforts toward adoption, allowances to deny services entirely for some parents, and shorter timeframes for parents to regain custody of their children. Importantly, ASFA focused on *child safety*, the second fundamental principle in this field.

The either-or debate between child protection and family preservation is, of course, misguided. Family preservation services can be targeted to the children who are at imminent risk of removal—those who have been harmed or who are at significant risk of imminent harm—but the odds that these families will make transformational changes in their life circumstances within a short timeframe are slim, and the likelihood that they can change before their children are hurt is also questionable. In other words, family preservation services can be offered to families at the edge of care, but given the very high thresholds for removal and the severity of families' needs upon the verge of care, family preservation services are not likely to have a robust effect. These are the children and families who have complex or long-standing problems and difficulties. Though family preservation services are likely to improve parenting,[18] they are unlikely to transform lives—and transformation is what may be required for families that have a long pattern of maltreatment or unsafe behaviors or who, themselves, have no role models for positive parenting. Families whose children are taken into foster care are, on average, very challenged with multiple, overlapping difficulties in life and in caring for their child.[19] They are a relatively small percentage of the population and may require extreme measures in order to change their parenting behaviors. Changing the socioeconomic and structural conditions surrounding their lives would also contribute greatly to their capacity to raise their children well.

How many children does this discussion concern? Is it indeed a small percentage of the population? As is the case in all matters pertaining to child welfare, it depends on the age of the child and on the child's race or ethnicity. Of the 6.6 million children referred to the hotline in 2014, about 265,000 children (4%) entered foster care, or less than 1% (0.3%) of the total US child population.[20] The numbers are consequential because all of these separations represent a dramatic act of state power and significant trauma in the lives of some children. Among the children entering care, almost half aren't even old enough for kindergarten.[21] And the disproportionalities by race that are evident in maltreatment reporting and substantiation are also apparent in entries to foster care. African American and Native American children are about twice as likely to be placed in foster care in any given year than White children.[22] These point-in-time estimates tell only one part of the story, though. If we look across childhood, the likelihood that a child will *ever* enter care obviously increases. Before age 18, about 5% of US children will spend some time in foster care. For Native American children, the rates may be as much as three times higher, and for African American children, the differences may be two times greater than for White children. [23]

When 10%–15% of a population group is at risk of a stay in foster care at some point during childhood, efforts to identify strategies to reduce these entries are urgently needed. Pro-preservation enthusiasts often view entries to care and the overall foster care caseload as a target for reform.[24] The fewer children placed in foster care, the more children whose family integrity will be maintained. But how child welfare agencies reduce the flow into foster care is tricky. States that have witnessed recent declines in their foster care caseload have generally heralded these changes as an unfettered success.[25] The nation's foster care caseload declined considerably from its peak in 1999 of over 550,000 children in care to a low of about 400,000 about a decade later.[26] But in many states, much of the change was attributed to large numbers of children exiting foster care rather than to a reduction in entries.[27] And a decline in entries is only beneficial if the children left at home are safe, a concern that current data systems are unable to address.

As discussed in Chapter 3, the number of children entering foster care is dwarfed by the number of children who could probably benefit from a service but who are turned away by the state, or who are currently served by the child welfare system, though little is known about the nature, quality, or duration of the services offered, or the outcomes. If a child maltreatment report at the hotline serves as a signal of concern, then we know that about 20% of all signals receive a response from a child welfare agency;[28] four fifths of signals are left unheeded. Some of these children could benefit from home-based services—help accessing financial supports, housing, food, parenting advice, drug or alcohol treatment—some intensive family services and others less intensive, of course, depending on the family's needs. These families may be amenable to, and responsive to services, but in our current system they are typically given nothing or very little in the way of help. These are the families for whom family preservation services might be more effectively deployed. And in fact, these are the families who, in some jurisdictions, are targeted for Differential or Alternative Response.

When family preservation, Differential, or Alternative Response approaches offer services to families *other than* those families who need a more protective intervention such as foster care, and do so without siphoning resources from an already resource-constrained, out-of-home care system, then we will have arrived in a new era of child welfare in the United States that has features not so different from our European neighbors. The child protection argument will prevail for those children whose safety requires a protective response. And the family preservation argument will prevail for those children whose family autonomy should not be disrupted. The marginal cases at the center, where reasonable people might assess risk and safety quite differently, will likely remain contested until our risk assessment tools grow in sophistication and accuracy.

The long-standing debate between child protection and family preservation is often posed as a tension in the field, but in fact, it's a false dichotomy. The integrity of family life is best preserved when children are protected from harm. And children are protected when the sanctity of their healthy family is preserved. Child protection resulting in out-of-home care should always be a last-resort option after other, less intrusive alternatives have been tried. But the values of child protection versus family preservation do not always play out neatly in practice. Sometimes the tug-of-war child welfare workers grapple with as they try to determine where a child will be best protected is anything but straightforward.

"Tonya"

Nobody likes it when cases have to transfer from one social worker to another. Clients don't want to interact with an endless string of different workers. And staff don't like a case reassigned if they've just developed a trusting relationship. But sometimes, you hope a case can be reassigned. If it's a high-profile case with a mentally ill mother who incessantly leaves voice messages, or a case that requires a restraining order between you and the client, you praise the day the case is re-assigned. One day last summer, a colleague of mine in the **Ongoing unit** was moved to the **Court unit** due to "agency need," and she handed me the Thompson case, with a smile. During our brief case consult, she warned me that the case would be trying and then she wished me well on my journey with them.

The Thompson family included Tonya, age 13, her two adult sisters, Cynthia (21) and Samantha (25), the mom (Robin), and Tonya's dad (John). When the case came to CPS, only Robin and Tonya were living in California. The rest of the family was on the East Coast. The case was opened originally due to general neglect. Tonya was removed from her mother because of her mother's extensive alcoholism and two recent alcohol-induced hospitalizations. During both hospitalizations, Tonya had nowhere to go. Their friendship circle was limited and the rest of her family lived out of state. When Tonya's mom was at home, things were pretty rocky. She usually drove Tonya to and from school, but Tonya wasn't very adept at determining when her mom had been drinking, and there were a lot of too-close incidents that were unsafe. Of course, that was when Robin was up and getting around. She spent days at a time in her room, leaving Tonya to take care of herself.

When the agency was alerted to their situation, Tonya was on her own. Reasonable efforts to prevent placement were not offered because Tonya needed an immediate place to stay. In court, the judge ordered drug treatment, therapy, and parenting classes for Robin. Tonya was initially placed in a county foster home, but within a month, Tonya's sister, Cynthia, returned to California so that she could become Tonya's foster parent.

As I began working with the family, the challenges my coworker had warned me about became more and more apparent. On the surface, I saw an extremely bright and well-accomplished family. Degrees from universities and assets well beyond the norm of most child welfare cases. I remember wondering, "How could a family like this be in this predicament? Surely, they'll get this cleaned up quickly." Sadly, this was not the case.

To say that this family had unresolved issues is an understatement. Just because they accomplished a lot in school doesn't mean they were high functioning. John ran some huge corporation. Both sisters were working professionals. And Tonya was excelling in school and hoped to follow the footsteps of her academically talented siblings. Robin was a long-time, skilled professional, laid off shortly after Tonya entered care, in part, due to her alcoholism.

Robin and John's relationship with their children was complicated. Samantha was the "golden child." Both Robin and John respected her life choices. Cynthia, however, was the vocal child, more aware than the rest of their dysfunctional family dynamics and willing to talk about it. John had effectively pushed Cynthia out of his life, and Robin didn't want much to do with her either. Cynthia resented her parents for their troubled family life, for favoring Samantha, and for their inadequacies in parenting her baby sister. Now, she wanted to be for Tonya what her parents were not.

John wanted to remain a distant father, but not look like one on paper. He went through all the legal motions, paid for his own legal representation, appeared for hearings, and attempted to meet with Tonya for occasional, awkward visits. Tonya, for her part, wished he wouldn't bother; she felt like her dad was only there for show and she had nothing to speak with him about.

Tonya's mother loved her deeply, and Tonya loved her mom. In fact, all Tonya wanted was to be home with her mother. But that's what makes child welfare so challenging: Sometimes we need to keep kids away from the parents they want to be with.

After Robin was laid off from work, her finances grew tight. Although she initially brought store-bought gourmet treats to her weekly visits with Tonya, she began baking goods to cater to Tonya's preferences. With the impairment of her alcoholism, though, she'd often misread instructions or expiration dates, or overlooked mold, showing up with moldy, strange, or expired treats for her daughter. Her alcoholism impaired every aspect of her life, coloring her judgment about even the simplest of tasks.

I wondered, often: Is Tonya better off living without her mother? Although I examined these questions privately, these are not the questions that lie at the heart of child welfare. In court, the question at hand is: Does this mother meet the criteria for a count under **WIC 300**? And does the court have continued jurisdiction to keep this child separated from her mother? The question isn't: "Will removal and foster care be more harmful than remaining with an alcoholic mother?" Our choices don't always correspond with a child's best interests, and it's so damn hard being caught in the middle of that.

As a social worker, I have to respond to so many actors that have nothing to do with Tonya and her mother. I have to respond to the court and the legal representatives in the room; I have to be sure that I use sound legal judgments when writing my court reports. I have to respond to my agency and consider the risks very carefully. Knowing that this child could go home and maybe die in a car crash, all because I made the wrong recommendation, weighs heavily in my every deliberation. And it's easy to get wrapped up in my relationship to the family. I want to show them that I believe in them, and I want to give them a chance.

I think a lot about why I do this work. I want to help people change and to help families "work." It's probably because my own family didn't "work." Do I want this family to "work" because it appears they have what it takes, or is it because my family didn't, and I wish someone would have given us the proper chance? So I fall back on the pages and pages of policies and procedures that line the shelves of the office, and I let these guide my decisions.

Those policies tell me to cancel Robin's visits if she fails to call in by 8:00 a.m. on the day of her appointed weekly visit. The policies tell me to remove her from the visitation list after two cancelled visits. And the policies tell me to recommend the termination of family reunification services if mom isn't visiting with her daughter. And so that's what I recommended, despite knowing that it takes an alcoholic more than 6 months to overcome a lifelong battle and that expecting an alcoholic to call each morning by 8:00 a.m. is not realistic. I watched as the policies and procedures of an agency triggered Robin to lose hope, drink more, and rehospitalize.

Toward the end of the case, Cynthia decided to return to the East Coast. Tonya, of course, wanted to move with her. Cynthia wasn't registered as a foster parent in her Eastern state, so Tonya had to move in with Samantha instead. I traveled with Tonya to get her settled with Samantha, watching her all the time bridle at the prospect of living with a sister she didn't really like, but who was nonetheless an approved placement. Not surprisingly, that arrangement fell apart quickly and Tonya was ultimately placed with Cynthia as soon as her foster parent license was granted. Three thousand miles away from her original home, Tonya could no longer visit with her mother, even if she wanted to. My case closed, and I transferred it to a new worker in a new state. I wonder, sometimes, how that worker felt when she was assigned the Thompson case.

I have to use my heart and my mind in this work. My heart to connect with and motivate others, and my mind to make really hard decisions based on policy and evidence. In Tonya's case, I had to use both when I came to realize she couldn't return to her alcoholic mother. But I question my decisions all the time.

I make these hard decisions over and over again, and get it all done in 40 hours each week, and then practice self-care and go to the lunch-time yoga class offered on Tuesdays that "really help" alleviate stress, so that I can work productively in this field for some 30 years. Honestly? It's hard.

I think a lot about my clients and about how we move them from place to place, and how this affects them. Tonya slept in her bed in her mom's house one night and then was told the next day that she could only see her mom 1 hour a week and had to live in a stranger's home for a time while she waited for her sister. Then she lived with her sister, just down the street from her mother, but we dictated when and where she could see her mom. Then we moved her to a new state. She rarely saw her mom after that. What did that do to Tonya? And is Tonya really better off having gone through all of that, rather than staying with her mom?

That's what makes my work really hard. That question right there.

Socorro Reynoso

Tonya's circumstances raise so many questions. The case hardly characterizes the bright contrasts that shape the family preservation/child protection debate. Instead, the case falls squarely in the middle, where reasonable people would likely draw different conclusions about the best course of action. Could Tonya have remained at home? Were there services that might have reduced Robin's drinking so that she could safely care for her daughter? Could the state have developed a professional circle of supports to replace the absence of informal support from friends or family? Tonya was older, so her risk of harm at home was generally low (except when her mom was driving drunk). But Tonya was isolated, and without an informal support network, and she had no one to care for her during her mother's stays in the hospital. Robin, too, was resistant to engaging in services, so an offer of voluntary Differential Response would have been ineffective. And there was much acrimony between the older sisters and their parents, so a voluntary placement with Cynthia but without court involvement would have quickly unraveled.

Finding the right path in a case such as Tonya's is typically elusive. Choosing the best approach available, however, often aligns with choosing a principled plan. The staff involved in Tonya's case, in attending to the first principle of child welfare, determined that Robin was not raising her daughter safely and that her circumstances warranted government involvement. Because Tonya was not *safe* (principle 2), she was placed with her sister, thus adhering to the principle that *children should be raised with their family of origin* (principle 3). At a minimum, Tonya was assured of her safety in her sister's home. But minimum is well short of ideal and in Tonya's case, the outcome was never ideal for anyone—not for Tonya, not for her mother, and not for her child welfare worker.

It's hard to guarantee safety in child welfare—not in a birth parent's home or in foster care. Sadly, both options entail risks. Risk assessment tools help, but many children who are left with their parent following a child maltreatment referral are later re-reported for a new incident. In fact, in one study of all infants reported for maltreatment in California, but left at home with their birth parent, over 50% were re-referred before their fifth birthday.[29] And reunification with a birth parent following a spell in foster care also entails risk. About 20% of all entries to care are actually re-entries following a return home from care.[30]

So is foster care safer? The evidence on the safety of foster care has generally suggested that the large majority of children are treated well. Studies eliciting the voice of youth in care typically show positive regard for caregivers and reciprocal feelings of attachment toward youth.[31] But foster care is not always safe and evidence from a range of studies indicates that a disturbing proportion of children and youth may be maltreated in out-of-home care. Official reports of maltreatment in foster care highlight the safety of care. According to the federal government, abuse in care occurs less than 1% of the time.[32] Yet other sources that rely on the retrospective views of youth who experienced care are sobering. Estimates range from 20% to 33% of youth experiencing neglect while in care, between 13% and 15% of youth experiencing physical abuse, and sexual abuse ranging from 2% to 8%.[33] And a recent study involving youth aging out of foster care indicates higher rates of maltreatment still.[34]

Child welfare workers, faced with cases involving ambiguity, don't always have great choices to select from. In spite of parents' best efforts, they may not be able to keep their children safe, kin who take care of children may be overstretched to care for children well, and child welfare agencies short on resources may not screen for the most capable foster parents to take care of kids. Armed with insufficient information and constrained resources, a pro-preservation or pro-protection stance doesn't always guide practice. Both philosophies are undergirded by child welfare principles of safety and family (principles 2 and 3), often in direct conflict with one another. In the following case, we see that sometimes there is no clear answer. Relying too much on the principle of family may unfairly compromise the rights of children to a safe childhood, and relying too much on the principle of safety may unfairly separate children who care deeply for their parents.

"Terry"

I was about to knock on her door to investigate another referral. I'd been here before; so had my colleagues. Molly was what we euphemistically called a "frequent flyer," a person who comes to the attention of my agency on a fairly regular basis. This time, it was a different house but the same person. I wondered how I'd be received.

When Molly opened the door she greeted me by name and invited me in. It was as though I were on a social call, except that we both knew I wasn't. Molly was friendly and chatted as if my presence were of no consequence. Her little boy, Terry, looked at me with big eyes. He was a petite toddler, quiet, and shy. He said a few words, but with his newly developing language skills, I didn't catch it all. Not very helpful when I was trying to figure out what was going on in the home.

I told Molly that my agency had received a phone call alleging excessive drug and alcohol use that posed a danger to her son. Molly laughed it off. She said that she didn't drink anymore and she didn't do drugs. She pointed to her son, a picture of health. It was obvious, she said, that she didn't neglect her son and that Terry was well taken care of.

Our friendly chat continued for quite some time. We talked about her son's father, no longer a presence in their lives. We talked about her recent involvement with the police and some pending charges. And we talked about her care for Terry. I pointed out that the referrals we kept receiving in our office probably signaled her need for a little help. I told her that we could offer her services to help strengthen her parenting, and that we could set up a voluntary agreement that would keep her out of court. She balked at the offer, though, and I left her house feeling as if we'd had a friendly visit, but one that resulted in little progress regarding her son's safety.

I returned to the office to discuss the case with my supervisor. She encouraged me to return to Molly's home and try to persuade her to engage with us in a voluntary case. I'm not quite sure why we thought Molly would say "yes." We'd been to her home so many times before.

We had talked with her. We had offered services in the past. And the allegations, this time, were similar.

But neither my supervisor nor I wanted to go to court, and we knew Molly certainly didn't want to face a court case. Of course, parents feel so much better when they control whether they'll accept services, rather than being forced. But voluntary cases are also a bit of a risk. If the parent initially engages, but then withdraws from services, our options aren't very good. We can either close the case or take the case to court. Closing the case means that the family didn't need that much from us, after all. But taking a voluntary case to court means that the initial voluntary offer wasn't really voluntary anyway. Parents probably know this when we make our initial offer, so I understand their skepticism.

I returned to Molly's home to talk with her again. She shared with me some of her recent struggles and told me she wanted to make a new start in life. To my surprise, she decided that accepting our invitation for services might help her get there.

We decided to start with an alcohol and drug assessment to determine the level of service she would need. The assessment indicated that residential treatment would be best. Molly was willing to try it, but she wanted her son to go with her. After calling various agencies, I found an appropriate treatment setting that would take them both. There, she would work on her sobriety goals while caring for Terry in a supportive environment. I was pleased with the easy transition. Molly didn't have a job and was looking for a new home anyway, so she just packed up, got in her car, and checked in. I visited and kept in regular contact, talked with the residential treatment staff, and communicated with the Probation Department so that they were aware of her transitional living situation.

Molly told me she worked diligently in her program, and all reports from the staff were positive. Her recovery was underway and she was caring for Terry attentively. Terry, too, seemed to be thriving. He was cheerful, chatty, and a bit less shy. He was obviously attached to his mother and went to her whenever he needed comfort.

After several weeks, Molly indicated that she was ready to go home. I spoke with staff who agreed that a transition to outpatient services was warranted. But where would she live? Molly wanted to return to her old neighborhood, where she had friends who could support her parenting. I worried, though, and tried to convince her that the old neighborhood might compromise her recovery and that she would face significant temptation to return to her old habits. She returned to her neighborhood in the end, enrolled in an outpatient program, reliably met with a local therapist, and started looking for work. I monitored the situation for a couple more months, regularly meeting with Molly and with Terry, who always appeared well cared for.

I finally determined it was time to close the case. Terry was safe, and Molly seemed aware that her behaviors were important to Terry's safety. I discussed the case with my supervisor, and she agreed. Then I met with Molly who was optimistic about the future and who agreed that it was no longer necessary for our agency to be involved with her family. We said good-bye and I left, feeling pleased that the case had closed successfully.

I was happy with the outcome of Molly's case. We'd kept her family together. Even though they experienced several residential changes, Terry always stayed with his mother, and Terry was safe. But the outcomes this family enjoyed were too short-lived. After about 2 years, the calls started coming in again.

Following one of these calls, I was assigned the case and I found myself knocking on Molly's front door again with some trepidation about how I would be greeted. It was a different house, but so much was the same. There were Molly and Terry, warmly welcoming me into their home as if it were another social call. Terry was about 4 years old now and much more communicative. Although it was clear to me that Molly had lost her fragile recovery and the circumstances of her home and parenting had deteriorated substantially, my assessment and the SDM risk assessment tool told me that she was providing minimally sufficient care for her son and there was no cause to open a case.

The referrals kept coming throughout the year, however, and although everyone who worked with the family was concerned about them, we did not have evidence to suggest a safety threat to Terry. One final call to the agency alleged drinking, physical violence, Molly's arrest, Terry being left with unsafe adults, and a series of other behaviors that put the little boy at risk. While conducting the investigation, I spoke with Terry, who told me he felt unsafe in his mother's home.

I reviewed all the circumstances with my supervisor, and I was assigned to detain Molly's son. Within 2 days we were in court. The judge reviewed the evidence and determined that Terry could not remain safely at home. Terry was separated from his mother and placed in foster care with his grandparents.

Molly was very upset that her son had been placed in care. She didn't believe there was a problem and minimized the risks she posed to Terry. But she was comforted to know Terry was living with relatives and would be well cared for while she sorted out the circumstances of her life. Once Terry was settled with his grandparents, I began the long process of supporting Molly in her efforts to reunify with her son.

Today, I wonder about cases like Molly's. Our agency received numerous referrals before we were able to engage her in voluntary services the first time. And the calls poured in again during our second episode with this family before a crisis finally demanded that we act. I think that our decision to keep Molly and Terry together in the first instance was right. But when we returned to her home 2 years later, their circumstances had declined substantially, and I wondered how long Terry had been living in this uncertain home trying to manage his safety largely on his own. Would things have turned out differently if we had insisted on a removal in the first instance? Or was there anything we could have done to hold this family together the second time? And how many times do we let parents keep trying while their children wait?

Viviana Colosimo-Blair

Terry spent the first 4 years of his life living with his mother, whom he obviously loved. Their family life, however, was often chaotic, sometimes frightening, and intermittently unsafe. The frequent calls that came to the child abuse hotline signaled community members' concerns about the family. Community members knew the family needed help and child welfare workers had, in the past, extended voluntary offers of assistance. But Molly rebuffed the offers several times before she finally engaged and said "yes" to residential treatment. When Molly and Terry were placed together in residential treatment, and for a time thereafter, Molly got a glimpse of the life she wanted for herself and her son. But her sobriety didn't last long; it was too fragile, and she relapsed into the habits that exposed her son to regular risks. Extended family had tried to help in the past, but Molly had burned many of those bridges by the time Terry was a preschooler. And the support she received from friends in the neighborhood amounted to shuttling her son to one home or another while Molly struggled with her addictions. By the time this worker was involved with the family again, Molly was in jail and there was no family of origin available to care for Terry at home. Strict adherence to the third principle, that *children should live with their family of origin,* was not possible in this instance. The second principle of *child safety* required a response.

Child welfare workers regularly wrestle with the dilemmas posed by conflicting principles. These are the cases that test their moral compass about what is right and that push their intellect to devise creative alternatives that can bridge the divide. Being aware of a bias toward a pro-preservationist or a pro-protectionist stance can help caseworkers remain clear-eyed about the options available to them and which principle they are likely to privilege (e.g., safety or family) given an ambiguous situation. But cases like Molly's remind us that strict adherence to one stance over another is usually unrealistic in practice. Each individual case is remarkably involved, and family life is never static, always ushering in new complexities over time. One principle can never prevail over another in all circumstances. Principled practice with each family instead requires close analysis and a customized response. Being a child welfare professional means living in a world of work that offers imperfect choices. And therein lies the challenge.

5

When We Say "No" to Family

ACROSS TIME AND CULTURES, extended family have often stepped in to care for children when parents were ill, incapacitated, or when they died or were otherwise unable to provide for their children.[1] This has been true in the United States for centuries, and it continues today. This was especially true for African American children in the United States, of course, during the period of slavery and thereafter when children were regularly separated from their parents. In these instances, extended relatives or unrelated adults typically assumed the responsibility for children's care.[2] According to some sources today, upwards of 3 million children in the United States live in the homes of their relatives without their parents present, usually for reasons associated with poverty, drug involvement, mental health or health concerns, or other issues.[3] Most child-sharing happens privately; families arrange for the care of children without the need of, or outside the gaze of, government officials. Some relatives care for their family's children at the behest of child welfare agencies and the courts, but that was not always the case.

The children at the center of the child welfare system have come to the attention of government agents due to maltreatment, and where these children should live has been a source of controversy in our field for decades. In the 18th and 19th centuries, children who were brought to the state's attention due to the death or incapacity of their parents typically were placed in institutions or orphanages for their care.[4] Later, it was determined that children were best served in families rather than institutions, but the families sought for children were usually those separated by socioeconomic class or by distance.[5] Indeed, for several decades in the late 19th and early 20th century, thousands of White children were sent on "orphan trains" hundreds of miles away from their parents where they would start entirely new lives in the homes of substitute caregivers.[6] The notion behind these stark disruptions was that children, if left in the environment of their families, would be negatively influenced by family members with questionable moral character or inappropriate behaviors. Family were considered part of the problem, certainly not the source of a solution.[7] Although the orphan trains ceased to exist in the early part of the 20th century, there was general agreement that children were best raised in the homes of families. Two-parent, heterosexual, racially matched nuclear foster families were typically sought out to care for children, privileging those families with a caregiver-breadwinner and a stay-at-home mom.[8] Parents and extended family members were often viewed as dangerous or threatening.[9]

In recent decades, the pendulum has changed direction, this time away from the homes of strangers and toward the homes of extended family. Several forces are implicated in the field's newly found enthusiasm for "kin." Regardless of separations between children and their original parents, significant evidence suggests that children don't leave families behind. Studies of children in foster care often report on children's longing for their parents and other family members.[10] And many children who leave foster care at age 18 (or 21) either want to, or actually return, to live with their birth families or relatives.[11] We also know from the anthropological literature that some kin show natural bonds of obligation and affection toward their relative children[12]—obligations that child welfare agencies might take advantage of to the benefit of children.

But significant shifts in practice usually involve other forces at play as well. The availability of federal funding and changes to federal guidelines have a tendency to shift state policies that trickle down to child welfare practitioners. In this case, the US Supreme Court ruled in the *Youakim v. Miller* decision[13] that states were required to pay foster care board rates to relatives who met foster care licensing requirements and were caring for children from very low-income families.[14] Later, Congress identified kin as a placement preference when children were removed to out-of-home care.[15] Some states have interpreted the federal government's signal of support for kin as an opportunity to place children with relatives who are unlicensed (or unable to be licensed) and therefore ineligible for foster care subsidies.[16] Surely a cost-cutting strategy, these measures speak to the spirit of the law (kin preference) with little regard for the actual costs associated with raising children.

Of course, out-of-home care is also subject to conditions of supply and demand. During the 1980s and 1990s the United States saw a very sharp rise in the foster care caseload. From 1985 to 2000, foster care caseloads doubled with the proportion of all US children in care rising from about 4.1 to 8.1 per 1,000.[17] Some evidence suggests that during this same time, many states and counties experienced a decline in the number of available foster homes.[18] The American economy was punishing to those families who aspired to the ideal foster family; economic forces pressed thousands of women into the labor market to make ends meet,[19] reducing the size of the available foster parent workforce. And although foster care agencies belatedly embraced single-parent families and LGBTQ families as the "new" foster family,[20] the demand side of foster care still required a more elastic supply of caregivers. Faced with a sharp increase in entries to care (demand), and a decline in homes for children (supply), agencies were eager to establish new resources in which to place children. Kinship care is an elastic resource that can be easily stretched when demand rises. In some states the definition of "kin" is extremely expansive; "kin" includes blood or legal relatives, "godparents, family friends, or others with a strong emotional bond to a child."[21]

Race politics also contributed to the shift toward kinship care. For decades, a lively debate raged about the "best" out-of-home care setting for children. In fact, part of the reason the orphan trains of the 19th century were finally curtailed was not so much that there was disagreement about sending children hundreds or thousands of miles from their parents, but because many of the immigrant children taken from parents were Catholic, and the large majority were eventually placed in Protestant homes.[22] These "unmatched" homes set the stage for later debates about racial matching for children in care. The debates were sharply articulated in 1972 when the National Association of Black Social Workers set out a position statement castigating transracial placements, suggesting that they represented a form of cultural genocide.[23]

The merits of same-race versus transracial placements were the subject of intense debate and research for a number of years[24] until the federal government finally entered the deliberations with a policy approach that, in effect, allowed transracial placements. The Multi-Ethnic Placement Act (MEPA: P.L. 103-82) (and the subsequent interethnic adoption provisions) pronounced that state child welfare agencies could not delay or deny foster or adoptive placements based on the race of the child or the caregiver,[25] essentially quieting the debate and directing child welfare workers to consider racially unmatched placements, when necessary. For child welfare workers concerned about children living in racially or ethnically consonant households, kinship care offered a natural solution absent the contentious debate.

Today, almost one third of children living in out-of-home care in the United States are cared for by relative foster parents,[26] most commonly maternal grandmothers and aunts.[27] In general, much of the research literature suggests that there are a number of benefits that accrue to children placed with their relatives. Children placed with kin are less likely to move from one placement to another compared to children placed with nonrelatives.[28] Placement instability is associated with a number of negative outcomes for children,[29] so efforts to offer children stability of care are important considerations. And for those children who are reunified following a stay in out-of-home care, re-entry appears to be less likely when the original placement was with kin.[30] When children live with their relatives, they visit with their parents more often, and they are more likely to be placed as a group with their other siblings, rather than being split up into separate foster homes.[31] For children who know and love their relatives, a move into their home is less disruptive and certainly less traumatic than when children are placed into the home of strangers, and when children have unique cultural, religious, or linguistic traditions, these are more likely to be preserved in the home of a relative than they might be if placed in a home outside the family.[32]

In spite of the benefits, there is research that some kin—particularly kinship grandparents—may need assistance in improving their caregiving practices with children. In Zinn's study of kinship care, caseworkers rated grandparents lowest in "fostering competence" compared to other relative caregivers.[33] Yet the services that might help these caregivers may not always be available. Consistent evidence suggests that kin caregivers request fewer services of child welfare agencies, but they are also less likely to be offered services, compared to nonkin caregivers.[34]

Long-term outcomes for children in kin and nonkin care are difficult to compare because it seems that the children who live with kin are, on average, less emotionally and behaviorally challenged.[35] But some permanency outcomes are the same. Children are equally likely to reunify with their birth parents if placed in kin or nonkin homes, but the pace of reunification appears to be slower and therefore the duration in care longer for children in kin care.[36] Among the children who are not reunified, children placed with kin are less likely to be adopted.[37] Some evidence suggests that kin may be reluctant to be involved in proceedings that terminate the parental rights of a daughter, sister, or other close relative.[38] Other evidence indicates that the take-up rate for adoption may have more to do with whether the option is presented to relatives.[39] Even so, kinship adoption is a rapidly growing phenomenon in the United States.[40] In 2000, about one in five US children adopted from foster care were adopted by relatives. Almost a decade later, that number had increased to 30%.[41]

We know that kinship foster parents are a fairly homogeneous group. Child welfare-involved families are disproportionately vulnerable both socially and economically. They are more likely than the average American family to be low income, to have lower-than-average education, and to have unstable employment.[42] Not surprisingly, then, kinship foster parents are also socially disadvantaged with large proportions living in poverty, having secured a high school diploma or less, and living in single-parent households.[43] Many suffer from serious and chronic health conditions such as heart disease, arthritis, obesity, and diabetes.[44] In general, then, where we see the greatest differences between kin and nonkin foster care settings is the substantial socioeconomic risks that children may experience when living in the care of their relatives, and the attendant disadvantages relating to educational attainment, health, and neighborhood context.[45]

The introduction of kin into today's child welfare system has not always been easy. Some child welfare workers harbor reservations about kin;[46] they worry that the challenges of parenting the first time around will spill over into the second round of parenting, or that the home, more generally, does not meet the well-being needs of the child. Findings relating to the intergenerational cycle of maltreatment suggest that children who are sexually abused or neglected may be more likely than their nonmaltreated peers to grow up and maltreat their own children.[47] This does not mean that the majority of maltreated children grow up to maltreat, however. The evidence suggests this is *not* the case.[48] However, due to the increased likelihood that challenged parenting behaviors may be learned, child welfare workers are appropriately considerate of kin caregivers and of their past parenting practices.

Efforts to diligently identify and search for kin have grown markedly with access to the Internet and its capacity to search using key terms. Kevin Campbell has pioneered efforts at "family finding" using a range of search databases, resulting in the identification of dozens of close and extended kin who may be related to a child.[49] Relatives are assessed for their interest and capacity to care for a child, and often a family team meeting is called to determine how several members of the family can be engaged to help support the child and her parents. While the evidence on the results of family finding are mixed, the strategies used in the family finding model represent positive social work practice.[50]

When kin are selected as children's caregivers, caseworkers must be aware of the complex family dynamics that may be at play and the complicated emotions caregivers may be experiencing. Relatives usually come to their caregiving role abruptly. Rather than plan, prepare, and train for the introduction of a child into their home, the call to draw on their services often comes with little notice. Caregivers often feel a combination of grief, loss, and anger—grief for their daughter or son who may be struggling to care for the child, loss of time and freedom, and anger at being asked to rise to a new level of commitment that was fully unanticipated.[51]

In spite of the practice challenges associated with kin, federal law is clear about prioritizing the fourth principle laid out in Chapter 1: *When children cannot live with family, they should live with extended relatives.* But how do child welfare workers manage the tension that arises when policy requires a diligent search for relatives and placement into kinship homes, with other policies pertaining to foster care? According to federal law, children's foster care placement should be in the "the least restrictive (most family like) and most appropriate setting available and in close proximity to the parent's home, consistent with the best interests and special needs of the child."[52] When relatives are selected who live far away, parents have significantly reduced opportunities to visit and show their efforts toward reunification. Or relatives may be willing and available, but insufficiently prepared to attend to a child's special needs. Quickly, we see that the simplicity of a fundamental principle is often complicated in real-life circumstances.

Under simple and ideal circumstances all cases would offer a clear hierarchy of options so that choices between competing policy requirements and principles—and children's competing needs—would not collide. If all kinship homes (least restrictive) offered a safe alternative for children (most appropriate setting), down the street from children's original home (close proximity), to promote regular visitation (reasonable efforts), child welfare workers' jobs would be much more straightforward. Too often that's not the case, and caseworkers must make tough choices between the competing and fundamental ideas of child welfare: children's needs for family, safety, proximity, and permanence.

"Shannon"

I'd been working with foster youth in local nonprofit agencies for 4 years, and one year as a **continuing worker** with the county. I had experience, I had specialized training, and I still had questions about the day-to-day work of child welfare. Almost at capacity in terms of my caseload size, I remember wishing that I had just a bit more time to devote to each family to build relationships and effect change. I was giving my cases all of my skill and my heart and there wasn't much left to give. Of course, at just about that time, I received an email from the control clerk assigning me a new **"pre-dispo" case**. Now, I was full to the brim.

A child had been temporarily removed from her parents' home and a **Dependency Investigations (DI) worker** was now examining the circumstances surrounding the removal so that she could prepare a detailed report for the **jurisdiction/disposition hearing**—a court hearing that would set the path for this child and her family. As a pre-dispo worker, I came on to the case to support the DI worker, to develop a collaborative approach, and to offer a warm handoff to the family before the DI worker transferred off the case. Following the court hearing, I would serve as the family's primary social worker, whether the child remained separated from her family on a plan of **Family Reunification** or went home on a plan of **Family Maintenance**.

The case included information about a family of three. The parents were recently separated, and the toddler had been detained in the spring, 3 months earlier. The family had been to court multiple times as the judge granted continuances in response to the father's lawyer's requests. The process was more arduous than normal because the father's attorney disputed the county's allegations and wording in several areas of the petition. The file that I read described multiple allegations, including domestic violence between the parents with the child present, methamphetamine addiction for both parents, and criminal history for both parents. The mother had assault and child endangerment convictions, and there were concerns about her mental health. The father had drug manufacturing, DUI, petty theft, and domestic violence/assault convictions, in addition to an allegation some years earlier relating to sexual abuse.

I called the DI social worker to get a fuller picture of the situation. She explained that there was a large age gap between the mother and father, the father being older. When the mother discovered she was pregnant, she moved in with the father and paternal grandparents. She had no friends or supports in the area beyond the paternal family. Both parents were using methamphetamines and getting into physical fights while holding the child. The grandfather was quite elderly and unwell, and the DI worker shared her concerns about the grandmother's mental health. The DI worker indicated that the relationship between all of the parties in the home was difficult and confusing. She believed that the paternal grandmother had an unrealistic view of her son, leading her to deny his drug-related and violence-related behaviors. The paternal grandfather, on the other hand, defended the mother and corroborated her version of events. The DI worker was unable to develop a safety plan with the family in part because neither the grandmother nor the father believed he was engaging in any risky behaviors.

I read the DI worker's detailed reports and related attachments, including police reports, restraining order applications, copies of threatening emails and text messages, and a request to the local probate court to grant guardianship of the child to relatives. In fact, when the case came before the probate court judge, she only granted a temporary 30-day guardianship and referred the case to child welfare for investigation because of the complicated safety concerns. Upon removal, the DI worker had considered placing the child with kin based on the paternal grandparents' willingness to care for the girl. However, because of the relationship between all of the parties, she determined that a kinship care placement in this case would be problematic. In the end, the DI worker had placed the child in a nonrelative foster home.

I attended the jurisdiction/disposition hearing and was introduced to the mother, Megan. She seemed downtrodden and depressed, vacillating between tears and stoic silence. The judge noted that Megan had been engaged in services voluntarily for almost 3 months and praised her for her commitment to her daughter. He ordered **Family Reunification Services** and asked that Megan return to court in 6 months to show progress on her case plan.

Samuel, the father, was not present at the hearing. The DI worker explained that the father had not visited the little girl in several weeks and that he had told the worker he did not want to participate in reunification services. Even so, because he could not make his wishes known to the judge directly, the judge ordered Samuel to participate in family reunification services as well. This, of course, worried me. Making "**reasonable efforts**" for an uncooperative or unwilling parent can be very time consuming, but I was hopeful I could encourage him to participate in services, after all.

Little Shannon was now in her third foster home in as many months. What, I wondered, could a toddler do to cause multiple placement disruptions? I learned that the first two sets of foster parents both wanted to adopt Shannon. They grew deeply attached quickly and couldn't imagine seeing her return to her parents' care. Each couple had decided to cut ties early to spare their grief at her loss. Shannon had no difficult behaviors, no medical issues, no delays, and yet she still experienced significant placement instability. Maybe she was too loveable.

My agency assertively pursues **concurrent planning** for very young children in foster care. Foster parents are selected to play a dual role with children—committed to adopt them if their parents are unable to reunify, but equally ready to give the children up if the family can be reunited. I feel for concurrent foster parents. It's brave, almost impossible, to commit your unconditional love to a stranger's child only to let them go, months or years later. I understand adults who become overwhelmed by the emotional risk and decide to have a child moved. I understand the loss they must experience. But I also know that adults usually have emotional resources to draw on—tools and skills to manage the emotional upset. What do children have? What do they learn from these experiences? Only that they live in an out-of-control world where nothing can be predicted.

Shannon was now in her third foster home. I was determined to be transparent with the foster parents to give them an accurate picture of the parents' progress and the likelihood that Shannon would leave care and return home. I didn't want them to claim surprise, and I certainly didn't want to see this placement disrupt.

I met Shannon in Mr. and Mrs. Caldwell's home and found her extremely shy at first. She seemed very comfortable with her foster parents, however, and soon showed her true colors as a friendly, creative child—even a ham, constantly trying to make others laugh. She clung to Mrs. Caldwell in one moment and was showing me her toys the next. I took this as a good sign; despite the moves, she was still able to build comforting relationships with new people. It was easy to see why the previous foster parents had fallen so deeply in love. Shannon was an adorable child.

I next met with Megan who, according to the requirements of her case plan, was living in transitional housing and was completing outpatient drug treatment. She was anxious and had many questions. She admitted her past violent convictions. She owned up to her addiction, and she vividly recounted the violence she'd experienced at the hands of Samuel. She also told me she feared that Samuel would take their child if she were given custody, detailing a previous incident when he had taken Shannon away for several days without revealing their whereabouts. She talked about the violence and neglect that she now understood surrounded her daughter. When she and Samuel were high, they completely neglected her needs. And when they fought violently, Shannon was often held between them. There was an authenticity about Megan, and her openness made me believe she was hiding nothing and was ready to make a change.

Because I had learned Samuel wanted to waive services, I anticipated the next 6 months would be replete with messages and letters, but no direct contact. To my surprise, he responded to my call. I explained that I was the new social worker and that at the last court hearing the county had been ordered to offer him services to help him reunify with his daughter. He told me the previous worker was biased against him and that he dropped out because he felt he would never get his little girl back. I assured him that my role was to help him reunify and we agreed to meet.

I met Samuel the next day, and we talked for about an hour. During that time he vehemently denied everything. He was not violent; the mother attacked him. He was not an addict; he used methamphetamine and marijuana on a recreational basis. He did not sexually abuse anyone and was adamant he was being framed. I listened attentively but explained that the court found all of the allegations to be true; he would need to show the court that they were no longer of concern in order for his daughter to be returned. He agreed to participate and wanted to set up his visits right away.

Samuel's greatest worry was that Shannon was living with strangers. He asked if she could instead live with his mother, the paternal grandmother. I knew the probate court and also the DI worker had already assessed her for placement, but I told him I would conduct my own assessment. There were so many issues to consider in this assessment. Clearly relatives are preferable over strangers. For practical, relational, and legal reasons, I was compelled to carefully review the possibility of placement with the paternal grandparents.

Closer examination, however, revealed concerns. I attempted to schedule a meeting with the grandmother at her home, but Samuel declined on several occasions, saying it wasn't a good time because of his parents' poor health. Their health concerns made me wonder whether either elderly caregiver would be agile enough to run after a toddler. Further, the father's reluctance to have me see the home made me suspicious that the house was unsuitable, as previously described by the DI worker and probate court investigator.

I reached the grandmother on the phone and asked her some questions about the home, her relationship with Shannon, and with her son. The grandmother denied that Samuel had any issues. These denials called into question her protective capacity. I also asked why she hadn't yet visited Shannon. The grandmother was unable to answer this or several of my other questions; it seemed that she did not understand my queries. I was worried about the possibility of a cognitive deficit or maybe dementia. My final consideration was that the father lived on the same property in an adjoining apartment, and I did not have confidence that the grandmother would enforce boundaries or uphold the expectation that the father live somewhere else.

I tried to reach out to other relatives, but there were none to speak of. Megan was an only child, so there were no aunts or uncles on her side of the family, and I did not consider Megan's mother—the maternal grandmother—as Megan described her as physically abusive and an active alcoholic. Samuel was estranged from all of his other family members, and none were described as appropriate for placement.

Other relatives surfaced, though. Megan's father and stepmother came to visit and met Shannon for the first time. They too wanted to be helpful and asked if Shannon could live with them rather than with her foster parents. Although these grandparents were active and healthy, and they posed no safety concerns, they lived several hundred miles away. I knew placement that far away would essentially eliminate visits with Samuel and Megan, and regular visitation is associated with reunification. Further, although they were blood relatives—a clear priority in policy and practice—Shannon knew them as strangers. Another move for her would be consequential. Megan was following the requirements of her case plan and, as a result, reunification looked promising within the next 6 months. Ultimately, I denied placement with all of Shannon's relatives and left her in the home of her foster parents.

Although Samuel was frustrated that his daughter was not living with his parents, he nonetheless engaged in some of his required services. He went to outpatient drug treatment for a couple of weeks, started drug testing, and was seeing his daughter regularly during supervised visits. I wanted to stagger his case plan so that he didn't experience an excessive burden of requirements, so I added a case plan component about a month into the case. I asked that he participate in regular therapy. The new requirement shut him down. He continued to visit his daughter fairly consistently, but he refused to engage in drug treatment, drug testing, or his other services any longer. His denial was deep, and the list of other people's problems was long. I really think he believed what he was telling me, but from my perspective it was clear that his reality did not reflect my reality. Our meetings always ended with him in tears, berating me, and accusing the agency of stealing his daughter. I provided opportunity after opportunity for him to participate, offering referrals that I knew he wouldn't utilize, but covering my bases so that no one could say I didn't do everything I could to try to help. What made it hardest was that I supervised hours of visits between Samuel and Shannon, and she clearly benefited from their relationship. But he couldn't see that his behaviors at home were a danger to her.

Although Samuel struggled participating in his case plan, Megan was an all-star, making my job easy. Her motivation to get her daughter back was deeply internal, and she harnessed that motivation. I gave her some tools and resources, but she's the one who made the most of the opportunities presented. She drug tested weekly, she attended all of her appointments, and she was engaged and participating. She was developing insight into what she had exposed her daughter to, the possible effects on her child, and how her actions could be changed to prevent further trauma to Shannon in the future. Megan's path wasn't easy. She struggled with housing challenges, job loss, and continued harassment from Samuel in attempts to regain power and control. But she was open and honest with me, and that helped me find the right resources for her. Given her progress, I felt comfortable shifting visits from supervised to unsupervised, and from hourly to several days per week, to frequent overnights. The gradual transition allowed Mr. and Mrs. Caldwell to share parenting with Megan over a period of several weeks so that Shannon could benefit from all of their love.

About mid-winter, we returned to court for the 6-month **Family Reunification Review**. Because of the delays in the beginning of the case, Shannon had been in foster care for about 9 months. I recommended to the judge that he terminate Samuel's reunification services and return Shannon to her mother with an additional 6 months of mandatory Family Maintenance services. Both parents attended court, but Samuel stalked out of the courthouse before the hearing was called, instructing his attorney to tell the court he had "no comment."

Shannon had lived with her foster parents for about 6 months. But how long does it take substitute parents to fall in love with a child? Clearly much less time than that. The couple had made Shannon a genuine part of their family. They loved her like a biological child, and Shannon was clearly attached to them. I gave them the news and let them have a final night with Shannon before I moved her home. When I arrived the next morning, everything was packed and ready to go. I asked if they would be open to continuing their relationship with Shannon and Megan, and they were overjoyed at the prospect.

I'll always remember that morning. It represents, for me, the essence of the lose-lose and the win-win that is the child welfare system. I had Mrs. Caldwell place Shannon in a car seat and we drove away. It was wrenching. There was Shannon, on her way to live with her mother, clutching her blanket and teddy bear, crying and calling out for her foster parents. I tried to soothe her, of course, but she eventually cried herself to sleep, awakening only when we reached her mother's apartment.[53]

It was difficult, at first. Shannon was anxious and clingy to Megan. She would often cry and ask for her foster parents, waking throughout the night with nightmares. Megan was horribly concerned that she was doing something wrong. I had to explain again and again that these were normal reactions, and that any move is stressful for a toddler. I encouraged her to be loving, consistent, and responsive—all things that she was already doing—and Shannon would grow to trust her again.

Megan found the adjustment to full-time parenting especially difficult because her recovery of 10 months was still fresh. She worried that she wasn't ready, that she didn't have everything in place, and that Shannon might be better off staying with the foster parents who had significant financial resources. I had to be a cheerleader, reinforcing her capabilities and reassuring her that the number-one thing a child needs is a mother's love and not material items. I encouraged Megan to lean on her support network during this transition, because a relapse would have been a huge setback for all involved. Megan rose to the challenge, and as the days and weeks progressed Shannon settled, slept through the night, and relied on Megan for her consistency and care. For their part, Mr. and Mrs. Caldwell maintained regular visits so that Shannon would not suffer another loss.

During the period of Family Reunification and 6 months of Family Maintenance services, Megan completed every component of her staggered case plan. In addition, she graduated from our voluntary drug court, found stable housing, and started working on a degree. Shannon was thriving. She was growing taller and chatting incessantly. She enjoyed supervised visits with her father, took regular outings with Mr. and Mrs. Caldwell, and started going to day care.

It was summer again. I had worked with the family for about a year. Megan had been clean and sober for 15 months, and Samuel was visiting. Megan and I sat together in the waiting room at court. I wanted to neatly sum up her accomplishments and give some essential reminders for future success, but instead, we had a heart-to-heart talk about where she started, the challenges in her life, the progress that she'd made, and my honest belief that she and Shannon would both thrive. Megan had important supports now built into her life—including the support of Mr. and Mrs. Caldwell—and Shannon had many people in her life who cared for her. I felt confident she would now be safe.

Cheerleader to the end, we entered the courtroom together, teary eyed. The bailiff called the case. The judge complimented Megan on her tenacity and hard work. I recommended he dismiss dependency with full legal and physical custody granted to Megan and continued supervised visits for Samuel. Five minutes after entering the courtroom, it was all over. Megan hugged her attorney, and we left the courtroom. I congratulated her, she hugged me, said thank you, and drove away.

All that's left are the files in my filing cabinet and a photo of Shannon that Megan gave me on our last home visit. The girl in the picture glows with confidence. I have so many hopes for this family—that Samuel will stay involved and that Megan will remain strong. But I hope especially that Shannon will enjoy a childhood free from further trauma and disruption and that she gets to keep all of the important relationships she's developed with her parents, her extended relatives, and her foster parents, all of whom love her dearly.

Alyssa Barkley

The child welfare worker who originally detained Shannon held concerns that her parents were not caring for her safely. Enacting the first principle of child welfare (*Parents who care for their children safely should be free from government intrusion in their family*), Megan and Samuel were met with a child welfare response. We don't know about the early interactions between the child welfare worker and the parents, but we know that the worker and the courts determined that Shannon was *unsafe* (principle 2) in the midst of domestic violence and parental drug use. The volatile situation and acrimony between the parents was severe, pitting the second principle of safety and third principle of family squarely in conflict. And the initial child welfare worker and this worker both tried to enact the fourth principle (*When children cannot live with family, they should live with extended relatives*), but the circumstances of the available kin created too much uncertainty. Indeed, a probate judge in an entirely different court also viewed the extended family member as problematic. Ultimately, Shannon was placed in foster care, though the experience was not without its hazards. Although her caregivers loved her, the turbulence in and out of three homes was far less than ideal. When Shannon returned home to Megan, the third principle of child welfare was again endorsed (*Children should be raised with their family of origin*), even though the Caldwells were eager to make a permanent commitment to the little girl. This child welfare worker's dedication to the child, Shannon's devoted mother, and the generosity of the Caldwells, insured that Shannon would experience the principles of family and permanency—not in conflict, but in harmony—an outcome in child welfare that is too often elusive to attain.

Child welfare work is often less than ideal and frequently complicated. Where children should live and with whom can be guided by policy proscriptions, but day-to-day practice suggests that these decisions are nuanced and must be implemented thoughtfully. Returning to the fundamental values guiding child welfare, children such as Shannon should be *raised with their family of origin*. But when temporary circumstances limit staff's capacities to keep children with their own family, children like Shannon should have the benefit of an alternative home. In the best-case scenario, children can be shared between parents, relatives, and foster parents, where they experience a thick circle of love that has nothing to do with the legal boundaries of relationship and has everything to do with people who would turn the world upside-down for one, individual child. Sometimes that can happen in child welfare; it takes a skilled child welfare worker to set the tone and context to make it happen.

6

Fighting for "Hard-to-Place" Kids

THE LONG HISTORY of child welfare in the United States is a story of opposing ideologies. This is, perhaps, no better exemplified than in the field's views of congregate care. Early efforts in child welfare emphasized the use of group care arrangements for children. Orphanages, centered on the care of a single racial or ethnic group, national origin, or religious group, were an improvement upon the adult-centered almshouses where children were housed in the early years of US history.[1] The term *orphanage* is really a misnomer, however, as most children had at least one living parent, typically unable to care for them due to extreme poverty, ill health, or other incapacities.[2] Orphanages reflected a common view that institutional care represented an appropriate model for children's care.[3] The strategy was considered optimal to inculcate religious teachings and to build moral character among children who were otherwise considered wayward.[4]

But over time, congregate care arrangements were supplanted by foster homes, first seen in the large-scale relocation of White immigrant children from the city centers of the East on "orphan trains" to western family and farm homes,[5] and also in Midwestern efforts to develop a viable child welfare system within newly created state government structures.[6] The 1909 White House Conference on the Care of Dependent Children established a consensus among child care professionals that children raised outside of their home of origin were best raised in families.[7] The data thereafter show a gradual decline in the use of residential care. In 1923, about two thirds of children in out-of-home care resided in congregate care settings; a decade later, the percentage had dropped to less than half; and by 1969, fewer than one fifth of children lived in residential institutions.[8]

The emergence of foster care as the preferred placement setting was as much a tilt toward a different paradigm as it was a rebuttal of what had heretofore been viewed as advantageous. Group living, rather than offering the promise of shared expectations for behavior and morality, instead was viewed as a setting for contagion, where the manners and norms of "deviant" children would be adopted by others.[9] Today, the principle that *children should be raised in families* prevails. We see increasing numbers of children placed with their relatives when substitute care is required (see Chapter 5), and when kin are unavailable or inappropriate for care, foster homes are typically pursued for children's temporary, and sometimes permanent, care. Group care is seen, in most states and even internationally, as a "last resort" placement setting, rather than a preferred starting point.[10]

The decline of group care has followed shifting principles and beliefs, but theory and research evidence also guard against its use. Developmental theory suggests that—at least for younger children—families are best suited to provide the consistency and attachment youngsters need.[11] And the evidence on the effectiveness of congregate care is mixed. Most studies are limited methodologically, but even the stronger studies point to disparate findings. Some research shows modest beneficial effects compared to community-based alternatives;[12] some show no effects;[13] while one study evidenced more positive effects for youth compared to treatment foster care.[14] Beneficial effects are typically noted as short term and do not, generally, appear to be sustained over time.[15] Because the evidence is mounting to indicate that many children otherwise served in group care or residential treatment could be served as effectively in well-supported treatment foster care homes,[16] the additional cost associated with congregate care and its greater degree of restrictiveness call into question its suitability for large proportions of children in out-of-home care.

Today, group care disproportionately serves boys, older youth, African American youth, [17] and children with behavior problems.[18] And unlike the majority of children who are placed in care for reasons relating to child maltreatment, children who are ultimately placed in a congregate care setting are much more likely to be removed from home because of "child behavior problems."[19] Common conceptions suggest that the majority of children "fail up"—that is, they are initially placed in kin or foster homes, and then through a series of placement disruptions move into more restrictive levels of care over time.[20] This is not necessarily the case. On average, children who are ever placed in congregate care have more variable patterns in their placement histories than children who are never placed in congregate care.[21] But their patterns of care are neither predictable nor vertical (from less restrictive to more restrictive levels of care).[22] One study examining a nationally representative sample shows that among all children placed in a congregate care setting over a 3-year period, fully half were placed directly into congregate care upon removal from their home.[23] In another study, children were most likely to be placed in group care, residential treatment, or an inpatient psychiatric facility within the first 2 to 3 months following entry to care.[24] Children with clinically significant behavioral or emotional needs were especially likely to be placed directly into a congregate care setting. And although the common view is that group care should only be used for children with substantial emotional or behavioral needs, many children in group care have a behavior profile not dissimilar to children placed in foster care.[25]

Why do we use group homes if there is general consensus that other options are preferable? Resource availability likely contributes to the utilization of group care, particularly for children or youth who do not need a more restrictive care setting.[26] Unlike foster care, congregate care is a relatively elastic commodity. Recruiting, screening, and training foster parents is arduous work and there is, as yet, no evidence base to guide agencies in successfully recruiting a robust supply of caregivers. As a result, the shortage of foster homes is acute in many jurisdictions, particularly for older youth. In Los Angeles County, for example, home of the largest child welfare system in the United States, the capacity of foster homes declined from approximately 22,000 beds to 9,000 in the most recent 15-year period.[27] And according to media accounts, foster home scarcity is a problem in most states and is reported in news outlets on almost a monthly basis.[28] In contrast to the difficulty in growing and supporting a large supply of foster homes to care for children, group homes can be relatively easily developed and staffed in response to surges in demand. Evidence from one state shows that group care placements often serve as a temporary solution to shortages in the foster caregiver census.[29]

A cross-section of all children in out-of-home care shows that about 14% live in a group home, residential treatment facility, or inpatient psychiatric facility[30]—a 37% decline since 2004.[31] But substantial state variation exists. In Colorado and South Carolina, for example, 35% and 22% of children, respectively, reside in congregate care settings, whereas in Oregon and Kansas, only 4% and 5% of children, respectively, are served in group care.[32] Variability in the utilization of group care across states is also seen as we examine the prevalence of young children in congregate care. Policies in some states guard against the use of congregate care for younger children, but in other states, over two thirds of the children in group care are under the age of 12.[33]

These point-in-time estimates only tell one side of the story, of course. When we examine children's experiences over time, a different narrative emerges. In fact, many children touched by the child welfare system are served in some type of group care setting—particularly older youth and those who have remained longer in care. A study of youth in care at age 17 showed that the large majority (75%) had spent some time in a residential treatment facility during their total stay in care. Almost one in two children had been in an inpatient psychiatric facility.[34] Stays in congregate care settings are usually relatively brief. Over one third of children stay for only 2 months or less; on average, children remain in group care for about 9 months or less.[35]

On the basis of the evidence, there is a growing consensus in the research community that limited use of congregate care settings targeted to children with specific needs, using evidence-based models, may be beneficial.[36] But moving from most preferred to least preferred does not address the complexity of the individual needs children bring to care; eliminating the availability of group care altogether can hardly be a responsible choice when the range of children's needs is so great. In fact, overreliance on the principle that *children should be raised in families* reduces the flexibility child welfare workers need to make the right judgements about children's best care settings. Instead, key to appropriate decision making is having tools and time to make accurate assessments of children and their needs, and an ample supply of caregiving options so that staff can select the best setting to meet each child's needs.

Treatment foster care is often suggested as the antidote to group care for children. Indeed, the research evidence on the effectiveness of treatment foster care—a foster care setting where caregivers are specially trained and supported to care for children with special needs, including mental health, emotional, or behavioral difficulties—is generally positive.[37] But just as agencies struggle to find and support a robust supply of traditional foster parents, efforts to recruit and support treatment foster care providers are equally under-developed.

With too few foster parents and treatment foster parents available, too often group care is used for "hard-to-place" kids when the bureaucracy neither has the time nor the resources to identify creatively an alternative placement resource. A recent national study found that about two fifths of children and youth placed in congregate care settings had no "clinical indicators."[38] Findings such as these suggest that decisions to use group care are sometimes motivated by factors other than need. Child welfare workers who want to resist the institutional pressures to overrely on group care may need fortitude and a good deal of tenacity to keep the child's needs at the center of their practice.

"Danny"

According to Danny's **Risk Profile**, he was a sexual perpetrator with mental health and behavioral challenges, and a history of violence toward adults and peers. He was what most child welfare workers would call a "difficult-to-place" child. I was told that the Risk Profile protects the agency from liability, as it informs the foster parents of risky behaviors, health issues, and mental health needs that the child may (or may not) have. The foster parents can then make an informed decision about whether or not they are able to meet the needs of the child. It makes sense, I suppose, from an agency standpoint. But what about the standpoint of the child?

Danny's parents had struggled with his behavior for some time. As early as preschool, Danny was assaulting teachers and peers, destroying property, and being highly disruptive in the classroom. There was a long history of domestic violence between his parents, as well as violence between Danny and his older brother. The history of allegations against his parents ran the gamut—emotional abuse, physical abuse, and neglect. In each investigation, however, his parents presented as dumbfounded as to why their son was behaving in such a manner. They often pointed to their older, well-adjusted son as proof that the problem must lie in Danny himself. At one point, they convinced themselves that Danny must have been molested as a very young child in child care, and that this was the cause of his anger and acting out.

About 6 months prior to my meeting Danny, his parents had sent him to live with relatives to see if a change of environment would be helpful. Danny did well with his relatives and didn't exhibit any of the behavioral challenges that his parents reported. But after a few months in his relatives' home, Danny displayed a new behavior that no one anticipated: Danny inappropriately touched a younger child in the home. Some would say that Danny "sexually perpetrated" or "molested" this young child, but I'm reluctant to use this terminology because it comes with a damaging label that can follow a child for a lifetime. It is certainly a label that gets highlighted with a star next to it on the Risk Profile, making it very difficult to get a foster parent to even consider accepting the child. Label aside, Danny's behavior was inappropriate and landed him in Juvenile Hall in the county where his relatives lived, several hours away from his parents and the community he called home. Even the staff at the Juvenile Hall were not pleased to have Danny in their custody, and they fought to have jurisdiction transferred to the Juvenile Dependency Court in the county where Danny's parents lived. The court held a hearing to determine whether Danny would be best served through Juvenile Dependency—otherwise known as child welfare (**WIC 300**)—or Juvenile Delinquency, known as juvenile justice (**WIC 600**). It was agreed that Danny would be best served through child welfare, and a petition was filed under WIC 300 (b), due to his parents failing to provide for his general needs, and WIC 300 (c), due to their inability to meet his emotional needs.

From the outset it was clear that Danny had experienced significant trauma in his life and his needs were complex. It was also clear that his parents were not able or willing to meet his needs. The looming questions that I was tasked to answer were what exactly were Danny's needs and who would be able to meet them and keep him safe in the process. Managers in my department informed me, early on, that Danny would need to be placed in a group home. The limited information we had available was not favorable, relatives were unwilling to care for him, and his behaviors were just too risky and his needs too high to recommend a foster home.

Juvenile Hall was obviously not the answer for Danny. As I made arrangements to transport Danny to his home county, staff at the Hall called every day to complain about his behavior and demand that he be picked up immediately. When I asked for clarification about the behaviors that Danny was displaying, it became clear that the issue was not Danny's unsafe behavior; rather, he was needy and was constantly seeking the attention of staff. To put it bluntly, Danny was annoying, and to be fair, the Juvenile Hall setting was not equipped to provide Danny with the emotional support he needed. It was not until my 4-hour-long car ride with Danny that I was able to fully understand why the Hall staff were so eager to move him out.

I'll admit that I was nervous about personally transporting Danny such a long distance. My knowledge of Danny was limited to the worst things written about him in his file, and the Juvenile Hall's eagerness to move him along made the pending trip unnerving. He was a large teenage boy with a history of violence, who for the first time in several weeks would be stepping out into the free world. What I was hoping for was a sullen teen with a chip on his shoulder who was too cool for me and unwilling to speak; at least that would be a quiet and uneventful drive. There is no way I could have guessed how it really turned out.

The Juvenile Hall caged van pulled up, and Danny emerged wearing the street clothes that he'd obviously worn when he was admitted. They hadn't been washed. Always managing risk, the Hall staff had removed his shoe laces and his belt (risk of strangulation), so he kept slipping out of his too-loose shoes and he struggled to keep his pants up while handcuffed. As we transferred Danny's belongings from the van to my sporty Chevy Malibu rental, courtesy of my employer, I wondered what the hulky, uniformed, and altogether intimidating Juvenile Hall officers were thinking. Of course, I brought my own reinforcement for protection: another female coworker, even smaller than I.

Danny, I was warned, was indeed a big boy, much bigger than me. I made sure to ask the Juvenile Hall staff if Danny had received his noon medications, meant to stabilize his mood and minimize the risk of experiencing angry outbursts, and asked what type of emotional state he was in.[39] Of course, he hadn't received the medications and he had slept the first 4 hours of the trip. Lucky for us, he was unmedicated and energized. I was relieved when he took his medication at my polite request with no resistance. After a moment of becoming reacquainted with his personal belongings, including his belt, we began our journey together.

Danny was talkative; very, very talkative, and he talked as if he had known us for years. In fact, most of his comments began with, "Did I ever tell you . . .?" He was incredibly excited about driving through San Francisco and seeing the Golden Gate Bridge, although he seemed equally excited about random other sightings on the road. Trucks, signs, bumper stickers, unique license plates, trees; he was easily amused. He talked about his hobbies and talents and genuinely speculated on whether he might be part African American because of his dancing, rapping, and basket weaving skills. He enjoyed listening to the radio, but became concerned when Alicia Keys' song "Girl on Fire" came on, at which point he commented that she should be careful because people might think she were an arsonist.

By the end of our trip, I'd only known Danny for 4 hours, but it felt like I had known him forever. He was sweet, funny, absolutely adorable, happy, had a surprisingly positive outlook on life, and wore his heart on his sleeve. I did understand, however, why the Juvenile Hall felt challenged by him. He was exhausting, needy, and starved for attention. He certainly had my attention at this point. In our 4 hours together he had melted my heart and made an impact on my life that I would never forget.

We placed Danny in a temporary foster home utilized for the sole purpose of housing foster children ages 10–17 until a longer term placement can be identified. It is our county's version of an emergency shelter or receiving home. Ms. Dickinson, a gentle-voiced foster mother with a heart of gold, lived in a lovely home on a beautiful stretch of land. It was a complete contrast from where he'd lived a day previously, and probably a drastic difference from his prior home environment as well. I hoped this change of environment would provide Danny what he needed to change the direction of his path in life.

Days went by and I received only positive reports from Ms. Dickinson. The only issue she raised was the need to offer multiple prompts for quiet time. Basically, he never stopped talking. I began to wonder if sending Danny to a group home was necessary, or at all appropriate, given the fact that he was showing stability in a regular foster home. When I asked Danny where he wanted to live, he told me he liked living with Ms. Dickinson and rejected living in a group home, as he feared it might be similar to his experience in Juvenile Hall. I was directed, however, to move forward with identifying a group home for Danny because there was no foster home willing to take him, given his alarming Risk Profile. Moreover, the school district refused to allow him back because of the previous incidents that had occurred while he was living at home with his parents. Even the County Mental Health Department agreed that Danny needed to be given a non–public school designation, meaning he needed to receive his education within the walls of a residential treatment facility.

When Danny lived with his parents, he struggled significantly and it seemed like he had burned every bridge that might lead to supportive services in the community. If I wanted to keep Danny out of a group home, I was going to have to advocate strongly against my own agency in addition to every other department in the county that would be providing services to Danny. As I spent more and more time with Danny, though, I decided that this was a battle worth fighting.

At first, I thought that my best line of defense would be to buy as much time as possible. The more time Danny stayed in Ms. Dickinson's temporary foster home and proved he was not just experiencing a "honeymoon," the better. I couldn't possibly be forced to send a kid to a group home after having perfect behavior in regular foster care for several weeks. Luckily, I had a very understanding supervisor who trusted my judgment and was willing to support my crusade. But unfortunately, it started to look like the battle was bigger than both of us combined. No matter how sympathetic others were to my cause, there was simply no foster home in the county willing to take Danny.

Or was there? Danny was doing very well in his current foster home, and Ms. Dickinson had expressed an interest in having him stay. In my county, allowing a temporary foster home to keep a child long term was a very touchy subject, taboo even, due to the fact that there was a shortage of this type of home. If the **Placement unit** got word that a social worker was trying to recruit a temporary foster home for a long-term placement, the social worker's head would be on a chopping block. I needed to buy more time, so I appealed to the Juvenile Court judge. Our judge had a tendency to micromanage many juvenile dependency cases—a dynamic I often found quite frustrating—but in this scenario, I hoped her style would work to my child's advantage. Ultimately, it did. The judge ordered that Danny not be sent to a group home without (1) a psychological evaluation in which the psychologist weighed in on the type of placement that would best meet Danny's needs, and (2) a court order allowing a group home placement.

The psychologist conducted an evaluation and determined that a group home would be the worst placement option and would increase his potential for victimization. She recommended a therapeutic foster home with no younger children present. Indeed, that was exactly where Danny was currently placed! I had already irritated staff in the Placement unit, so I did the unspeakable: I encouraged Ms. Dickinson to make the call, to say that she wanted to become a long-term foster home, and to keep Danny. At first, I thought we'd won. But then I realized that all of us lost: me, Danny, and all the other foster children who could have thrived in her care. The **Foster Family Agency** with which she was affiliated felt very strongly about keeping her as an emergency caregiver and set up numerous hurdles for her to jump. The back and forth took its toll, and in the end she decided to withdraw as a foster parent altogether.

When a system tasked to protect children cannot stay focused on the child, who wants to be part of that system? Who can stand by and watch while a child's needs take a backseat to the needs of an agency? Danny's foster mother couldn't, and as a result she simply left. I wanted to keep fighting for Danny, but I couldn't do it alone. It would take a team to care for him, and I didn't even have a foster parent on Danny's team anymore.

I began to see clearly the discrepancy that sometimes lies between what is in the best interest of a child and what is in the interest of the agency. But shouldn't the best interest of the child prevail? From that point on, the best interest of the agency seemed to prevail.

My supervisor and I got nowhere in our continued efforts to persuade others to take our view. After putting in some effort with the school district and mental health department, our manager ultimately decided that the situation was not worth the potential of damaging our agency's relationship with other county agencies. I was officially given the directive to place Danny in the group home that the Placement unit had secured for him. While the judge was powerful, she couldn't materialize a foster home that would take Danny, and I still had no options.

I felt lost. It was the first time I cried at work. At least I made it to the parking lot before I broke down. I called my supervisor from my car, and she did her best to be empathetic while gently making it clear that she had to support our manager's decision. I told her that I could not ethically sign the paperwork, and I did not think I could bring myself to take Danny to the group home. She reminded me that while I felt powerless, Danny still needed me to be strong for him and make the best of the situation for him. I could not stomach the thought of letting Danny know that he would have to go to a group home even though he had thrived in his foster home. I didn't even know if I could do it without weeping myself. It felt like I had his future in my hands, and I was being forced to lead him down the wrong road. I felt physically sick. I had worked in high-level group homes for many years before becoming a social worker. In fact, I was inspired to become a social worker in an effort to keep kids out of group homes when they didn't need to be there. Here I was, part of the problem I'd hoped to prevent.

I vividly remember driving to the foster home to break the news. Like all the other times I visited him, Danny was cheerful, in good spirits, and excited to show me his newest arts and crafts creations. I sat down with him and as gently as possible told him of the transition ahead. I'll never forget his response. He said that at least he would be able to go to the harvest festival, which was close to the city where the group home was located. I didn't know whether to laugh or burst into tears. After all Danny had been through, he was still able to look on the bright side of everything!

I took my supervisor's advice and did my best to make Danny's transition as smooth as possible. I didn't sign the placement paperwork, however, as it felt like an ethical breach. My colleagues knew I was struggling, and even staff in the Placement unit began to feel bad for me.

To my surprise and eternal gratitude, one of them gave me the heads-up that a foster mother and father with a history of working with some of our most challenging kids recently had a child move out, and they had an opening. Suddenly I felt a ray of hope. Usually, staff in the Placement unit pitch a child to our foster parents, but there was no way I was letting that happen. I needed these foster parents to see Danny through my eyes, not read about him in the Risk Profile.

I called and told them all about Danny. I hid nothing. I knew I would be required to share the Risk Profile with them and obtain their signature, so there was no reason to sugarcoat his history. We talked about his sexualized behavior, about the challenges with the school district and with the Department of Mental Health, and I made it clear that it might take some time to work out a service plan to meet his needs. But in our conversation I emphasized who Danny really was and how he was doing with Ms. Dickinson. I provided my assessment that many of Danny's prior behaviors were the result of a chaotic and traumatic home environment and that I was hopeful he would continue to do well in a supportive, nurturing, and structured home. I was open and honest about all of the unknowns. It didn't take long before they made their decision; they let me know that they wanted to give Danny a chance and open their home to him.

Typically, I hand off my cases to an ongoing worker as soon as the **disposition hearing** is over. In this case, my supervisor allowed me to keep Danny's case past the disposition hearing so that I could support the transition to his new foster home. The day he moved was the last time I had contact with Danny. I lingered a little longer than needed and when we said goodbye I selfishly asked that he remember me, knowing full well that his memory of me would be lost in the mix of all the other social workers that he was likely to encounter through the life of his case. To my delight, he responded that he would definitely remember me, but not as the social worker who saved him from going into a group home; rather, as the girl who was bitten by a golden retriever. I couldn't help laughing as I remembered the story I'd shared with him about a golden retriever that bit me in the face, leaving a small scar in the smile line on my cheek. He had found it particularly amusing that out of all dogs, it was a golden retriever that bit me. I honestly didn't care what it was he remembered about me, just as long as it was a positive memory that might bring him a smile some day. I think about Danny often and it certainly brings a smile to my face, scar and all.

Monica Montury

This child welfare worker fought hard to keep her child out of group care, thus enacting the principle that *children should be raised in families* (principle 5). Danny was not *safe* (principle 2) and could not live *with his family of origin* (principle 3). And *extended relatives* (principle 4) were unavailable for his care. Although the child welfare worker enjoyed the support of a compassionate supervisor, she still needed to exert tremendous efforts to help others in her agency see the value of the fundamental principle of *family* (principle 5). The lesson, of course, is that sometimes agency priorities can become cloudy when a simple path isn't readily available. And the role of the child welfare worker in serving as a fierce advocate pursuing a principled path may be required more frequently than might be expected.

Children with challenging behaviors or mental health needs typically require a level of effort that goes beyond the average. They have complicated problems that sometimes require complex solutions. For some, group care may be the best alternative to secure the principle of *safety*—especially those with deep scars and fragile mental health. Some children, victims of profound maltreatment, have been significantly traumatized by their experiences in families and struggle with extreme mental health issues that challenge their capacities to live peaceably in any environment. Some evidence suggests that over one third of children involved with the child welfare system have emotional or behavioral problems; among older children, over half manifest these problems in the clinical range.[40] For these children, the aspirations of our foundational principle of family is tested; a family-based placement may be impractical, and it may conflict with the pragmatism of caregiver availability and the limits of parents' own capacities. Sometimes an evidence-based congregate care setting[41] may provide the rehabilitative environment a child needs to promote his or her well-being. But as we see in the following illustration, efforts to secure the services some children need—whether in a foster home or group home setting—sometimes conflict with other principles we hold of equal value.

"Luke"

It was my first year as a child welfare worker when I was assigned to Luke's case, a 13-year-old boy, initially raised by his mother in the Midwest. His mother suffered from a severe addiction, and she neglected Luke's needs entirely. In addition to neglecting Luke's care, her inattention to her young son exposed him to repeated sexual abuse by a number of her acquaintances. Luke's mother eventually lost physical and legal custody of her son and later abandoned Luke altogether. When I met him, Luke told me he hated his mother, but it was also clear that he felt a range of other emotions about her and was troubled that he had no information about her whereabouts or how he might contact her.

As a result of the chronic abuse and neglect he experienced in his early childhood, Luke was challenged by significant mental health concerns. According to the psychological evaluations in his file, Luke suffered from posttraumatic stress disorder (PTSD), attention-deficit/hyperactivity disorder (ADHD), conduct disorder, depression, and a severe and debilitating anxiety disorder. At the center of his fears were his constant worries that he would be abandoned again. In addition to his mental health challenges, Luke had a disabling condition requiring accommodations. As a result, he also worried that the adults responsible for his care might not be sensitive to his physical disability or that he would not be cared for properly.

Prior to meeting me, Luke had spent a good part of his childhood in and out of foster care outside of California. While in care, he had experienced multiple changes in placement from group homes to foster homes to residential treatment as he and the adults around him struggled to manage the behavioral issues caused by his anxiety. After he was placed in a special day school where he received therapeutic services for his mental health needs and a predictable routine that helped him manage his anxiety, Luke became stable enough to live with his father, Mark, and stepmother, Lisa. When the family later moved to California, Mark was taken aback at how the move destabilized their fragile family stasis. Faced with a seemingly unending string of behavioral problems, Mark and Lisa struggled to address the boy's conduct appropriately. A child maltreatment report was filed when Lisa shoved Luke, temporarily exacerbating the symptoms associated with his disability.

Mark fought the physical abuse allegations in court over a period of about 6 months. He argued that he and Lisa were busy and hardworking, that they loved Luke, were committed to supporting him, and knew what was best for him. Although Mark conceded that they needed help managing Luke's behavior, he also believed that the state had no right to remove the boy from their custody. He also claimed that the child welfare services offered to his son, to date, had been ineffective or, worse, harmful. Luke, he contended, needed a therapeutic group home to attend to his mental health needs. In short, their family needed help because of Luke's needs—not because he and his wife had maltreated their son.

I was assigned to Luke's case as a **Family Reunification** worker after the court had taken jurisdiction and assigned Luke to out-of-home care. My role was to support Luke and his needs while also assisting the parents' efforts to strengthen their skills in managing their son's behaviors. The goal was to reunify the family and return custody to Mark and Lisa. Of course, the irony of the situation was that Mark had never wanted to lose legal custody of his son in the first place.

The initial months of Luke's stay in out-of-home care were fraught. Motivated simultaneously by a desire to place Luke in a family-like setting but also deterred by the enormous costs of therapeutic care, my supervisor encouraged me to place Luke in a series of foster homes, with largely disastrous results. With at least five placements over six months, Luke was moved repeatedly for reasons ranging from cruelty to animals to inappropriate sexual conduct with other children. Ultimately, Luke found stability in a group home specializing in the care and treatment of youth with severe emotional disturbance. There, Luke seemed to find comfort in a predictable 24-hour schedule and the therapy he received from an attentive clinician who deeply understood him, his history, and the ways that his past shaped his current behavior. In addition, the therapist worked with Luke's father to develop skills in monitoring and managing his son without physical punishment. I was encouraged as I observed Luke's increased emotional stability, his engagement in treatment, and his father's dedication to his son.

After Luke had been in care for 12 months, I was forced to make an impossible choice: recommend that Luke return home to his father or recommend Luke's permanent plan as remaining in the group home. These binary options didn't suit the needs of this family, but they were the options available to me, given the structure of the law and the principles upon which these laws are based. Luke could certainly return home, but he would need a high level of daily support in school and at home to help with his therapeutic needs. Both Mark and I clamored to bring such support into his home, but neither the child welfare agency could provide these high-level in-home services, nor could a juvenile court judge impose these requirements on mental health or educational agencies outside its purview. Alternatively, if Luke remained in his group home, where his therapeutic and educational needs were met, his father would lose access to the services that were supporting the family and—ultimately—he might lose his parental rights to Luke as well.

While encouraged by the family's progress, I was still deeply concerned that Luke and his family would not do well without the additional supports provided by a structured educational and mental health milieu. Both Mark and I had tried to secure these services through the child welfare, mental health, and educational systems but to no avail, and Mark did not have the financial means to pay for these services privately. Hoping that Mark would be able to petition the court at a later date if circumstances changed, I recommended at the **permanency** planning hearing that services to Luke's family be terminated with a permanent plan for Luke to stay in the group home where he was receiving therapeutic support.

It shouldn't have surprised me, perhaps, but everything fell apart after that. Losing services and the state's confidence in their family, Mark and Lisa seemed to lose faith, too. They decided abruptly to move, determining that the cost of living was too high and that they could live more affordably in a community about 100 miles away from Luke. Luke was devastated. His original fears of abandonment resurfaced, and the resulting fear, anger, and sadness were overwhelming. Over the next few months, I was often called to pick up Luke from Juvenile Hall following incidents of vandalism, drugs, or violence. Of course, these behaviors also made it more difficult to reconnect Luke with his father, even though a connection was what he craved most.

The futility of Luke's case never left me. Luke needed the services and supports that a therapeutic group home could provide, but to secure those services Mark and Lisa had to be labeled poor parents, unable to control their son. The services, once provided, were time limited. To continue intensive services for Luke, a "permanent plan" of sustained residence in the group home was required and the services that supported this fragile family were withdrawn. In the end I was left wondering why we couldn't just help Luke and his family—providing services for as long as it took, and without conditions. For a spell, Luke had found stability, happiness, and a connection with his father. Ultimately cured of his mental health concerns or not, I wish that we had helped him hold on to that.

Wendy Wiegmann

We'll never know if Luke could have lived somewhere other than a group home. Certainly this child welfare worker tried to help him live in a *family* (principle 5) before resorting to a more restrictive level of care. But the *parent's voice* (principle 8, which will be discussed in a later chapter) was loud and insistent: Mark had seen how ill served his son had been in foster homes outside California and within. He felt certain that his son needed the structure and support of a therapeutic group home, and the child welfare worker tried diligently to honor his voice in the process of serving his son. Once the boy's safety and well-being were secured, however, the push to determine Luke's *permanency* needs (principle 6, also discussed in detail later), unraveled all of the hard work. Mark lost what tenuous faith he had put into the system, and Luke lost faith in his father.

Indeed, *children should be raised in families.* In line with our principle, most children thrive in families. But some children need an alternative care setting, at least for a period of time, to stabilize their behavior and attend to acute mental health needs. In some cases, congregate care provides safety to children and to their caregivers; in others, group care can attend to children's well-being needs as their behavior and mental health are stabilized prior to stepping down to a lower level of care. Reducing reliance on group care is certainly warranted in states and jurisdictions that see higher than average rates of utilization; that regularly use group care for longer-than-average stays in care; or that rely on group care for young children. The challenge for child welfare professionals is in balancing the foundational principle of family with other equally important principles. Recognizing that there is infrequently one single path forward, and that different cases will call upon staff to maximize different principles, the centerpiece of child welfare is revealed. Navigating these competing spaces is at the heart of the profession.

7

The Quest for a Forever Family

FAMILY IS A central feature of human existence. It has social, economic, political, legal, and ideological dimensions. In addition to its centrality to the human condition, it is undergoing rapid change.[1] Although original conceptions of family were rooted in biological ties between the birth mother and child, and the legal relationship of birth father and child, these narrow definitions have been profoundly reshaped in most modern societies.[2] Today's families, to borrow a definition from Galvin and associates, are "networks of people who share their lives over long periods of time bound by marriage, blood, or commitment, legal or otherwise, who consider themselves as family and who share a significant history and anticipated futures of functioning in a family relationship."[3] These new definitions are welcome in the field of child welfare, where family may be constructed by blood, history, relationship, or legal bonds.

Traditional family configurations are being replaced by a variety of alternative family arrangements across the United States. Today, one half of all US children will spend some part of their childhood in a single-parent household.[4] Ten percent of US children are being raised in grandparent-headed households.[5] And some estimates indicate that almost two fifths of lesbian, gay, or bisexual adults have previously or are currently raising a child.[6] Among low-income families, children's experiences of family are even more varied. Edin and Nelson's studies show that family relationships among low-income households are much more complex than average US families, often characterized by adults with sequential relationships and including many stepchildren.[7]

Foster youth, many of whom hale from complex, low-income families, move into family situations that are also highly varied. As such, we ask them to be extremely flexible, sometimes responsive to a series of evolving household types and arrangements, before they return to their birth families or are placed in new, permanent homes.

But regardless of the shape or boundaries of family type, the family serves as an institutional frame for most modern societies and is most surely the site for rearing children. Child welfare is nested in this institutional frame, fixated on children in the context of families. Whether the role of the child welfare worker is in supporting or finding family (as described in Chapter 3), redirecting children from unsafe families (Chapter 4), or reaching out to extended families (Chapter 5), caseworkers are on the front lines of shaping children's family experiences when family life is in trouble.

Perhaps because of a core belief in the importance of family, in the duration of family relationships, and in the shared history and future that families bring to children, child welfare workers are also dedicated to the concept of permanency for children—*that the caregivers they live with will care for them permanently.* The notion of permanency was featured prominently in the Adoption and Safe Families Act of 1997[8] and has had, until recently, a uniquely American meaning.[9]

Today's legal experts consider permanence in terms of its legally binding qualities or "an enduring relationship that is legally enforceable."[10] Not surprisingly, efforts to support permanency for children begin within days of a child's entrance to out-of-home care. The first permanency goal, of course, is to return children to the birth parent from whose home they were removed. This happens for about half of the children who enter care, though we see variability, depending on the age of the child, the type of maltreatment the child sustained, and other factors.[11] When reunification cannot be achieved, other permanency options are explored with children's relatives, either through adoption or guardianship. [12] And when relatives are neither available nor appropriate, nonkin caregivers are sought out to support children's quest for permanency, most frequently through the avenue of adoption.

The United States has been called an "adoption nation"[13] because we have a higher rate of adoption than any other country. This includes adoption through foster care, international adoption, and private adoption. The most recent estimates indicate that over 136,000 children are adopted annually,[14] and foster care adoptions account for about 40% of all adoptions in the United States.[15] To pause and consider our European counterparts, we see that adoption is infrequently invoked in many other countries. In Denmark and

Norway, for example, adoption is legal, but it is rarely invoked;[16] in Sweden, it can only be granted with parental consent.[17] Adoption raises important questions about the human and legal rights of the birth parent and because many adoptions from foster care in the United States are involuntary—that is, they occur without the consent of the parents—adoption represents an extreme form of state power and should therefore be invoked with considerable caution. Adoption requires the termination of the birth parent's legal rights to the child and it transfers these care and custodial rights to an alternative adult. For the child, adoption confers a number of important material advantages, including greater financial security and rights to inheritance, but there are affective dimensions as well. Adoption offers children a critical sense of stability and belonging[18] that they may otherwise lack in foster care, and many scholars point to adoption as both lasting and binding.[19]

Children subject to legal guardianship, usually with a kinship caregiver, also experience the benefits of legal permanence. Although parents may petition the court to return their child if warranted, it appears that these requests come to the courts infrequently. Children living with their legal guardians experience greater placement stability than children living in foster care, and children report an important sense of psychological or affective permanence while being raised by their relative guardians. Child welfare professionals and judicial officers are in general agreement that adoption is preferred over legal guardianship when reunification has been ruled out, [20] but the availability of subsidized guardianship for kin, made possible through the Fostering Connections to Success Act,[21] has opened a door to another permanency option to families for whom adoption would neither be preferred nor appropriate.

Staff who navigate the complex work of child welfare must attend to all aspects of children's permanency needs. Children require legal permanency, of course (what Mark Testa refers to as "binding" permanence),[22] but children also need to feel as though they are wanted; that they belong; that they are part of a family; and that their home for now will be there into the future—"lasting" permanence.[23] For many children, there is no distinction between types of permanency—where and with whom they live is obviously permanent, emotionally, psychologically, physically, and legally. But one child welfare worker describes how the simple principle of permanency is sometimes difficult to execute in practice. How to proceed when children's legal and affective permanency needs may be in conflict is highlighted in the following case.

"Ethan"

I live and work in a rural area of California. The large majority of people here are White and Christian, and they have common interests in outdoor activities like swimming, boating, hiking, hunting, and fishing. A nearby prison regularly releases parolees at our bus station without buying them a ticket home, so the community has its share of convicted felons. The community's conservative mindset and skepticism about how to respond to homelessness and poverty make it an interesting place to be a social worker trying to support families. Although there's little diversity, the homogeneity of the population simplifies the matching process when you're looking for a foster home that would have commonalities with a child.

Because of my previous career as a middle school teacher, I was given a position in the Intensive Services unit of our agency, where we work primarily with youth whose behaviors land them in a group home or put them at risk of going to one. These children often act out. They run away, get arrested, or engage in dangerous activities, which means that they need a lot more attention than a "typical baby case," when an infant is safely placed in a foster home, or with a relative or a family friend who loves them.

Ethan joined my caseload about 3 years ago. He's currently 10 years old and in the fourth grade. He likes soccer, video games, swimming, and watching movies. He shares his snacks and loves to show off his newest toys. He's good at reading and math, but lazy with homework, and he wants to be a forest ranger when he grows up. In other words, he's a seemingly typical little boy, right?

Ethan entered foster care at age 6 after his stepfather was arrested for possession of extensive child pornography, and the home was found in deplorable unsanitary condition, the details of which I will omit to spare the reader. Drugs and related paraphernalia were out in the open and in Ethan's reach, and Ethan's mother severely neglected her son. Further investigation revealed that Ethan had been molested by his stepfather.

Shortly after Ethan was removed to care, his mother relocated to her home state, making visitation sporadic and reunification efforts very difficult. She was pregnant with twins at the time and thought that if she remained in California, her children would automatically be removed from her care at birth. Ethan's stepfather, and father of the twins, was in prison, so there was little that held Ethan's mother here. An **ICPC (interstate compact for the placement of children)** application was completed to assess whether Ethan could be placed with either his mother or maternal grandmother in the other state. Social workers in that state conducted an assessment and determined that neither was able to care adequately for him. The grandmother had an extensive history of abusing her own children and continued to struggle with alcoholism, while the mother suffered from debilitating mental health conditions.

In spite of the distance, Ethan's mother worked hard to respond to the requirements of her case plan. Except for visitation, she completed all of the court ordered services toward reunification. The court found, however, that the objectives of providing ongoing stability for Ethan were not met. Her mental health, her continued communication with the child's father, and her own childhood trauma made it impossible for her to prove that she was capable of protecting Ethan in the future. Further, she now had twin babies she was raising. She was eligible for Social Security due to her diagnosed mental health condition, but this limited income made it hard for her to function and provide for her family. For Ethan, the situation was confusing. His mother had tried to get her son back, but the court was unmoved; she was sufficiently "safe" to raise two young babies, but was "unsafe" to raise her young boy. The judge and child welfare worker felt that Ethan's mother could not meet his emotional needs and that she was likely to expose him to future trauma. The fate of the twins, raised in another state where the judge had no jurisdiction, could not be a subject of our concern, whether we wanted to help her raise those children or not.

Ethan was moved from one foster placement to another five times over the course of a year; twice because of his behavior, twice because foster parents mistreated him, and finally to a low-level group home for boys under age 12. Although policy and practice guard against the use of group care for children under age 12, it was believed at the time that there were no other options available to this little boy. Ethan was assigned to my caseload because my unit specialized in "high-risk" youth who needed intensive services to treat maladaptive behaviors.

For 2 years, I visited Ethan once a month and watched him grow into his own person. Ethan was a good student but pestered his peers. He wanted to see his family but mostly for the presents they gave him.

His mother would visit when she could afford it, but because the court had terminated her reunification services, the agency's focus was only on Ethan and his plans for permanency. I continued to ask the mother about her relatives, hoping we could identify another family member to care for Ethan. I also asked our agency's family finder to look for extended relatives who might be related to the birth father. No results. My coworkers thought my efforts were futile. "Group home kids are not adoptable" is the common mantra among many seasoned staff.

Ethan's mother still had her legal parental rights intact and wanted to reunify with her son. I encouraged her, because I feared that she was Ethan's only chance at permanency, as he was getting older and his behaviors had intensified. She returned to California for awhile and tried to find housing. The long wait lists for subsidized housing made it difficult, and she could not afford rent, so she stayed in a motel with her twin toddlers. She tried to engage with her son, but with limited income, twins to care for, and no one in the area to provide help or support, she ran out of money after about 2 months and gave up. My supervisor and I refused to believe that a cute, smiley, intelligent 8-year-old boy could be deemed unadoptable. We worried that Ethan would bounce around in foster care for the next 10 years if we gave up on our hope for permanency. He needed a parent, and while he was becoming more and more attached to the group home director as a mother figure, he and I knew that she could never really be that permanent person for him. Ethan's legal parent remained his mother, but there was no "permanency" in their relationship. In fact, he had neither a legal or affective relationship with any adult in his life that he or I could describe as "permanent."

The search started for a forever family who would be a "good fit" for Ethan. I asked the adoptions unit to search for families who were looking for someone like Ethan, using their national confidential online databases. No good matches were found. Then, a local couple was identified who had an interest in adopting. It was a same-sex male couple who had already helped raise a friend's teenage daughter.

I held a **full disclosure meeting**, during which all the pertinent details of Ethan's family history, physical health, mental health, and behaviors were shared with the prospective adoptive family. I shared what I knew about this little boy, Ethan's therapist disclosed details of his past and of his challenging behaviors, and the public health nurse who managed his health file told them what she knew about his physical health. The foster parents were very excited to meet Ethan, and we made a plan for them to develop a "**family book**" as a means of introducing themselves to Ethan. But 2 months later, they contacted me to let me know they decided against the adoption. I felt grateful that they made this decision early on before meeting and then abandoning him. The adoptions unit saw this as their last option, however. Ethan's permanency was again put on hold. His case was brought to court again, and the judge ordered a permanent plan of long-term foster care because no permanent home had been identified.

I was determined that Ethan would not be raised in a group home. I returned to our agency's licensing unit and called the local foster family agencies to determine if there was a foster home available for a great kid. The unfortunate truth is that many social workers would have been less optimistic than I about finding a home for Ethan, but optimism seemed to pay off. I got a call in early summer and was told that a family had just completed the licensing process with the intention of adopting a young boy. I arranged to meet Mr. and Mrs. Wilson, and I told them about Ethan.

Ethan moved in with the Wilsons that winter, after a 4-month transition process. I initially introduced Ethan to the family by way of a photo album. Then I brought them to visit Ethan in the group home. They went on various outings, and then brought him home for a day, then a weekend, then holiday breaks. All the while, I continued to educate them about his several "odd" behaviors: needing the bathroom door to always remain open a bit, regularly refusing to shower, overeating, and needing lots of hugs. The effects of Ethan's early traumas were still evident, and it was important that they show sensitivity to his needs for safety.

The Wilsons were retired and had invested wisely, so their home was beautiful, with a pool, and a TV in Ethan's room. Ethan enjoyed special privileges such as playing games on his tablet after he completed his homework. He enjoyed their dogs and felt like he was part of the family. He got along with their other son but the age difference was too great for them to really play together. The Wilsons had a house in the mountains where they spent their summers, and Ethan attended a camp where he learned all about nature. And they understood that Ethan was, and would always be, attached to his mother. He could talk with her anytime by phone, though he typically chose not to. And he occasionally spoke with the group home administrator so the ties to the important people in his life were still secure—everything according to my plan. Ethan developed a great affection for the Wilsons and told me he wanted to live there forever.

About 8 months after Ethan moved in, the Wilsons left me a voicemail message stating that they needed to speak with me urgently. I returned the call, and Mrs. Wilson explained that they could no longer adopt Ethan. She said that she and her husband stayed up all night talking about it, and they just didn't think they had the patience to handle some of his behaviors. She said Ethan still craved sugar all the time, he didn't change clothes even once during the summer camp, he tended to tell lies to get his way, and he argued about small requests that were made of him. She told me that she understood it would take time to find him a new home, so his move was not imminent, but it was time to start looking for an alternative.

I hung up in utter disbelief. This news, when the court hearing to terminate parental rights was only 1 week away! I experienced a rush of thoughts and emotions. The behaviors Mrs. Wilson described sounded somewhat typical for a 10-year-old boy with a history of significant trauma. I'd witnessed her show tremendous patience toward Ethan. Was this excuse a cover-up for some other issue? Where was their commitment to this little boy? How would I find a new home? I called our attorney and asked her to postpone the hearing.

A week later, a new phone call from the Wilsons suggested they had changed their minds again. Could I now trust these people to raise this special child? If the adoption moved ahead, would they truly commit to serving as a forever family? If I moved him now, could I find a new home? How much damage would I cause if he had to move in with new strangers again?

I discussed the situation with my colleagues, and there were opinions on all sides. After careful consideration I decided that the bigger risk to Ethan's well-being and attachment would be to move him yet again without even giving this family a chance to explain their fears.

I called a **team meeting** to determine a path forward. I attended along with the Wilsons, the adoption social worker, Ethan's therapist, and a member from the **wraparound services** team. The Wilsons explained that they were having family problems and were blindly misdirecting their frustrations onto Ethan. They said they loved Ethan and that they were committed to him. They had spent the weekend talking to our foster parent liaison about their trepidations and realized that they might need to sort out their own family issues before going through with the adoption. I validated their fears and assured them that a person who does not analyze such big decisions probably is not thinking things through thoroughly enough. In the end, we made a plan to include the Wilsons in Ethan's therapy sessions, to engage the wraparound team to provide added support in managing Ethan's behaviors, and to revisit the prospect of adoption at another scheduled team meeting.

We decided to keep Ethan at home with the Wilsons but indefinitely postpone the adoption. I rescheduled the court hearing and went through with my recommendation to terminate parental rights. I called Ethan's birth mother to explain what was happening and why I was moving forward with the termination proceedings. She said she understood and said she was glad he was getting a life she couldn't give him. She asked if she might receive from the Wilsons notes and photos on occasion, and I assured her I would encourage them to honor her wishes. Her attorney later appealed the termination, and so we wait. I'm sure the attorney thought it was the right thing to do—a strategy to delay and give her one last chance to reconsider.

Today, Ethan still isn't adopted. Although he lacks legal permanency at this time, I feel confident he's secured a deep relationship with the Wilsons that gives him a sense of affective permanency. The Wilsons say they are fully committed to being his parents. I still harbor worries that they don't fully understand Ethan's traumatic childhood and how this will likely impact the rest of his life. But they are committed to trying. They are working out their own parenting differences, with help from Ethan's therapist. Mrs. Wilson went back to work part-time, and Mr. Wilson is begrudgingly doing the homework shift. Ethan hates writing and therefore avoids homework adamantly. Ethan is taking a low dose of ADHD medications and says he likes sitting separately from the other kids in class because it makes him "listen better." Every month when I leave Ethan's foster home, he walks me out to my car and gives me at least three hugs. Ethan still needs a nightlight, he lies about silly things for attention, and he's adamant that the shower curtain remain open so he can be assured there are no monsters in there. Ethan now calls Mr. and Mrs. Wilson "Mom" and "Dad," which makes them happy to hear. The rest of the story is yet to be told.

Hanna Rashkovsky

This child welfare worker, determined to enact the principles of *family* (principle 5) and *permanency* (principle 6), had to exert considerable effort to find the right home for this little boy. But the child welfare worker recounting this story sits with considerable uncertainty, unsure whether Ethan's permanency will last, limited in a next-best option if the Wilson's can't hold on to Ethan, and insufficiently content with the current degree of permanency she's secured. There were days when Ethan's permanency felt secure and therefore lasting, but without a legal agreement, there was no certainty that it was binding. Nevertheless, it was the best deal this social worker could broker for Ethan, in spite of its considerable limitations. And if the child welfare worker's experience is both frustrating and unsettling, imagine Ethan's. What's more, Ethan must manage his feelings of insecurity largely on his own. He has no siblings to buffer the situation, and while his child welfare worker and group home administrator try their best, his isolation is, in fact, profound.

Unlike Ethan, some children come to foster care along with their siblings. In fact, many children placed in foster care come from large families.[24] Their narrative of connection is often strong, but their permanency requirements can be especially difficult to secure. Data from one state suggest that only about half of children in foster care reside in a home with all of their siblings. For child welfare workers, finding a home to accommodate a large sibling group can be especially challenging.[25] Not surprisingly, the larger the sibling group, the less likely children can live together.[26]

Information on siblings in foster care is relatively sparse, but the data that are available speak to deep connections of affection.[27] Some evidence suggests that children who are not placed with their siblings miss their brothers and sisters more than they miss their birth parents. When placed together with at least one of their siblings, children typically feel more positive toward their foster family.[28] But for children who are initially placed with a sibling and then separated, many develop behavior problems in care.[29] Often, siblings are the thread that binds troubled families together; some children serve as protectors of younger children, and other siblings take on the role of parent when the original parent is unable to play this role.

Given the importance of siblings to children in care, securing their permanence together is surely in their best interests. But attending to the permanency needs of more than one child doubles or sometimes exponentially complicates an already challenging situation. The strategies child welfare workers employ to adhere to the fundamental principle of permanence, with both legal and affective dimensions, for all children in a sibling group can seem herculean.

"Olivia, Ronald, Vanessa, Chloe, and Nathaniel"

I'd been a child welfare worker in the adoption unit for about 10 months when I prepared to meet a sibling set of three: Olivia, age 14; Ronald, age 10; and Vanessa, age 9. The three children had been placed together in a group home about a year-and-a-half earlier. The children had two half-siblings: Chloe, age 4, and Nathaniel, age 3, who were living in a foster home about 30 miles away with caregivers who were intending to adopt. In California, these are referred to as "**fost-adopt**" homes. Before the children were removed to out-of-home care, they'd all lived together with their mother and with Chloe and Nathaniel's father. The initial child welfare worker on the case removed the children based on allegations of child neglect, substance abuse, sexual abuse, and domestic violence. Immediately upon their removal, the children were split up. The three oldest children went to the county's **emergency shelter** and the younger two were placed in an **emergency foster home**.

In line with policy and practice imperatives, the child welfare worker assessed relatives to determine if appropriate kin could take in the children. A maternal aunt was identified who had an existing relationship with the three older children, but had only met Chloe and Nathaniel three times over the course of their lives. Aunt Shari lived approximately 3 hours away and had a range of personal circumstances that kept her from taking in the children right away. In addition, because she lived so far away, the social worker was reluctant to consider her home as a placement option because the distance would interfere with the children's need to visit with their mother during the period of reunification services.

A fost-adopt home was identified, but the caregiver was willing to accept only two children, so Chloe and Nathaniel were sent to live there while the child welfare worker looked for a different fost-adopt home for the older children. Such homes are scarce for older, larger sibling groups. It's sometimes difficult even to find a temporary foster home willing to take a sibling set of three. Ultimately, Olivia, Ronald, and Vanessa were placed in a low-level group home. The group home included a set of two individual homes on a quiet street with a rec room, a garden, and playground. The five siblings visited regularly over the next several months, but Ronald and Chloe started experiencing difficulties before and after their reunions, so visits were put on hold.

The younger sibling set were under the age of 3 at the time they were admitted to care. In line with state policy, their mother and father were offered 6 months of services toward the goal of reunification. The father was incarcerated, however, shortly after the children's removal and was not expected to return home for some time. At the 6-month hearing, finding that the mother had not made progress on her case plan and was unable to safely care for her children, the judge ordered reunification services terminated. Adoption was identified as the younger children's permanent plan.

The law pertaining to the older siblings allowed for their mother to receive 12 months of reunification services. Even with the additional time, their mother couldn't engage in her case plan and a 12-month court hearing found, once again, that she was unable to care for the older children safely. Reunification services for these children were also terminated, and the court ordered a "planned permanent living arrangement" for Olivia, Ronald, and Vanessa—a new term for what we used to call "long-term foster care."

Shortly after the 12-month hearing, Chloe and Nathaniel's placement fell apart. The judge ruled that the children had a continuing, beneficial relationship with their mother. As such, he declared that terminating the children's legal relationship with their mother would be detrimental to their well-being. Rather than move toward adoption, the judge left the mother's parental rights intact and ordered a permanent plan of **guardianship** for the children. Chloe and Nathaniel's foster parents had developed a close bond with the children and intended to adopt them; an outcome of guardianship did not feel like the family they were pursuing. Deflated by the judge's order and upset by the outcome of the proceedings, they gave a 7-day notice, asking that the children be placed elsewhere.

All five children needed to secure a permanent home when I was assigned the three older children to my caseload. (The two younger children had always been assigned a different worker.) Olivia, Ronald, and Vanessa had been visiting with their Aunt Shari over the previous year. She had expressed an interest in having these children live with her; she had even discussed the possibility of caring for all five children. My role was to assess whether Aunt Shari was appropriate for placement and, if so, to help the children transition into her home, to reestablish connections between the sibling groups, and to finalize a legal guardianship or adoption with the aunt. The two sibling sets—at that time—had not seen each other for approximately a year.

As I prepared to meet Olivia, Ronald, and Vanessa, I was struck by how confused they must feel about their circumstances. They were separated from their younger siblings and while they were ostensibly living "together," Ronald actually lived in the house next door to his sisters because of foster care regulations regarding gender differences. Although the law indicates that children should be placed in the "least restrictive, most family-like placement," how could these children experience their group home as "family-like" if they lived in different homes?

I arrived at the group home and met three extremely shy children. Their bashfulness was only outpaced by their obvious anxiety at meeting yet another new adult. This was understandable and not entirely unusual among children I met for the first time. Typically, children warm to me and I'm able to engage them in conversation. It was different with these children. They hardly acknowledged my presence, and Vanessa hid underneath the table during the entire visit, only speaking in what could best be described as baby talk.

Over the next several months I made small in-roads with the children, and they grew to trust me. I learned more about the children—their strengths, needs, challenges, and wishes. I learned that they had been told by other children in the group home that they would likely grow up there until their 18th birthday. In the past, this had been true, and many children had "aged out" of this group home. Recent changes in state policy, however, were shifting the way my agency used group homes and, as a result, I was getting pressure to move the children. Group homes were only appropriate for children whose behavior warranted a high level of intensive care. Given that Olivia and Vanessa had no behavioral challenges and family reunification services had terminated, I was directed to identify a foster home instead.

The children had lived in their group home for the previous year and a half, and they had established relationships with the other children and with the staff. This was home, and it provided the stability they had wanted their entire lives. They wanted to stay. But the children's understanding of their future was murky. Their mother told them that if they could not live with her or in the group home, they would live with their Aunt Cathy. But I knew that Aunt Cathy had lost parental rights to her own children and had been ruled out as a possible placement resource early on in this case. When I talked with the children about the possibility of moving in with their Aunt Shari, they were visibly shaken and angry.

Given her status as a preferred relative, I assessed Shari for placement of the three older children. Shari had a relationship with the children prior to their involvement with CPS and had been visiting them monthly for the past 6 months. She lived in a small, two-bedroom home and was employed intermittently. Shari had never been married and had no children or previous parenting experience. I spoke with her about her expectations for raising three preteen children, one with especially heightened behavioral concerns, and her responses suggested that she was unaware of children's general needs or the effects of trauma on children.

Shari told me that her sister had recently called and asked her to take all five of the children. We spoke at length about what this would require. She had doubts right away but wanted to consider it. Shari felt the familial tug of obligation toward her nieces and nephews, but Shari still harbored concerns about introducing five children into her life. When I returned to the office, I spoke with Chloe and Nathaniel's child welfare worker about Shari's suitability as a caregiver for the three, or for the five, children. I expressed my concerns about multiple issues. I felt that she needed parenting support and education. I also was worried about her lack of social and familial support. She was estranged from her family, and her closest friends were those she worked with at her occasional job. I realized that I would feel more secure about the situation if she were certified as a foster parent from the local **Foster Family Agency**; that way, she would be assured of receiving more regular support than I could give from 3 hours away. I was also worried that her income and irregular work schedule would make caring for five children very difficult. She would probably need to move, get a bigger car, and be available to take five children to at least three different schools, due to their ages and levels of education. I realized as we spoke that although I felt comfortable placing the three older children in her care, I felt uncomfortable about placing all five children; that doing so would likely set her up for failure. My coworker expressed her relief when I shared my views and stated that she was in complete agreement with my assessment.

Our legal, philosophical, and practical goal was to maintain family continuity for these children. Ideally, this meant placing all five of the children with an approved relative who was known to them all. This was impossible, of course, as there was no such relative available for placement. Coworkers and supervisors now engaged in a series of lengthy conversations to review the various options available for these children. Some argued that the older Ronald and the younger Chloe should be placed together in a group home or intensive therapeutic foster home, given their extensive therapeutic needs, while sending the remaining three children to live with Shari. The notion was that Shari would likely succeed in caring for less challenging children; if more difficult children were placed in her home, she might not be able to care for them, and their placement together might cost the other three their permanency. My supervisor's view was different. She preferred that all five children be placed with Shari. She counseled me to talk with Shari and to guide her toward accepting the agency's decision in spite of her own reservations.

With multiple possibilities under consideration, I had to reflect on what I defined as "family" and what would be least traumatic for the five children under these circumstances. The sibling sets had now been separated for almost 2 years. Chloe had slight memories of living with the older children, but Nathaniel had no recollections at all. When the older children visited their siblings, Olivia and Ronald slipped back into their parentified roles with the younger children despite intervention and support, while Vanessa's behavior regressed during and after visits. Olivia, Ronald, and Vanessa had never lived without one another and neither had Chloe and Nathaniel.

The children's sense of family helped me understand what I needed to do. It became clear to me that placing all five children together with Shari would be unlikely to succeed. It also became clear that the sibling sets should remain intact. For Olivia, Ronald, and Vanessa, placement with Aunt Shari was inevitable. Shari wanted the three older children with whom she had a relationship, and the agency had no grounds to deny her request. Because Shari lived so far away, and Chloe and Nathaniel still needed a home, I spoke with my coworker about finding a foster home in a town nearby, to help maintain and nurture the sibling relationship. We agreed that this plan was in the best interest of all of the children. We met with our supervisors to discuss our decision and to argue the reasons behind it.

I facilitated a slow transition into Aunt Shari's home for Olivia, Ronald, and Vanessa. They completed their school year where they were, and they visited with Shari almost every weekend. During this time, Shari was certified as a foster parent through a foster family agency and took parenting education as well as classes on how trauma affects children. In spite of our best intentions, the transition was hard on the older children. To the very end, they still didn't want to leave their group home.

Chloe and Nathaniel were placed in a fost-adopt home in a city only 20 minutes from their siblings. The transition was fairly smooth for them and they adjusted rather quickly. Shari met with Chloe and Nathaniel's foster parents, and they all agreed to meet monthly for sibling visits with hopes that over time a relationship could develop which would allow for more liberal visitation and an extended family-like atmosphere for all of the children.

It's been over a year since the children moved into their new homes. Olivia, Ronald, and Vanessa are enrolled in private school and they're engaged in a variety of extracurricular activities, which they thoroughly enjoy. All three children have become more self-confident, engage with adults and peers with ease, and they express themselves openly. As soon as the children moved in, Aunt Shari benefited from **wraparound services** from her foster family agency; these services helped her better manage some of the behaviors and challenges that accompanied the transition into her home. Each of the children also sees a therapist on a weekly basis. Today, Olivia, Ronald, and Vanessa tell me that they're happy that they're living with their Aunt Shari and that they want to be adopted. The agency recommended and the court ordered the termination of parental rights for their mother. She initially appealed the decision, but didn't follow through, so the older children's adoption is now imminent.

Chloe and Nathaniel also appear to be doing well. Chloe says that she enjoys school, and Nathaniel is preparing to begin kindergarten in the fall. Their family was also offered wraparound services to help during the early months of transition and, as a result, Nathaniel's challenging behaviors have declined considerably. Nathaniel and Chloe refer to their foster parents as "Mom" and "Dad" and have told their social worker and me that they're happy in their home.

The younger children's permanency is now secure, too. The foster parents were recently granted legal guardianship status by the court. Although the agency again recommended the termination of parental rights and adoption for the children, the mother appealed the agency's request. This time, however, the foster parents were prepared, and they have committed to care for the children regardless of the nature of their legal relationship. Undeterred, they will also continue to push for adoption.

The children see each other on a monthly basis and seem to genuinely enjoy their visits. In my continued work with Olivia, Ronald, and Vanessa, I have helped them adjust to their new relationship with Shari. Rather than see her as an occasional aunt, they now rely on her as their parent. Olivia, especially, has found relief in allowing an adult to take on this position in the family, and she's relished her new role as simply a proud big sister and as a relatively carefree child. They now understand why Chloe and Nathaniel don't live with them, but they also know they share a bond that time and distance cannot break.

And it's been hard. At one point, it was very challenging for the older children to hear Chloe and Nathaniel call their foster parents "Mom" and "Dad"; and they were hurt when the younger children said their foster siblings were going to be their "real" sisters after their adoption. I've tried to help them redefine what "family" means so that they can make sense of their situation. For them, "family" is who you live with and who you love; it can be both/and. The younger children still refer to the older siblings as "Sissy" and "Brother," and Chloe and Nathaniel's foster parents talk about all of the children as brothers and sisters.

As a child welfare worker, I sometimes have to make choices that are difficult and not as clear cut as I'd like. I can only do the best with the information that I have. Could Shari have cared for all five children successfully on her own? Maybe. Would Olivia, Ronald, and Vanessa have blossomed as they did if they had to share their caregiver with two other children? Maybe. Would the older children have resumed their parental role in a home with five children, losing the childhood that they otherwise gained? Maybe. I'll never know the answers to these questions. I know I made the most reasoned decisions that I could to support the best interests of the children, based on the information that I had at the time. In the end, that's all any of us can do in child welfare.

Traci Bernal

Five children; a kin caregiver capable of caring for some, but not all; siblings who had different levels of attachment with one another based on where they'd lived previously or their age; and a need to secure permanency for them all. Any child welfare worker assuming that the fundamental principles would sketch a clear, simple path forward in this case would be mistaken. Enacting the fourth principle (*children should live with extended relatives*), was only possible for some, but not all of the children. And permanence (principle 6) could only be enacted if the children were separated, thus partially breaching the principle that *children should be raised with their family of origin* (principle 3). As in so many cases in child welfare, efforts to maximize one principle for a family inevitably clashed with another, equally important principle of practice.

Of course, children should live in permanent homes with caregivers whom they view as family forever. The troubled lives of the children who come to the child welfare system, however, rarely bring in tow tidy lives that can be arranged in simple boxes. The creative efforts of child welfare workers to look for expansive solutions to children's permanency needs often mean settling for a best resolution under uncertain conditions. Staff such as these, who remember that children are most likely to thrive when they experience the stability of caregivers who love them, will at least find a partial solution to children's needs in the murky context of child welfare.

8

Culture Clash and the Power of the State

THE ORIGIN OF the child welfare state in the United States, as we learned in Chapter 4, is typically traced back to the legend of Mary Ellen in 1874.[1] Some of the features of the Mary Ellen story speak to the power of the state vis-à-vis vulnerable families; in particular, Mary Ellen's parentage (she was probably orphaned and no longer had birth parents to claim her) and her "ethnicity" likely contributed to the state's involvement in her well-being and care. Although some evidence suggests that the state was reluctant to become engaged in family life, in general at that time, Mary Ellen, it is believed, was the child of immigrant parents, originally from Ireland. Her "ethnicity" signaled her "otherness" and made more palatable the state's intrusion into her family. Using today's racial lens, a child of Irish parents would hardly be considered "ethnic," but under the standards of the day, Irish Catholics were considered foreign to the dominant, Protestant majority.

Along similar lines, Charles Loring Brace's efforts to remove thousands of children and youth from New York to farms in the Midwest by way of the orphan trains (noted in Chapters 5 and 6) is also a story about the child-saving movement and the disproportionate number of children taken from immigrant parents.[2] In short, the founding of the modern child welfare system was a response, in part, to the mass migration of European immigrants to the Eastern states with the accompanying confusion and social instability that attended.[3] Records from Charles Loring Brace and the Children's Aid Society show large numbers of children sent to the West who came from Irish, Southern European, or Eastern European backgrounds—Catholic backgrounds—that were different from the majority Protestant population and that were considered "ethnic" at the time.[4]

These early examples of state involvement in immigrant family life stand in stark contrast to the state's interest in African American children during the 1700s and 1800s. In the North, where slavery was prohibited, African American children's needs typically were ignored by the state and were recognized and responded to by the African American community. A number of orphanages in New York and Philadelphia, in particular, were sponsored and managed by African American members of the community.[5] In the 18th and 19th centuries, and even well into the 20th century, children of different races did not mix, nor did children of different religious backgrounds.[6] While orphanages were used for some children's care, much of the alternative care African American children received came in the form of informal child-sharing rather than institutional support.[7]

In the South under slavery, African American children were, of course, entirely under the control of the state as the law sanctioned total power over children, their parents, and their families.[8] The degree to which the state was in control of family life among slaves in the South represents an odious stain on US history. At the dawn of the Civil War, it's estimated that there were 4 million slaves in the South, half of whom were children.[9] Put simply, from the beginning, the state's relationship to the African American child in the United States was simultaneously a statement about underinvolvement in the North and overinvolvement in the South.

For a brief period following the civil war, the federal government played a limited role in the lives and well-being of African American children. Under the Freedman's Bureau, a number of orphanages were established to care for destitute African American children. But the federal initiative rapidly collapsed—the Freedman's Bureau was only authorized for 7 years—and African American children's needs thereafter largely fell to the African American community, to religious groups, to the settlement houses, and to mutual aid societies.[10] Private and religious institutions were free to discriminate against whole groups of children based on characteristics of race, religion, or national origin. A count in 1923 from 31 Northern states indicated that among a total of 1,070 agencies serving children, 35 were exclusively for African American children; another 264 claimed to accept all children. The remaining 72% of agencies served only White children or other non-White children except for African Americans.[11]

Initial state involvement in African American children's lives appears to have taken root in the 1920s and 1930s when social workers advocated for the establishment of separate public services for African American families,[12] and when racially matched foster homes were deployed in response to children's needs.[13] But the enormous expansion of state involvement in the lives of African American children seems to have coincided with the vast inclusion of African American families into the public welfare system in the 1960s.[14] The rights-based approach to expand eligibility for all public services to African American families during the civil rights movement brought many children and families to the attention of public authorities who had heretofore been excluded. Later, the crack-cocaine epidemic of the 1980s and 1990s and the related increase in female incarceration saw a veritable explosion in the foster care census nationwide.[15] African American children—especially African American babies—were at the top of that trend line and tens of thousands of African American families saw their children removed to foster care during that period.[16]

Today, African American children are dramatically overrepresented in the child welfare system in comparison to their representation in the general population. About one quarter of all children in the US foster care system are African American,[17] though African American children only represent about 14% of the total US child population.[18] African American children are more than twice as likely as White children to be reported for maltreatment, substantiated for maltreatment, and removed from their birth parents' home.[19] Most sobering, over 10% of all African American children in the United States will spend some part of their childhood living in foster care.[20]

The disproportionalities we see among African American children are repeated for American Indian and Alaska Native children as well, and the history of overinclusion is similarly patterned for both groups. The long and deeply troubling relationship between the state and Native American families has always been a story of significant power and control relating to race and nationality.[21] Our early history saw the state's sanction of slaughter and forced migration of tribal families.[22] Then in the last century, thousands of children were taken from their parents, sent far away, and enrolled in boarding schools, where their language, culture, and traditions were eradicated.[23] Tribal children were routinely taken from their parents; in the early 1970s, some estimates indicate that at least one quarter of Native American children spent some or all of their childhood in out-of-home care.[24]

The state's involvement in Native American children's foster care and adoption was a sharp contrast to the racial-matching practices of the 1940s and 1950s for African American children. Although early efforts to identify adoptive homes for African American children focused on race matching, federal efforts to encourage foster care and adoption for Native American children resulted in large numbers of racially unmatched placements. Some estimates indicate that upward of 85% of all tribal children in foster or adoptive homes were living with nonindigenous families in the 1960s and 1970s[25] as an intentional strategy to assimilate Native American children into the majority culture.

In 1978, the federal government developed policy explicitly targeting American Indian children (Indian Child Welfare Act, P.L. 95-608), devolving authority for child welfare decision making to the tribes and identifying family and tribal placement preferences if children were removed from their birth homes. Substantial progress has been made,[26] but in spite of the benefits of the law, large numbers of Native American children continue to have contact with the child welfare system.

Current estimates indicate that 16.5 per 1,000 American Indian and Alaska Native children are reported for maltreatment compared to about 11 per 1,000 for White children. The data further suggest that Native American/Alaska Native children are about 1.6 times more likely to be confirmed as "victims" of maltreatment and 1.6 times more likely to enter foster care than their representation in the population would suggest.[27] Although many more Native American children today are reared in their family of origin than in our recent past, foster care is still a prevalent feature of the Native American experience. Estimates indicate that up to 15% of Native American children will be placed in foster care before they reach adulthood.[28]

The importance of race to child welfare history and current practice cannot be overstated.[29] But what explains these disproportionalities? Do all racial and ethnic groups experience similar overrepresentation in the child welfare system? Asian American children are actually underrepresented in child welfare. And how can child welfare workers contribute to a service response that is sensitive to the fundamental principles laid out in Chapter 1? Child welfare workers are charged with keeping children safe and supporting their families, but importantly, these tasks must occur in the context of another of our principles: *Families' cultural heritage should be respected.*

As described in Chapter 1, contact with the child welfare system is not an equal-opportunity experience in the United States: African American and Native American children are much more likely than other children to be reported, substantiated, and removed from their parents' homes to foster care.[30] But the reasons for disproportionate representation in child welfare are complex and passionately disputed. One line of argument suggests that disproportionate need explains much of the difference. That because of institutional racism and our long history of racialized policies, African Americans today suffer greater social disadvantages than other groups, increasing the likelihood they will live in poverty and to suffer from a range of other family challenges.[31] Another line of argument indicates that racial bias among individual staff is to blame.[32] Whether or not we will ever be able to pinpoint the exact origins of disproportionate representation, or the degree to which one line of argument is a contributing factor, is unlikely. Depending on the case, the worker, the context, and many other factors, racial bias may sometimes contribute greatly to the racialization of the child welfare system; at other times, disproportionate need may be the culprit. Because the causes are complex, the solutions are, too.

Fuel for the bias argument comes from the historical record of unequal treatment and evidence from many sources pointing to racial bias as part of the human condition, and as part of many aspects of US society.[33] In child welfare, a seminal study—conducted four times over the past few decades—also pointed to the likelihood of bias as a significant contributing factor. The National Incidence Studies of Child Abuse and Neglect (NIS) attempt to uncover the actual incidence of maltreatment in the United States as distinct from the rate of official reporting. The studies take place every 7–10 years. The early NIS studies showed that African American and White children were maltreated at equivalent rates,[34] yet official reports of maltreatment and contacts with all aspects of the child welfare system showed disproportionate involvement for African American children. Findings from the NIS studies suggested that if maltreatment were equally distributed between African American and White children, yet their representation in the child welfare system was different, racial bias might be the central cause.[35]

Findings from the NIS-4—the most recent study—offered an apparent reversal from the previous studies. It showed differential rates of maltreatment, with African American children suffering a significantly greater likelihood of maltreatment than White children.[36] Moreover, subsequent reanalyses of the NIS-2 and NIS-3 data showed that these differential rates had been evident all along.[37] The new analyses did not negate the implications of bias, but they raised questions about other factors that might also be at play in explaining differential rates of child welfare exposure.

Efforts to unpack the origins and the meaning of bias are complicated, of course. Which staff actions are intentional versus unintentional? When are decisions made based on ill-formed assumptions about a group? When a single decision is made in error, how are subsequent decisions affected? And efforts by child welfare workers to embody the principle—*families' cultural heritage should be respected*—are sometimes thwarted by others with little understanding and considerable power, but usually by professionals attempting to enact another fundamental principle: *Children should be safe.*

"Mario"

I was in my cubicle doing paperwork, on call for the next emergency referral that would come into the hotline. Around lunchtime, a school teacher called reporting that her 4-year-old student was complaining about pain in his abdomen. The teacher indicated that there was a language barrier between her and the child, but she understood the essence of the boy's message: His dad hit him. There was a bruise, and it appeared to be a fresh injury.

The hotline social worker passed the information along to me. As an **Emergency Response** social worker in the bilingual unit, my Spanish-speaking colleagues and I were assigned all of the calls involving Spanish-speaking clients. I checked in with the Supervisor of the Day to let her know where I was headed and told her I'd call if I needed to consult with her. I then conducted a quick search in our child welfare record system and determined that this family had no prior CPS history in the state.

I drove out to a small town at the edge of the county. I arrived at the elementary school during their lunch break. Office staff called 4-year-old Mario to the office and gave us a private room to meet. It appeared that Mario's primary language was Spanish, but I asked him, just to make sure. I offered some paper and markers to make him feel comfortable, and started with small talk—simple topics like school, friends, and family. Once he grew comfortable, he became a talkative and active child. He began rubbing his abdomen over his shirt, so I asked about it. He told me that his father had hit him with a belt. He showed me a large green and blue bruise on his abdomen. Mario had delayed language development, so it was hard to understand everything he said. I asked him to repeat himself so that I was sure I understood completely. He told me that on the previous day, his mother brought his father the belt. His father meant to spank Mario on the bottom, but as he grabbed his son by the hand, Mario jumped out of the way and the belt hit Mario's stomach instead. Mario was an animated storyteller; he acted out the incident while explaining it to me. He said that the belt buckle—not the leather—hit him. He told me that his mother went to him right away, consoled him, and treated his injury with ice and ointment. He also told me that his mother had never hit him, but that his father had. Mario was very "matter of fact" in his telling of the situation, and it was clear that this was how he was disciplined in his family.

I left him drawing pictures while I called his parents and asked them to come to the school to talk about the injury. After that, I made the phone call I was dreading: the call to law enforcement. Child welfare workers are required to notify law enforcement whenever there is an injury of any kind, even small bruises or accidental injuries, because they need to determine whether a crime was committed. In cases such as this, where a social worker has the lead in the investigation, they typically take photographs of the injury and hear the social worker's assessment. Then, the social worker and police officer come up with a follow-up plan together that is documented in a police report. However, I occasionally encountered officers that did not collaborate and preferred their own independent investigation; this was my biggest worry in cases with language barriers and cultural differences. Based on my previous experiences, I assumed I'd be done speaking with the parents by the time the Sheriff's Deputy arrived.

I was talking with the principal about identifying a private room for my conversation with Mario's parents, Juana and Miguel, when they arrived. Mario saw his parents, flashed a huge smile, and ran toward them, leaping into his father's arms. Mario was obviously thrilled to see his parents. To my great disappointment, the Sheriff's Deputy walked in moments later. I was hoping to interview the parents alone and then relay the information to her, but instead, the Deputy insisted that we do the interview together because she did not speak Spanish. I called to consult with my supervisor, and she advised me to proceed with the interview, including the Deputy. I felt the parents' apprehension; they seemed especially intimidated by the presence of law enforcement in the room.

Juana and Miguel were monolingual Spanish speaking. They reported that they arrived from Mexico a few years ago and were lucky to have had relatives already here to help them get established. Miguel had a good, full-time job, and Juana worked part-time. They reported no prior interaction with law enforcement. Miguel admitted hitting Mario with a belt. Mario's behavior had become increasingly unsafe, and Miguel had warned several times that he would use the belt if Mario did not stop. He emphasized that it was an accident; he was aiming for his bottom, but Mario moved and the belt buckle slipped and inadvertently hit his abdomen. Both parents reported that Mario is hyperactive and constantly climbs on countertops, tables, and chairs to open the front door. They did not think they did anything wrong, in general, by sometimes disciplining Mario with a leather belt.

When I told them what constitutes "physical abuse" in California, the parents looked confused. Juana said, "I don't understand. Am I supposed to let him do what he wants? What were we supposed to do?" I explained that although their culture uses corporal punishment as a normal form of discipline, in the United States, leaving any marks or bruises crosses the line into physical abuse. I validated their concerns but tried to help them see that their traditional strategies for disciplining their child would need to change if they lived in California. Even though they were surprised and bewildered by this new information, they appeared receptive to services. I let them know that I would be providing a referral for in-home parenting education to help them.

I relayed to the Deputy—in English—what the parents had told me; I also emphasized that they were cooperative and willing to learn new parenting techniques. I then stepped outside to consult with my supervisor, and so did the Deputy.

In situations like this, I take several factors into consideration, such as the receptiveness of the parents to work with CPS, the support system around the child, the likelihood of imminent danger to the child, their CPS or criminal history, and what the **Structured Decision Making (SDM)** tool that we're required to complete recommends. I then review the case with my supervisor and ultimately make a decision. I had a few options to consider: (1) Make a referral for in-home parenting services and close the case. (2) Open a **Voluntary Family Maintenance** case, which means the family voluntarily agrees to 6 months of services from CPS with social worker supervision, but with no court involvement. (3) Take the case to court and recommend a **Court Family Maintenance** case, with the child remaining at home while the parents participate in mandatory services. Or (4) take the case to court and recommend a **Court Family Reunification** case, with the child placed out of the home while the parents receive services.

After further conversation with the parents, they indicated that they were willing to sign a **safety plan**. The plan noted that Miguel would temporarily move out of the home while he and his wife participated in parent education services, and that both parents would withhold from using any type of physical discipline. Reflecting again on my options, I rejected options 1 and 2. In both cases, participation in parent education services would be voluntary, and given the age of the child and the severity and location of the injury, I was concerned that these options left the child vulnerable to too great a risk. Option 4 seemed overly intrusive as the parents were remorseful about the injury, cooperative about working with the agency, had a strong support system, and the family was clearly attached and loving toward one another.

Ultimately, I determined that Court Family Maintenance was the most appropriate option for the family. The parents were willing to do whatever was needed to keep the child at home, but I could not ignore the severity of the injury. Also, I felt that having court supervision would avoid any risk of noncompliance the moment I walked away. We make our decisions in Emergency Response investigations with the little information we have at that moment. I didn't know this family. What if they left the area after I made a recommendation for voluntary services? Maybe they found child welfare intervention frightening and would want to flee. How could I be sure, in that case, that the child was safe? Even if they stayed in the area but decided to reject services, after all, our agency would have no recourse. There would be nothing we could do to compel them to participate in services and to learn new parenting approaches. I felt I couldn't take that chance.

What happened next came as a surprise. The Deputy told me that her Sergeant gave her orders to arrest Miguel for the injury.

I've had prior investigations where one of the parents was arrested for abuse, but those parents typically lied about the injury, had no guilt about it, or minimized it. I've even had investigations where I felt that a parent should have been arrested for a severe injury but wasn't. This was the first time when an arrest caught me completely off guard. The deputy herself admitted to me that she felt it was an accidental injury and that the parents were forthcoming and receptive. However, she was overruled by her superior and had no choice.

She told the parents. Miguel remained calm and cooperative, but Juana was visibly worried. She kissed him, hugged him, and told him she loved him and would see him soon. We waited in the principal's office until classes were dismissed and most children had left the campus, before the Deputy took Miguel into custody. The arrest didn't change my recommendation; if anything, it actually reinforced it because I knew my supervisor would now insist on a mandatory court case for the family.

The next day, I visited Juana and Mario in their home to let her know the details about the Juvenile Court hearing that would occur the following day. Miguel's parents—who also lived in the home—met me. Juana's eyes were swollen, signaling that she'd been crying. She shared her worries about her husband. She was visibly stressed about their living situation given her husband's role as the main breadwinner in their home. The grandparents were willing to step in to help supervise Mario while she went to work, but she was so fearful of him getting any bruises, even if they were from playing, that she refused to let anyone else watch him. Consequently, she had no plans to return to work until she knew what was going to happen. The only thing more frightening than losing her husband, was the prospect of losing her son.

I let her know that the in-home parent educator would be coming to her home later that week to begin services. Mario was there while we were talking, and it was quickly evident how hyperactive he was. He put a chair by the front door and ran outside before Juana could catch him. Juana and I spent the next 20 minutes trying to talk him off the roof of a truck. This was a challenging boy who would require a range of positive parenting strategies to engage and focus him; it didn't surprise me that his behaviors sometimes made his parents very frustrated.

The **detention hearing** was held the next day, 48 hours after the arrest. Previous to this case, all my court case recommendations had been approved by the judge. I knew there was a problem this time, however, when the **social work court officer**—the social worker who stands in for us in court—showed up at my cubicle shortly afterward. She told me that the child's attorney had contested my decision to keep Mario in the home. Miguel's attorney, Juana's attorney, and **County Counsel** (the attorney for the child welfare agency) had all supported my recommendation, but the child's attorney felt the child was in danger living at home with Juana. The judge scheduled a trial for the next day, and I was called to testify to defend my recommendation. I was blown away.

I've always taken great pride in my assessment skills, my ability to remain neutral and calm while a child discloses graphic abuse, my ability to stay cool and collected in moments of crisis, and most of all, my ability to leave work at work. I could always go home trusting my decisions and knowing that if something happened overnight, it was not because of anything I did wrong. That sense of confidence was shattered in a moment. I spent the next several hours going over my notes and reviewing the incident over and over in my head. I consulted with every social worker I trusted and with my supervisor.

I was surprised to learn that some of the social workers from the other Emergency Response unit, who only investigate English-speaking families, stated they would have removed the child from the home. They felt that because Juana provided the belt and allowed the physical discipline to occur regularly, it made her as guilty as Miguel and, thus, a danger to the child. I was puzzled by this US-centered and culturally insensitive response. In many Latino families, the father is the primary disciplinarian, and corporal punishment is considered normative. I argued that if corporal discipline were all you knew, and it was accepted in your community, it would be disorienting to learn that it was considered illegal in a new country context. In many of my investigations, I often found myself counseling immigrant families about the need to adopt US parenting practices. Many of the immigrant families I worked with feared jeopardizing their future in the United States or being arrested and deported. Although a lot of immigrant parents have shared with me their concerns that US parenting undermines the authority of parents over children, they always seemed receptive to adapting to American practices. My conversations with my English-speaking colleagues made me feel uneasy. What if the judge harbored similar views? What if Mario were separated from his parents because of a cultural misunderstanding?

Before the trial the next day I met with County Counsel to review the questions the child's attorney might ask. I had considered raising the issue of this family's cultural context but decided instead to focus on the basics of child welfare: safety and risk. The courtroom was, as usual, crowded.

Moments after the hearing began, the judge requested a meeting in his chambers. I sat in a small circle with the judge and the various attorneys. The child's attorney was adamant that Mario be removed from the home. I answered several questions, focusing on the child's safety. I stated the facts: Miguel committed the offense and he was arrested. He had now been released and had agreed to follow a safety plan, living for the time being at his brother's home. Juana had never used corporal punishment on the child and was willing to work with

CPS. I also recounted how happy Mario was when he saw his parents at the school, surely an indicator of their family's bond. I told them that we had already removed Miguel from the home. We were keeping the perpetrator away from the child, but it was causing stress on the family. If we were to remove Mario, we'd be doing greater harm than good to this family. I reminded everyone that the parents were cooperative and willing to jump through hoops to keep Mario at home. Miguel's attorney even said that Miguel was willing to stay away and not have *any* contact with the family if that could secure Mario's place at home with his mother. It was Juana's attorney that ultimately raised the important issue about the clash of culture that I was so concerned about. She reminded everyone about this family's culture and spoke about the role of physical discipline in some Latino parenting. Mario's attorney countered, arguing that the cultural argument was being used to justify the injury. But there was no minimizing the injury; even though it was accidental, we all agreed it was a significant bruise in a sensitive location of the child's body. But if Miguel was genuinely remorseful, willing to learn other discipline options, and be supervised by the court for the next 6 to 18 months, why weren't we willing to work with him?

The judge pondered the arguments laid before him. Finally, he asked the child's attorney if she wanted to move forward with the trial, though he warned that the prior conversation hinted at a decision in line with my recommendation. She looked at everyone in the room, all of whom were supportive of keeping Mario at home. She finally said she would agree to leave the child in the home, as long as Miguel followed the safety plan.

The judge ordered 6 months of court-supervised family maintenance services. There would be a review hearing in 6 months to assess the progress and the need to close or extend the case. Within minutes, the hearing was over. Once outside, Juana and Miguel kept their distance from one another, fearful that any contact would jeopardize their case and the safety plan. Once the attorneys explained that the safety plan only applied to Mario, and that the parents were allowed contact with each other, they embraced and held hands all the way out of the building.

I felt relief. I had been so scared for this family. I've had to take children into custody many times, but always because there was no other way to keep the child safe at home. Mario's case was different. It was the first time I saw language, culture, and the power of the state collide to the detriment of the family. Thankfully, it's never happened again during my time at CPS. But the case stays with me as a reminder of the impact I can have on children and families and, sometimes, the limited impact I can have on well-meaning colleagues and other professionals, all of whom care about the safety of children.

Angelica Rodriguez

Mario was a challenging little boy whose behaviors stretched these parents' range of strategies to rein him in and keep him safe. In fact, it was because they feared for their son's safety that these parents used a disciplinary practice that was ultimately viewed by the state as unsafe. This clash, between the family's cultural traditions, their need for their child's safety, and the state's need to secure that same child's safety, brought the child welfare principles into conflict. Two groups valued the second principle (*Children should be safe*), but their interpretation of the principle was filtered through their own cultural lens. As a result, the first principle (*Parents who care for their children should be free from government intrusion in their lives*) was in question, and this family was taken through a worrisome and probably life-changing interaction with law enforcement, child welfare, and the courts. If not for the advocacy of this child welfare worker, and her deep regard for the seventh principle (*Families' cultural heritage should be respected*), Mario might have been removed from his parents' home and placed in foster care, a significant state overreach and a deep injustice to the family.

Mario's story reminds us of the power of the state to shape and disrupt family life sometimes to cruel and devastating effect. Child welfare workers' and other public actors' views about families and misunderstandings about culture can result in significant harm. These harms, when perpetrated against an individual family, are disturbing and suggest considerable caution is warranted when a family's cultural traditions and heritage present as different from that of a child welfare worker or her supervisor. When these injustices occur with frequency, or when whole communities feel the sting of biased decisions, the damage reverberates with force.[38]

In many jurisdictions, the majority of the child welfare workers, lawyers, and judges are White. They may not be prepared to understand or assess accurately the needs and behaviors, or the values and cultural traditions, of immigrant groups or of families from a culture other than their own.[39] In states where immigration rates are high, the importance of understanding the cultural practices and traditions of immigrant groups, in addition to understanding their language, cannot be overstated.

Immigration is a constant in American life. Historically, we have accepted vast waves of immigrants. Today, the United States has more foreign-born individuals than any other country on the globe.[40] Of these, Latinos represent the largest immigrant group. Latinos are the fastest growing ethnic group in the United States; since 1990, the Latino population has grown by more than 60%,[41] and more and more of the immigrant population includes children and families.[42] Compared to non-Latino immigrants, Latino immigrants have lower educational attainment, lower incomes, and are more likely to live in poverty;[43] low-income Latino immigrant parents also describe considerable challenges accessing the food, health care services, and other supports their children need[44]—all factors that put families at increased risk for maltreatment.[45] Migration itself is also associated with a number of difficulties as individuals acculturate to new cultural expectations and traditions. These adaptations are often accompanied by high rates of stress, fear, isolation, and anxiety.[46] The strains are amplified when language barriers are at play.[47] And undocumented families often experience many of the strains described herein, but their concerns are also intensified by the fear of discovery and exploitation.[48] Recent immigrant parents may suffer chronic stress associated with the migration experience that is compounded by parenting in an unfamiliar context. Parenting stress may be high and parenting self-confidence low as caregivers attempt to use traditional parenting strategies in a context with children that is undergoing rapid change and transformation.[49]

In line with the growing proportion of Latino immigrants in the United States, the percentage of all children reported and verified as maltreated who are Latino has steadily risen. In 1995, 10% of all child victims of maltreatment were Latino, rising to 17% a decade later.[50] Today, the figure stands at 23%.[51] But the gross disproportionalities we see for African American and Native American children are not evident for the Latino population in most jurisdictions. And although recent immigrants experience many difficulties associated with their arrival in the United States, rates of contact with the child welfare system for Latino children roughly mirror rates we see for White children.[52]

In fact, our understanding of the risk of child welfare contact for the Latino population can be further unpacked. Among Latino children whose parent was born outside the United States, research consistently shows very low rates of contact with child welfare. [53] In a national study, researchers found that although non-native-born Latino families were more likely to be living in poverty than native-born Latino families, the immigrant families showed lower levels of family stress, lower levels of drug use, and were less likely to utilize poor parenting skills. They also lived in communities where they experienced a high degree of informal support.[54] In another study, Latino children born to US-born mothers faced about a 1.55 greater risk of contact with the child welfare system than White children, though Latino children of non-US-born mothers had a significantly decreased risk of child welfare involvement. And the story is more complicated still: Latino children raised in high-poverty areas (urban areas of high poverty or rural areas of high poverty) are also more likely to be referred for maltreatment.[55] These data suggest that an array of factors are associated with both risk and protection. Family poverty and neighborhood poverty exert a powerful and negative influence on parenting, but protective factors within the family and community may also buffer against these potent strains.[56]

Findings from studies of Latino families' contact with the child welfare system raise questions about the strength of the racial bias argument in fully explaining differential rates of child welfare contact. Bias sometimes occurs, as we saw in Mario's experience. But other contributing factors are also likely at play.[57] In particular, the argument that some communities experience disproportionate need has gained ascendance in the field in recent years and may explain some of the racially based differences in child welfare contact.

Children of color are, on average, more likely to live in poverty in the United States. About one in five US children were living in poverty in 2010, yet almost two fifths (38%) of African American children and almost one third (32%) of Latino children were living in poverty at that time.[58] Further, poverty is unevenly distributed geographically. African American children are about 14 times more likely than White children to grow up in a neighborhood with high rates of child poverty.[59] And various studies have indicated that the risk of maltreatment varies considerably by geography.[60] Significant evidence suggests that poverty is correlated with a number of other risk factors for children, placing low-income children at high risk for maltreatment and other untoward outcomes.[61] Poverty, combined with lack of informal support, substance use, mental health concerns, and family instability, can contribute to a toxic environment for childrearing. In fact, when the risks associated with poverty are combined with other sociocultural risks to children, we see the likelihood of contact with the child welfare system rise.[62]

In short, a complex interplay of multiple factors place children at risk of maltreatment and child welfare involvement. The distribution of risk in the United States is not at all even and, thus, different racial/ethnic groups face disproportionate need for services to support their families. The challenge for child welfare workers is to accurately and appropriately assess risk—heeding the principle that *children should be safe*—at the same time that they accurately and appropriately respond to the cultural and familial context in which children are embedded so that *families' cultural heritage should be respected.*

When child welfare agency staff respond to bureaucratic needs relating to risk, rather than children's needs relating to safety, all of the fundamental principles are lost, and we revert to a system based upon power and oppression that makes none of us proud.

"Pablo and Yessi"

I was impatient and exhausted the first time I met with Marilyn and Ricardo. I'd been dealing with a rising caseload; two social workers quit the week before, and I was less than a year into my career. The Fernandez case was one of the six new files that landed on my desk that Monday morning. Not a usual situation but also not unheard of. In order to triage the multiple crises on my desk, I saw that this one was relatively new—children detained 3 weeks prior, awaiting a contested court hearing in 2 weeks. Court dates had started to feel like deadlines, and real deadlines had started to seem more like "suggestions." Considering the chaotic state of my other cases, I opted to slide the Fernandez's case to the "deal with later" side of the desk. I had 2 weeks, after all, while I had only 3 days left to find a new foster home for another child, 2 days to see the last seven children of my 30-child caseload, and the time-consuming task of sending a case to closure. Closing a case meant three fewer children I needed to see that month, freeing my time to do more for my other families; this took priority over Ricardo and Marilyn's anxious calls to our Spanish interpreter in the office, Lupe.

When I met with Marilyn and Ricardo, it was a week and a half after their case was assigned to me and two and half weeks since they had last spoken to a social worker. I have to admit, I was not in my finest form. I had about an hour before my next meeting, and I had hoped to fill out my "historical information" questionnaire that would allow me to write a skeletal report to present to the judge at the upcoming hearing. Lupe was sick, and since I don't speak Spanish, an interpreter with no CPS experience came to the office to assist me.

"Escúchenos, por favor." Please, listen to us. I introduced myself, and both parents immediately made their plea: Please, listen to us.

Their two children, Pablo and Yessi, had been taken from them 4 weeks prior. On the day of their removal, Pablo and his mother had fought. Sixteen-year-old Pablo was her eldest child, a child she had left behind in Central America when she immigrated to the United States. Raised by his grandparents, Pablo was 14 before his mother could bring him stateside. Pablo struggled with the new country, the new language, and his new family. They fought that morning because Pablo was being disrespectful; further, he was moving so slowly he'd missed the bus to school. It would be an inconsequential and rather typical argument in most families.

When Pablo arrived at school, he was near tears and shaking with anger. A chain of events followed: A teacher called CPS. An English-speaking social worker arrived at the school. Pablo showed the social worker his bruised knuckles and ineloquently spoke about his mother hurting him. The social worker then visited his baby sister at her day care. She saw red, circular marks on the little girls' leg. Within a few hours Pablo and his sister were in the back of a car being driven to separate foster homes, the homes of strangers, hours away from their parents. In Pablo's group home and Yessi's foster home, their primary caregivers spoke English, a language neither spoke. Allegations of physical abuse move quickly in an understaffed county. Detain the child and let the judge sort it out. Perhaps the continuing social worker will have more time to gather additional information.

A no-contact order was issued by the judge pending my continued investigation, a fact that shocked me at the time but turned out to be almost routine. The orders—in my view—were made out of convenience so that testimony by children would be uncontaminated; they also helped children remain safe in particularly dangerous situations, though traumatized in instances when we got it wrong.

"Please," they begged me.

They understood that Pablo was having a hard time in the United States, and that maybe they handled this issue incorrectly. But where was their baby girl? Why couldn't she come home? No one had ever hurt their daughter. They just wanted to talk to their children, to see them. They had no idea where their children had been placed or if they were okay.

I left the meeting far too soon, with no information to offer them or promises to make besides "I will look into that for you." They seemed more anxious than when they came in, suspicious of my pledge to see their children in person that same week. Ricardo, in the last moments of the meeting, asked if his little girl could return home if he left the family and cut contact with his wife of 10 years. Marilyn remained silent, accused of hurting her son and daughter. I had no answers for them.

The public health nurse determined the marks on the 3-year-old Yessi's legs were "inconclusive." The foster mother swore that she believed they were cigarette burns. The 3-year-old child spoke primarily Spanish; the foster mother, the public health nurse, and I spoke only English. The only Spanish speaker in the household was the 13-year-old girl who claimed Yessi said her mom burned her. Two weeks after receiving the original case, I got in a county car with our interpreter, Lupe, and drove 2 hours and two counties away to see the children face to face.

When I met Pablo, he was quiet and unhappy. When he spoke, Lupe struggled to make sense of what he said. He spoke slowly, metaphorically. Lupe said he spoke like an old man, not unusual given that he had been raised most of his childhood by his grandparents in Central America. His English was nonexistent, and his Spanish was unsophisticated. Lupe described his speech as "working man" language, and he had difficulty speaking clearly about emotional versus physical pain.

Yes, he said, his mother hurt him. Whether it was physical or not, he couldn't say. He struggled to clearly differentiate his emotional turmoil from a corporeal injury. He described himself as "red inside" at school and very sad. He showed me where the bruises had been and mimed punching. He punched a wall, Lupe interpreted, because he was mad at his mother. In response to that, his mother had hit him with her sandal. Pablo said the shoe did not leave a mark. He desperately wanted to go home and asked where his sister was, and if they could return. Lupe spoke to him in a low, comforting voice for a few minutes while I struggled to keep up with my high school–level Spanish.

"He feels very guilty," Lupe said. "It's his fault he disobeyed his mother, and his fault his sister is in foster care. He doesn't think he was abused, and no one has ever hurt his sister. He wants to go home."

On the drive to meet with Pablo's young sister, living in a home even further away than her brother, I thought through what I knew about the case. A young man, new to the country, frustrated with culture shock, angry with his mother both for being absent his entire childhood and for disrupting his adolescent life abroad. They fought, and in the fight he sustained injuries to his hands. His emotional way of describing events made understanding the difference between corporal injury and spiritual injury difficult. Lupe had to ask many questions to determine that "feeling red" was an emotion, not a physical mark. The original social workers' quick investigation saw a very angry boy who said he didn't want to go home, said his mother hit him, and had bruises on his hands and arms. I glanced at my notes. The investigating social worker didn't speak any more Spanish than I did and had relied on interpretation from someone at Pablo's school.

We met with Yessi in the cavernous living room of the foster home. The first thing the 3-year-old told us was how much she liked the house, bigger than her parents' apartment by several times. Lupe spoke with her in small words and short sentences, playing with a doll while we spoke. Who lives at home with you? Who are your mommy and daddy? Are you a good girl? Is your brother a good boy? What happens when you do something nice? What happens when you do something bad? Has your brother ever teased you? Has your mother ever hurt you?

"Si!" Yessi was emphatic. Her mother hurt her before.

When asked how, Yessi described her father holding her while her mother hurt her leg. She rolled up her pants to show us the round, red marks, two right next to one another on her left calf. "Mommy did that," she said, seemingly unperturbed.

It took us over an hour to put together a narrative about her injuries. An hour is often more than a social worker has available to spend on an interview, and often longer than a child's attention span can last. I spent the extra time as much out of guilt for delaying my investigation as a sense of duty.

According to Yessi, her mother had "helped" her by hurting her leg. Apparently, a spider or mosquito had bitten her and it had become infected. Her mother heated a needle with a cigarette lighter, which she then used to lance the infected bite. The scars that remained were round and red where Yessi had scratched them while healing.

Lupe was anxious on our drive back to our office. She asked me an endless stream of questions: Would I present this information to the court? Would I ask for the no-contact order to be lifted? When could the children go home? Were we right to remove them in the first place? What was I going to do?

As a new social worker, I was in a difficult position. A senior social worker, a supervisor, and a judge had all decided that the facts of the case as they were presented were enough to remove these children from their parents' care. We were fast approaching the **jurisdiction hearing**, where the facts of the petition alleging abuse would be either found true or amended. In a county as conservative as this one, my chances of having the case dismissed were abysmal, and at the same time, where was the justice in having these two children separated from their parents and each other in out-of-home care?

I requested a **continuance** and spent 2 weeks building my case to present to the judge. I worked with my supervisor and the county's attorney to present the facts as plainly and unambiguously as possible. I then took the case to a meeting with a panel of supervisors and the manager of our division, asking them to review my argument for dismissal based on a lack of factual evidence of abuse.

"We can't dismiss the case." The **Emergency Response supervisor** was looking at her phone during the case review. She had signed off on the original **detention** petition. "There's something going on in that house. They admitted to fighting and to hitting him with the sandal."

"What about returning at least his sister to their care?" Another supervisor was trying to grasp at alternatives. "This seems to be a parent–teen conflict, not really something that affects their ability to parent a toddler."

"Didn't she have injuries as well?" My division manager looked tired. There had been a child death in another division of the agency less than a month ago. The effects were far reaching.

"Accidental," I said. "I really believe that, especially after interviewing her in Spanish with Lupe. I think there's been a significant amount of miscommunication."

"The judge won't dismiss it." The Emergency Response supervisor shook her head. "How about you recommend releasing them with a court-ordered **Family Maintenance Plan**? They'll be home, but we can still say we have an eye on things."

They quickly ended the meeting, seeing **Family Maintenance** as the best of both worlds—a child returned home after a cursory investigation was proved inaccurate but also a recommendation that was likely to be accepted by the court.

I didn't feel satisfied, and I was certainly unconvinced of the morality of this decision. I felt that the underlying message from these staff was that risk could never be truly eliminated—there was always a reason for us to be involved, if we looked hard enough. I didn't think an English-speaking family would have struggled as much with this investigation or been taken so far down the legal path.

I escalated the case. I took it to more meetings. The attorneys began to avoid me and my phone calls, tired of telling me the "standard procedure" for these cases. Eventually, I was granted the right to make a slightly different recommendation. I could ask the judge to dismiss the case, as long as I provided voluntary services with a full case plan, including parenting classes and therapy. The family would be required to comply with the case plan or else risk returning to court. "Voluntary" was, perhaps, not the best word for the approach.

In the meantime, I continued to meet with Marilyn and Ricardo. I organized a family meeting that included their entire extended family. I met aunts, cousins, nieces, and nephews. Most spoke some English, and all were desperate for information. Pablo was a good kid, they told me, but he was conflicted! Marilyn was a good mother, they said, but she was struggling! Ricardo was a good man, they said, but his hands were tied because Pablo was not his son!

An aunt asked to take Pablo into her own home, if he couldn't go home with his mother. A niece volunteered to move in with the family to keep the peace should Pablo return home. She had grown up in Central America as well and knew what it was like to be a young person in a foreign place with a family that didn't feel like family, she said. A grandmother offered to stop in once a day to talk to Pablo alone, to make sure he was being taken care of. The whole family watched me the entire meeting, knowing as well as I did the enormous power I held over these two children and their family. And here I'd spent the last couple of weeks feeling powerless myself, trying to persuade people with much more power than I to be appropriately responsive to this family. I tried to remain positive and courteous to the large clan in front of me, knowing that my power was only to put their case in front of a judge and hope that the facts spoke the volumes to him that they did to me.

I met again with Pablo, accompanied by Lupe. He'd been in foster care for 6 weeks. He told us he spoke to the staff at the group home by sitting with a cell phone between them using Google translate to talk about how depressed he felt, how guilty he was, and how much he wanted to go home. He asked me in halting English, "When can me, Yessi, go home? Today? Tomorrow?" Still, he was not allowed to talk to his parents on the phone or see them. His sister had begun to act out at the foster home, throwing nightly tantrums and crying herself to sleep. Their parents left me daily voice mails, both in Spanish and in highly scripted, pleading English.

While this case developed into a messy, time-consuming juggernaut, I remained the case manager of 28 other children with their own needs. A mother who didn't show up to three visits calling to demand another chance, a child in need of tutoring services, a teenager who ran away, another teenager asking for permission to dye her hair. Therapists needing me to sign releases, teachers needing signatures for special education, foster parents desperate for child care. Part of my job was also to see all of these children in person at least once a month, so in between hassled meetings with attorneys and cornering my division manager in hallways to talk about the Fernandez case, I was also driving up to 6 hours a day to see children living in far-flung foster homes, and I was staying until six or seven at night to see the parents of families who worked. It was unsustainable, and my coworkers and I spent many hours worrying about when reinforcements would come—a slow process for a profession based on civil service exams.

On top of everything, I had to write a report to the court to summarize my findings and recommendations on the Fernandez case. Memorandums to the court are usually short, fewer than five pages. My memorandum regarding the Fernandez children was 18 pages, plus an additional eight-page case plan. I had it proofed by two attorneys, one of whom was utterly convinced from the beginning that my request was an exercise in futility. After all, the mother admitted to hitting her son with a flip-flop, and the boy admitted to feeling frustrated. That was enough for a judge in the dark atmosphere that spreads through the Juvenile Court following a child death on somebody else's watch. What may have been a simple dismissal at another time became an arduous battle in that climate of fear. Judges, social workers, and supervisors are all human, and they feel the terror that follows this profession. What if I say a child is safe and then that child dies?

Staff in the agency made this point explicitly clear to me as I advocated for the case's dismissal: Should something go wrong, should a child be hurt, should police need to go take those children again, it would be my fault. I would have placed them in danger. And not only would it be my fault, but it would open the agency to severely increased liability. This weighed on me as I struggled to create a **safety plan** for the family.

This family's safety plan included all of the members of their extended family. The family cared deeply about these children, and everyone was now alerted to the problems and their role in offering support. With their engagement, combined with family counseling, I felt the children would be safe if they went home.

In California, children over the age of 12 are entitled to attend court, if they choose. Pablo wanted to be there, so the day of the court hearing I drove him there myself. We spoke in broken Spanglish, and I let him choose the radio stations. He was thinner than he had been when I first met him, and he didn't look like he'd slept well. His mother was waiting for us at the courthouse, and he ran to her; they both began to cry. Ricardo was unable to attend the hearing as he had already taken off several days' work to attend other court hearings and various meetings. Pablo and his mother hadn't seen each other in 7 weeks. They had missed Christmas. She had a bag with her, with some small Christmas presents. We sat, waiting for the case to be called.

It took the judge 40 minutes from the time of initial statements to make his ruling, an unusually lengthy hearing for our court. He spoke to Marilyn at length through the court interpreter. While the interpreter crisply presented Marilyn's statements for the court, Marilyn seemed lost. She tried to understand the judge's statements as the incredibly fast, sophisticated Spanish poured into one ear without any pause in the proceedings. The children's attorney was skeptical of my assessment. Who was I, after all? Brand new, unseasoned. The last interaction she had with the children had been when they were placed, crying, into foster care, and she had been one of the individuals convinced that something nefarious was happening in the home. But my facts were whole and correct, and my proposal was compelling. Dismiss the petition against this family, give them the opportunity to engage in "voluntary" services, and order our agency to present the case to the court again should the family fail to comply. It didn't feel like justice, but it felt like a way for Pablo not to say a weeping goodbye to his mother. The same mother who lost both of her children because in a moment of frustration she hit her son with a flip-flop.

"The standing of all parties?" The judge asked, waiting to hear the opinions of the attorneys on my proposal.

"Submitted." The county attorney looked at me and gave a small thumbs-up under the table.

"Submitted, with the understanding that failure to comply with the proposed voluntary plan will result in the department revisiting the court eligibility of this case." The child's attorney patted Pablo on the back while he struggled to follow the fast, crisp, and complicated interpretation given in Spanish.

"Submitted. This mother has done everything she can and agrees to comply with the voluntary plan." The mother's attorney barely looked up from his phone, already preparing for his next case.

"The court is willing to adopt this recommendation as written. It is so ordered. The department is ordered to have the younger child transported to the court so that both may be released into the custody of their mother with no delay."

When I got back to the office, there were two more cases on my desk.

Sasha McGowan

The harried and time-taxed child welfare worker in this case could have easily accepted the prior worker's assessment of this family's circumstances and determined that she too should invoke the second principle of *child safety*. But instead, she listened carefully to the parents, to the teenager, and even to the preschooler, Yessi (invoking principle 8, discussed in the next chapter). She listened, in spite of the fact that the language barrier between them made understanding difficult. And as she heard their story, she enacted the seventh principle, that *families' cultural heritage should be respected*. Because of her understanding, she fought hard to keep these *children with their family of origin* (principle 3). She did this, of course, against an agency backdrop where not only the previous worker but all of the other actors were privileging the second principle (*children should be safe*), largely as a response to community pressure intolerant of a mistake made in the recent past.

A number of studies suggest that parents' contact with the child welfare system can be experienced as disempowering and frightening.[63] Child welfare workers are seen as possessing significant power, and parents often feel as though they are unheard and misunderstood.[64] The power differentials between trained professional child welfare workers and vulnerable, low-income adults are amplified when issues of race and ethnicity are at play.

The stories of Pablo, Yessi, and Mario speak to the gulf of confusion that can result in consequential outcomes for children and families. These examples, highlighting the experience of recent immigrants to the United States, could have been told, replacing "immigrant" with another racial, ethnic, or cultural group, with a religious orientation different from the majority culture, or with a sexual orientation or gender identification that presented as "different" from the majority culture. The historical and ongoing disparate representation of African American and Native American children, in particular, certainly points to service system responses that may not always be based on issues of safety alone. Because of the dramatic overrepresentation of these groups in the child welfare system, our knowledge that racial bias is implicated in many of our interactions with others, and the awesome power differential between agents of the state and many mothers and fathers of color, caution in decision making is warranted, and fierce advocacy to fight for families may be sometimes required.

The United States is a racially and ethnically diverse nation, and forces associated with globalization are likely to intensify these trends.[65] As the United States grows more diverse, the likelihood that child welfare workers will encounter families from a wide range of backgrounds will increase; in these instances, the possibility that parents' experience of disempowerment and misunderstanding will be heightened. Child welfare workers wield a tremendous degree of power—the power to separate a child from his parent. When child welfare workers use that power inappropriately, without the cultural humility required to truly listen and understand children and families, they lose sight of the fundamental principle that must undergird this work. Keeping children safe is always at the forefront in child welfare, but balancing safety with respect for a family's cultural heritage requires thoughtful professionals willing to fight for a just response.

9

Whose Voice Counts?

IN SEVERAL OF our previous stories, parents and children were often insistent about being heard. In Chapter 8, Pablo tried to make his views clear: Child welfare workers had misunderstood his mother's intent; he was safe. In Chapter 7, we met Ethan, who told his child welfare worker that he loved the Wilsons and wanted them to become his forever parents. Luke's father, described in Chapter 6, tried to convince the child welfare worker, the judge, and the mental health providers that his son needed a therapeutic group home to recover from his years of trauma. In each of these and the other stories, parents and children tried to make their needs known; they tried to direct the course of events in their lives; they wanted to maintain some semblance of control, or at least engage with child welfare workers as partners to shape the trajectory of their lives.

Parents and children usually want to be engaged actors when their circumstances come to the attention of child welfare professionals. But often there is a disjuncture between families' wishes and their opportunities for engagement. Parents involved in the child welfare system have typically made serious missteps in their parenting. But even when children are separated from parents and placed in foster care, parents and children still retain important rights. So what rights are and should be retained when families engage with a system designed to help? The key, of course, is that this is a system designed to help families. When the paradigm for child welfare was one of punishment, as it was for many decades historically,[1] then the question of maintaining family rights to direct the course of services was less salient. For good or ill, child welfare workers were viewed as the professional experts and families were essentially pawns moved at the discretion of the professional. But today, child welfare is designed as a model for helping those it serves. In that light, shouldn't the recipients we're trying to help be asked what they want and need? Here, the eighth principle comes into play: *Parents and children (of a certain age and maturity) should have a say in the decisions that affect their lives.*

The notion of engaging family members as participants in decision making goes beyond the concept of helping. Given the intrusive nature of many child welfare services, these state-level actions must be viewed as reasonable in the eyes of the participants and among the citizenry at large. Important evidence suggests that too often birth parents do not view child welfare workers' decisions as fair, and they question the role of the state in their lives.[2] But intrusive state actions must be valid and appropriate, and legitimacy is better ensured when the recipients of state actions are included as decision makers.[3]

"Family-centered services," a term used frequently in the field, attempts to capture the essence of family participation in child welfare practice. The model demands a more egalitarian relationship between child welfare workers and families.[4] It requires "engaging, empowering, and partnering with families throughout the decision- and goal-making process."[5] And it entails sharing power and information with parents and children in a relationship where mutual trust may be thin and where respect may take some time to be earned.

The paradigm shift that requires caseworkers to engage parents, listen, and respond to their voice is largely regarded as a best practice in the field, but it is difficult to enact in practice. Talking to parents and truly listening is time consuming, and in busy agencies where caseloads may be high, the push to produce an accountable outcome may take priority over a process that is inclusive. Some agencies are turning the corner on embracing this paradigm shift, but institutional biases against parents[6] or traditional perspectives on the wisdom of the professional may still prevail in agency culture.[7] Thus, where we see caseworkers engage with parents, they largely do so using their professional discretion.[8] When child welfare workers rely on their individual preferences to determine the nature of their work with parents, both their skill and attitudes may need encouragement and support from thoughtful coworkers and supervisors.[9] Without an institutional frame to support family engagement, or without foundational principles to guide practice, individual discretion will continue to prevail, and some families will experience an invitation to participate in the details of their case and others will be excluded.

International comparisons hint at differences in parent participation across countries, in part reflecting the legislative frame in which child welfare work is conducted. In the United States, child welfare workers may be inclined to engage parents when the requirements of the case focus on information gathering; in the family-support-oriented child welfare systems of the

Nordic countries, parents may be more likely engaged to determine their service needs.[10]

The variability in worker behaviors is felt by parents.[11] Some child welfare workers are better listeners than others, some take more time with clients than others, some offer parents more choice in decision making than others. In general, the research literature indicates that many parents do not feel as though they were heard in child welfare deliberations about their family. For parents whose children have been taken from them and placed in foster care, their sense of powerlessness may be profound.[12] Efforts to engage parents as participants in decision making about their families' needs can help to restore parents' sense of capability and protection toward their children. The how-to part of this work is not complicated. Parents indicate that approaches that are nonjudgmental, nonstigmatizing, authentic, personal, and respectful are much more likely to result in responsive engagement on their part,[13] but these attitudes are not necessarily universally held. And much of the literature relating to parent participation is highly gendered; fathers, in particular, feel notably excluded from the decision-making processes about their children.[14]

When parents are consulted about what they need, benefits may accrue to the family. Some evidence indicates that parents who participate in decision making are more likely to engage in child welfare services, pursuing their goals, and complying with their case plan.[15] And importantly, parents are more satisfied with their overall experience in child welfare if they feel they have been heard and that staff have responded to their needs.[16]

If it's so difficult, how do child welfare workers begin the process of changing their practice behaviors to draw parents into the work as genuine partners? It probably starts with an attitude of respect and dignity,[17] something that many budding child welfare workers bring to the work initially, and that may need to be supported and encouraged as they mature in their role.

Since the research literature generally suggests that authentic inclusion of parents is not yet a hallmark of typical child welfare practice,[18] one can imagine that giving children a voice in child welfare is more exceptional still. At issue in engaging parents is *how,* but at issue with children may be *why.* In the United States, views about whether and how children should be included as participants in decision making vary considerably. These questions, contested in the United States, have been resolved by law in many other countries.

In several other countries, the framework for child welfare policy is based upon the principles set forth in the United Nations Convention on the Rights of the Child. The Convention has been ratified by every country in the world but the United States.[19] It serves as a framework for many countries to guide legislation regarding programs and policies affecting children. In the United States, hesitation to sign the Convention has revolved around issues of religious freedom, the fact that many of the principles are already embedded in much US legislation, and—not surprisingly, perhaps—the conflicts that arise when children's rights come into conflict with parents' rights.[20] The Convention reflects a major step forward for children. For centuries, children were viewed legally and culturally as the property of their father.[21] And, of course, children's status in the family is one of a dependent; their ultimate independence usually represents their readiness to leave the family home. The Convention shifts political and cultural views about children, elevating their status within families and within society as individuals with unique human and legal rights. It is, as such, a very modern invention in human history.[22]

The Convention is a multipart document, but Article 12 is especially relevant to child welfare, as it states that "children shall be provided the opportunity to be heard in any judicial or administrative proceedings affecting the child, either directly, or through a representative or an appropriate body, in a manner consistent with the procedural rules of national law."[23] It goes on to suggest: "Children should be involved to the extent that they are heard, that their perspectives and interests are included and considered, and that they are given sufficient information to make informed choices about their circumstances and their options."[24] The Council of Europe has used the Convention as a platform to develop guidelines for professionals who work with children in administrative or court proceedings. These include children's right to representation, participation, information, and protection. Importantly, the guidelines highlight the value of respecting children's rights such that they do not hinder the rights of others,[25] a hint at the very conflict at the center of much child welfare practice. Although the United States does not rely on the Convention or the Council of Europe's guidelines, the ideas undergirding these documents speak to one of the fundamental principles of child welfare regarding family participation in decision making.

Soliciting children's voice in child welfare when their family and their home are threatened may seem self-evident. Children's wishes are routinely sought in child custody decisions relating to divorce, when similar threats are at play.[26] But it's challenging to draw children into the decision-making process in child welfare. What is meant by participation? Are there different types of participation laced with different meanings? In California, for example, child welfare workers are required to meet with and speak with the child who is the focus of a maltreatment allegation (depending on age and maturity). The purpose of the meeting is to interview the child about the allegation of maltreatment and to determine its veracity. This, of course, might be a necessary practice, but it would not be considered sufficient as a measure of the child's voice in directing the future. In other countries, child welfare workers might place greater emphasis on eliciting a child's wishes or feelings about the current situation, or about their needs.[27]

These different dimensions of participation help to illustrate the various ways in which children might be included as full participants. Some authors have conceived of children's participation in decision making as a ladder, moving from the lower rungs of inauthentic participation (e.g., manipulation, decoration, or tokenism), to more broad and meaningful participation (e.g., being consulted and informed), to full and authentic participation that is child initiated and directed.[28] Others have taken this model of participation and adapted it to account for greater cultural diversity. Rather than a vertical ladder, perhaps the notion of participation should be viewed as a circle; children's experience of participation may depend upon their starting point and the contextual risks they might encounter if their starting point is too high.[29] And still others, considering the meaning of child participation specifically in the context of child welfare, have proposed the metaphor of a series of bricks.[30] In this visual representation, children's participation in child welfare decision making is mediated by a number of factors, including the degree of choice or number of options available, the accessibility of complete information, and the amount and source of support available to assist the child.

Of course, as with child welfare workers' practice with parents, work with children in this area is highly variable. Hurried child welfare workers often do their best to meet the best practice standards of child welfare and include children, to the extent possible, in child welfare decisions. Some caseworkers are expert at soliciting the trust and partnership required to engage collaboratively with children, whereas others may need support to develop these skills. And the principle of soliciting children's voice may be commonly shared, but the task of accomplishing that goal may be seen as someone else's job. Federal law indicates that children involved in child welfare proceedings be appointed a guardian ad litem (GAL). The GAL may be an attorney or a Court Appointed Special Advocate (CASA), a community volunteer specially trained to assume this role.[31] These legal advisors are required to represent children's best interests, and presumably the best way to recognize children's interests is to meet and talk.[32] When policy dictates that children's legal representatives are responsible for representing their best interests, it makes murky the role of the child welfare worker in determining children's wishes for their family.

But children tell us that the child welfare workers who show they care are extremely important. Children notice when staff listen to their needs and stick with them through difficult times. They see the difference between staff who show dedication—those whose actions show they are interested in children as individuals and hear them talk about their lives—and those who push paper or rush through a checklist of questions. And they appreciate staff for engaging with them, for taking their calls, and for responding to them with authenticity.[33]

The principle, that *children should have a say in the decisions that affect their lives*, coupled with children's views about the importance of expressing their voice and being heard, suggests that child welfare workers should be engaged in soliciting children's voice, regardless of the challenges entailed. And in doing so, we should anticipate that sometimes, if not infrequently, the wishes of the child will conflict with their own best interests. The most common clash arises, of course, in the placement decision itself. Many children—even those who may be abused by their parents—are reluctant to leave the home that they know for the unknowns of foster care.[34] Their wishes might include staying at home, whereas their best interest might require separation from their parents for awhile. How child welfare workers manage these competing choices—when their goal is to give the child voice in the process, but when their requests are unlikely to be honored—requires skill and sensitivity.

Further, our eighth principle, focused on client voice, includes both children *and* parents. But how can a child welfare worker honor a parent's wishes if it conflicts directly with that of a child's? A child welfare worker tells her story about a case that was particularly vexing in part because of her efforts to attend to a girl's wishes, at the same time that she was trying to be responsive to the mother's goals for her family, while also carrying the notion of fulfilling a "best interests" standard for the child.

"Alison"

The day my supervisor handed me Alison's case file her only words were, "This case goes to court a lot."

Every child welfare worker begins case work from a different perspective. Some workers choose to review the file in depth before contacting the child, foster parent, family members, therapists, and others assigned to the case. Working in the long-term foster care unit, the children who join my caseload typically have been in care for quite some time and their file is thick. When I receive a new file, I skim through the most recent material first, identify all the major parties, gather information as to the reason the child is in custody, and then I start making phone calls. The case file only tells part of the story and can be biased by previous workers' assumptions or judgements. The people at the center of the case are the experts.

I quickly learned some facts about the case. Alison originally lived with her two parents, Camila and Devon. Their financial circumstances were sometimes precarious as they struggled with occasional job loss, but they mostly found their financial footing and got by as a family. The parents were deeply connected to their faith and to their faith community, and they relied on a large network of family support. Even though Camila and Devon generally felt close to their relatives, only a very few extended relatives were aware of the circumstances surrounding their daughter.

Alison was an intelligent, artistic girl of 11 years. Her parents had enrolled her in music classes and swimming, both activities she excelled at and enjoyed. Alison did well academically and was a prolific reader. In spite of her many strengths, she had difficulty making friends, and I came to learn that she was troubled by mental health issues.

Approximately 1 year before entering foster care, the county received an allegation of abuse relating to emotional maltreatment, but the child welfare worker at the time assessed the situation, offered some support services, and eventually closed the case. Months later, a new allegation of child abuse arose, this time for physical and sexual abuse by the father. Alison told the child welfare worker that she had informed her mother, but that Camila did nothing. The girl was especially frustrated that her mother did not believe her. She told the worker that her father also had a drinking problem and because of her father's actions and her mother's inactions, Alison refused to go home. The worker's investigation resulted in an immediate removal into protective custody.

Both parents claimed the allegations were false and reported that Alison was being influenced by a friend from school who was in foster care and also had trouble with her family. The parents stated that Alison had recently been given a consequence for not completing homework and she was just angry. The parents repeatedly asked the child welfare worker to speak to administrative personnel at the school regarding the other child's potential role in the allegations. That may have happened.

The social worker before me may have been very thorough in all aspects of her investigation, but the file I read didn't show any documentation that school personnel were contacted, so neither the parents nor I knew much about the evidence that was collected to substantiate the case.

By the time I received the case, Alison had been in care for approximately 1 year. It had been a litigious year filled with anger, frustration, and a complete loss of trust. As I reflect on the case now, I see that trust was absent among everyone. The parents and child did not trust each other, the parents did not trust the agency, and initially the agency staff didn't seem to trust the parents or the child.

Alison adamantly refused to have contact with her parents or participate in supervised visitation. She repeated with me the behaviors she exhibited with her first child welfare worker: Whenever I brought up the subject of visitation, she would start to cry and recount stories of past incidents of abuse. At times she would try to negotiate the terms of visitation, dictating that she would only visit if her mother left the marriage. But visitation is usually ordered by the courts to promote reunification and it's a nonnegotiable activity. I was flummoxed.

When I first called Camila, her voice was cold. I knew that she and the prior child welfare worker had been at odds, that the child welfare worker did not support reunification, and that the mother had fought tenaciously to get a second and third chance in the courts. Every hearing, it seemed, was contested as Camila tried to prove to the courts that she could safely parent her daughter, and the agency social worker sided with Alison who indicated time and again that she did not feel safe with her parents.

My goal was to rebuild Camila's trust so that we could work together to help Alison. Instinctively, I knew that our first meeting had to be on her terms, so I asked her to bring someone for support to our meeting. That first meeting was challenging. Camila assumed the worst in me and in the agency; she assumed our motivations were to keep her daughter from her, and because of this she felt distant, cold, and hopeless. She lodged a number of complaints about the process, about the agency, and about the courts, but she saved her strongest criticism for Alison's foster parent, who, she believed, was turning Alison against her. Before we left the meeting, I asked about her ultimate goal. It was simple: She wanted Alison returned home.

By the time a case reaches my desk, the end goal of family reunification is rare. Courts and social workers have long since abandoned efforts to help families reunite, and my time is usually spent focused on the child and his or her needs. But it was obvious to me that Camila loved her daughter, and if I was going to be true to the ultimate goals of child welfare, I knew I needed to support Camila and Alison's fractured relationship.

A few days later, I made my first visit to Alison's foster home. I remember the day vividly. Alison sat on the couch with her foster parent, Mrs. Nicolette, and a social worker from the local **Foster Family Agency** as she recounted the trauma at the hands of her parents. Domestic violence, and emotional, physical, and sexual abuse were all part of Alison's personal story. Mrs. Nicolette was warm and supportive, conveying a deep empathic response to Alison and her concerns. Alison was adamant about not having contact with any family members; her foster mother nodded in agreement, and after hearing her personal accounts, I too was persuaded that contact could be problematic.

When Alison removed to her bedroom, Mrs. Nicolette's affect changed markedly. Where she had shown warmth and concern about Alison in her presence, she now exhibited a very cool demeanor, telling me all of Alison's weaknesses and faults. She and the social worker insisted that Alison should not be forced to have contact with her family. The argument regarding telephone contact and visitation had been going on for months in lengthy court hearings and had not yet been resolved. I suggested that phone contact be resumed, but Mrs. Nicolette advised that phone calls upset Alison deeply and impacted Alison's behavior in her home. She wanted contact to be restricted or eliminated altogether.

I left Alison's foster home feeling uneasy. I couldn't pinpoint my concerns, but I knew I felt uncomfortable about what I had witnessed. The emotional tenor of the home, the foster parent's fierce demands, the vague sense of threat that hung in the air—all of it left me apprehensive. I returned to the office and called Camila so that she could hear news of her daughter. Camila's callous voice faded, and the sadness and frustration of the past 18 months came to the fore. She'd finally received word about her daughter, an experience that had eluded her in previous contacts with my agency. The previous worker, out of deference to Alison's wishes, had kept silent about Alison's well-being, and Camila knew very little about her girl.

I discussed the case at length with colleagues and with my supervisor in the hope of determining the best step forward. I went to the three-volume case file and combed through all of the details, page by page. It occurred to me that a crucial oversight had been made early on in the case that needed further investigation. The agency is responsible for diligently searching for and identifying possible family members for placement. I found limited information, though, about extended family in the case file. I wanted to know more.

I went to visit Alison a few weeks later. I learned that her behaviors were becoming increasingly odd and challenging. Her grades were falling in school, her relationships with peers were highly problematic, and she was beginning to rock and shake. Although Alison was going to regular therapy sessions, her behavior was deteriorating. The therapist remained convinced that Alison's mental health issues were related to the trauma she had sustained in her family and that her wishes to refrain from contact with family members should be supported.

I shared what I learned about Alison's increasingly troubled behaviors with her mother; I wanted to understand if these were historical or new behaviors. Camila was grateful to have any information about her child and, in the process, brought Devon into the conversation. Both parents expressed concern about the home where Alison was placed. They asked why their child was not placed with willing and able family members and I—frankly—had no good answer. Since the case file didn't document a search for relatives, I had offered the option to Alison, but she refused. She told me she wanted to live permanently with her foster parent and even spoke of adoption.

The arguments between Alison, her parents, and Mrs. Nicolette were constant. I served as mediator, but I don't know that any progress was made. Alison felt sure that her parents denied her allegations of sexual abuse and that the divide could never be bridged. Alison's ultimatums became more pitched: If Camila wanted any contact, she would have to leave Devon. Camila wanted the family to work through their issues, acknowledging that their disciplinary practices had sometimes been too harsh, and still baffled by the sexual abuse allegation. After months of encouragement, I arranged a therapeutic meeting between Camila and Alison. Although the meeting went well, soon thereafter their relationship deteriorated again.

At the following 6-month court hearing, the lawyer for the parents and Alison's lawyer both turned on me: "Are you allowing a child to dictate the case, or are you making the decisions?" "You don't believe the child because you are permitting visits with family members!"

Whose wishes was I supposed to support? The parents'? The child's? Not "the family" when they were a single unit in name only. I felt buffeted between two opposing camps. Should I support the child's wishes and feelings—clearly and loudly articulated to me and to all who would listen? Or should I support a "child's best interests" principle and work toward reunification with family or at least some connection to an extended family member? And how could I honor Camila's views to at least reestablish a basic relationship with her daughter?

As time passed, my inarticulate misgivings about the foster home continued. Finally, my suspicions were confirmed. A state investigator called to notify me that they were closing the foster home. The investigator reported a litany of concerns, including locked refrigerators, emotional abuse, and a series of other offences. I was directed to remove Alison immediately. Alison tried to refuse, but her efforts were futile. Again her wishes were perfectly clear. She impressed on me the importance of placing her anywhere but with family members.

I wanted to respect Alison's wishes, but I also knew the law. I wasn't convinced that diligent efforts had ever been made to identify kin, and I couldn't ignore these possibilities. I asked Camila and Devon to create a list of all possible relatives, and I also received help from a local nonprofit agency that provides **family finding** services. I had a large list of names to work from and began to make my calls.

But Alison was now an emerging teenager with strong, well-articulated opinions. She convinced her lawyer that placement with family members would not be in her best interest, and the judge ordered her next placement in another nonkin foster family home. That worked out for awhile, but within 3 months, the foster mother could no longer manage Alison's behaviors. Alison was clearly struggling with a range of mental health issues, and they were all playing out in her foster home. She and her caregiver battled constantly about hygiene, food, and school and I got the call, asking that Alison be placed elsewhere.

The placement unit had, upon my request and insistence, identified an extended family member who was interested in welcoming Alison into her home. The relative was aware of Alison's history and wanted to protect her. Alison spoke with her relative on the phone and decided that a trial visit was possible.

The first few months were difficult, probably even more than she and her caregiver ever admitted to me. But the situation improved with time. Within 6 months, Alison invited her mother and me to watch her high school performance. I enjoyed Alison's incredible talents, but it was Camila who held my attention that night as I watched her beam with pride and love for her daughter.

Alison settled in to her kinship foster home and stayed there long term. Over time, and with the help of her extended relative, Alison slowly reconnected with her mother (though not with her father). Alison and Camila were never able to live together again, though. Too much time had passed, too many questions remained unanswered; but Alison and her mother rebuilt a relationship that had been almost lost.

The circumstances of that case still leave me feeling perplexed. I'll never know what really happened in the family to warrant a call to CPS. I'll never know if the allegations were true, or if Alison's understanding of her world was clouded by serious mental health concerns. I'll never know if the family could have healed from their wounds and reunified if they'd been given a chance. I'll never know if Alison's views about her family were largely motivated by the foster parent, or if there was a kernel of truth in her need for a complete separation. And I'll never know if it's always better to follow the wishes of the child or to follow the best interests of the child—especially when they don't converge.

In my last 2 weeks at the agency, I arranged to have a meal with each child on my caseload. With Alison, I arranged a dinner with her, Camila, and her kinship caregiver. My memory of that evening is so clear. Her caregiver was happy, her mother was happy, and Alison was happy, too.

Freny Dessai

Surely Alison was old enough to be a participant in her case. She was represented by an able lawyer, and she appeared as an autonomous force with the support of her foster parent and a private agency social worker confirming the appropriateness of her wishes. But did she warrant an exclusive right to have her wishes honored? This social worker, attempting to abide by the eighth principle, gave Alison a voice in the circumstances of her case. But in doing so initially, she was dishonoring Camila's views about how her family should be treated. When the social worker took the case, she also realized that in an effort to honor Alison's voice (principle 8), the fourth principle (*when children cannot live with family, they should live with extended relatives*), had been ignored. And in her reliance on privileging the eighth principle, this social worker had—for awhile—quieted her own internal misgivings when she believed that the second principle (*children should be safe*), might be at stake in Mrs. Nicolette's home.

Adherence to the eighth principle puts in sharp relief the fact that there are individual parties at the center of most child welfare cases. The language of the principle—parents *and* children should have a say in the decisions that affect their lives—is intentional. Too often, we gloss over the interests of the individual in child welfare by suggesting that *the family* should have a voice in decision making. But family is too diffuse an entity. Indeed, in child welfare, the family can encapsulate many people who may be related by blood, law, or relationship. Talk of "the family" can be helpful in some instances, but the eighth principle of child welfare requires a much more nuanced approach, sensitive to the unique views of each family member. It attends to the views of parents—both of whom may disagree with one another—and to children—who may disagree with their parent(s) and also with siblings.

All child welfare principles are in conflict. As is evident in the previous story, the eighth and final principle may sometimes be at odds with itself! But this is hardly an excuse for a retreat. Principled practice is complex, nuanced, and difficult. It requires thoughtful practitioners who are willing to embrace that challenge with passion for the families and sensitivity to their multifaceted needs. The complexity of principled practice should be recognized, articulated, and endorsed if we intend to be honest with families and candid with the public about the real work of child welfare.

10

Contested Principles on the Front Lines

MANY PROFESSIONS USE principles to guide their work. In medicine, doctors, nurses, and other staff turn to the Hippocratic oath—first do no harm[1]—as a fundamental principle of practice. Other examples come from the field of engineering, where a code of ethics guides engineers' obligations to society and to clients.[2] And in education, teachers are guided in their work with students by eight fundamental principles.[3] The larger field of social work also has a code of ethics that sets a frame for practice.[4] But the NASW Code of Ethics is far too large and generalized to guide the targeted decision making required in child welfare. As a unique subspecialty of social work, child welfare needs a set of principles that goes beyond the Code of Ethics. These principles are outlined herein, and they regularly shape practice and policy.[5]

Child welfare workers who use these principles as a guide will find that the guise of simplicity—a feature that makes each principle so attractive—masks a much more complicated field. Efforts to maximize one principle often result in a direct collision with efforts to maximize another. These values-based collisions lie at the heart of child welfare, they typify many cases, and their product is a series of morally precarious choices. Deciding what's "right" when attempting to maximize one value at the expense of another is contested territory, and it is ethically complicated. Each of the previous chapters has illustrated how and when our principles contradict and the tremendous challenge child welfare workers face as they attempt to balance competing needs and capitalize on the benefits of some principles over others.

Sometimes, however, child welfare workers are handed a case that is much more straightforward, where the fundamental principles not only guide the work, but each principle appears to seamlessly complement the others. These cases are the exception rather than the norm, as in the following.

"Joaquin"

Hospital personnel called the hotline to report a baby, born at 36 weeks' gestation. The mother tested positive for marijuana, amphetamine, and methamphetamine use and had not had any prenatal care prior to delivery. The child, unnamed, was known only as Baby Boy and was born with methamphetamines and amphetamines in his system, "pos-tox," as we say. He was born with poor tone and abnormal features, was lethargic, and possibly had sepsis. Baby Boy's father was present at the birth and told the nurses that he and his girlfriend were homeless and that he was concerned about their ability to care for the child. The baby's mother told hospital staff that she was in the process of losing another child to the system and was considering putting Baby Boy up for adoption.

The investigative social worker responded immediately after the agency received the report. He first met with hospital staff to gather information about the situation and learned from the delivering doctor that the mother arrived at the very late stages of delivery. She came in screaming, "The baby is coming out!" but refused to push, claiming that she had a critical medical condition that prevented her from being able to do so. An emergency C-section was immediately performed. The mother claimed to have had frequent visits to a prenatal clinic, but when nurses called the clinic for confirmation, they were told that she was never seen for prenatal care. According to the hospital doctor, the mother reported being prescribed medication for seizures and pain, but she denied ever using any drugs—including her prescribed medication—despite positive blood and urine tests for her and the baby. The mother also reported a history of seizures triggered by chronic pain, but she said that she could control the seizures if given powerful opioid medication, which she asked for by name. The contradictory information provided was concerning and the doctor suspected drug-seeking behavior.

After gathering information from hospital staff, the social worker introduced himself to the mother, Suze. He noticed that she presented as anxious, and he had difficulty keeping her focused on the conversation about her baby. Suze reported that the father, Jack, had left the hospital to secure housing so that they had some place to bring the baby home.

Suze did not want to be interviewed by the investigating social worker. She had a lengthy history with the agency and the courts, as a child and as an adult, and was in the process of contesting the agency's recommendation to terminate her parental rights to her preschool-age child. When questioned by the social worker, she made it clear that she did not trust or want to work with the agency. When asked questions about Baby Boy, the pregnancy, and labor, Suze was evasive; she angrily talked about her experience in foster care as a child and hating social workers, and she was focused on getting attention only on her current medical conditions. Suze denied that she had ever used drugs and claimed that she had previously entered residential substance abuse treatment only to appease the social worker, but that she had never really needed treatment. Suze reported that although she was allowed to visit her preschooler, she chose not to, to avoid the emotional pain associated with seeing the child.

The social worker asked Suze about her current drug use and positive tests, but she again denied ever using drugs. She claimed that her premature labor was triggered by household cleaner she inhaled while trying to clean the bug-infested hotel room where she and Jack were staying. The baby, she said, had drugs in his system because the father's friends were using drugs in the hotel room prior to the delivery. Suze also denied any prescription drug abuse and stated that she was prescribed methadone for migraines but that she stopped taking it when she found out she was pregnant.

When the social worker asked about her prenatal care, Suze initially reported that she had several appointments with the local clinic, but that the doctor had rescheduled them, causing her to miss some. After further questioning, Suze ultimately admitted that she was only seen at the clinic once during her pregnancy, and that the appointment was not for prenatal care but for pain medicine after an injury. She also mentioned that the doctor she saw had previously prescribed antidepressants for her, to treat postpartum depression relating to her first child. Suze talked at length about her seizures and chronic pain from various car accidents and physical traumas. The social worker asked if he could contact some of her previous medical providers to confirm the extensive and worrisome medical information she was providing, but Suze refused to give consent for him to do so.

Although she was adamant about not trusting the child welfare agency, Suze volunteered a lot of personal information. She revealed that she had been raised in foster care due to her mother's drug and alcohol addiction and mental illness. She described a difficult childhood filled with trauma, abandonment by her mentally ill mother, abuse by relative caregivers, then bouncing around in foster care.

The social worker next reached out to Suze's aunt. Speaking with the social worker by telephone, the aunt shared her concerns about Suze, indicating that Suze had initially reached out to tell her about the pregnancy and her intent to put the child up for adoption. The aunt reported that she wanted to be able to visit the baby and that she and her husband had considered adopting him themselves, but they decided they could not because it would result in Suze having too great a presence in their lives. Suze, she said, had a long history and had burnt many bridges with her original family.

The social worker spoke with the baby's father, Jack, by telephone after he twice refused to meet in person. The father reported that he met Suze a year before, after she had lost custody of her firstborn child. Jack told the social worker that he wanted to help Suze during that very difficult experience, and he had tried to be supportive of her. Jack said he was surprised that Suze tested positive for methamphetamines as he was unaware that she was using.

Jack was much older than Suze and had a teenage son from a previous marriage. Jack had moved to California some years before to be close to his boy. When he arrived, however, he was unprepared for the high cost of living. After struggling to pay rent, he made temporary plans to "camp out" while he saved money, but this turned into a long-term problem with homelessness. His goal, now, was to find a home for him, Suze, and the baby.

Four days after Baby Boy's birth, the social worker consulted again with hospital staff. Although Suze had asked about the child's well-being earlier that day—the first time since delivery—staff were worried that she had not shown other signs of attention or caregiving, and they were concerned about releasing Baby Boy to her care. The baby had ongoing medical issues that required clean surroundings; the parents' housing instability, coupled with Suze's substance abuse, mental health, and lack of prenatal care raised serious questions about the parents' ability to safely care for the child.

After completing the SDM risk and safety assessments and consulting with his supervisor and manager, the social worker substantiated allegations of general neglect against both the mother and father. The safety concerns that presented an ongoing danger to the infant were the mother's substance abuse and mental illness, her refusal to acknowledge the evidence of her drug use, the fact that the father denied knowing anything about the mother's drug use despite having lived with her throughout the pregnancy, the parents' homelessness and inability to provide for the child's basic and special medical needs, and, very significantly, the parents' ambivalence about caring for their son long term. Thus, it was determined that a petition would be filed with the court to remove Baby Boy from his parents' care.

A **detention hearing** was held the following business day. At the hearing, Jack's attorney notified **County Counsel** that he intended to relinquish the child for adoption. Relinquishing meant that Jack would voluntarily give up his parental rights, thus freeing Baby Boy for adoption. The judge accepted the social worker's recommendation and removed Baby Boy from his parents' care; however, due to his ongoing medical needs, the baby continued to reside in the hospital.

Although Suze's aunt was initially contacted and considered as a relative foster parent, she was unwilling to serve and—according to Jack and Suze—there were no other relatives able or willing to care for the child. The social worker made additional inquiries and found a paternal relative who might be suitable, but the relative declined the placement. When extended family could not serve as the baby's caregivers, the social worker identified a concurrent foster home—a home where the parents have indicated an interest in adoption if the child cannot be reunified with his parents. This family had been certified as a foster family only a week previously and knew something about child welfare, having adopted their older daughter years before.

I was assigned to Baby Boy's case after the detention hearing. During my first home visit with Baby Boy, his foster parents, Mr. and Mrs. Jaffe, made it clear that they wanted to support reunification between the infant and his parents, if that was the best thing for him. If that was not possible, they were eager to adopt the little boy.

Mr. and Mrs. Jaffe had begun to call the baby Joaquin, a nod to Mr. Jaffe's cultural heritage. Mrs. Jaffe immediately asked if they could meet Baby Boy's parents, as they wanted to get to know them and start building a relationship. They hoped that if adoption were pursued, everyone would agree to an open adoption.

I arranged for an **ice-breaker meeting**, where Jack, Suze, and Mr. and Mrs. Jaffe could meet and talk about Baby Boy—his needs, temperament, and anything else that might help with the baby's transition into foster care. Jack indicated that he was interested in participating, but he missed the meeting altogether and shared with me his deep ambivalence about the caregivers and the potential adoption. Suze also spoke with me by phone and said that they were trying to make the right decision for their child, that they knew they could not care for him, but that she also had mixed feelings about relinquishing him for adoption. I explained to them that relinquishment was a decision that they had to make on their own, but I understood it was not one that would be made lightly.

After many telephone calls, I finally arranged an in-person meeting with the parents and foster parents. I reminded everyone that the purpose of the meeting was to connect and to focus on the baby's care, not to make any long-term decisions. The conversation was sensitive, candid, and respectful. Mr. and Mrs. Jaffe assured Jack and Suze that they were in full support of reunification; they also talked about their affection for the baby and their capacity to take care of him forever, if needed. They talked about their adopted older daughter and about the benefits of an open arrangement for the birth parents, adoptive parents, and the child. Jack asked several questions of Mr. and Mrs. Jaffe; about their family history and motivation for wanting to adopt. Suze had been quiet for much of the meeting, holding the baby and seemingly disengaged in the conversation. Then, she abruptly stood up, and holding the infant in his blanket, walked over to Mrs. Jaffe and put the baby in her arms. Suze hugged Mrs. Jaffe and said "thank you." The moment was both surprising and touching, and although I thought this signaled an important new trajectory for the case, the path forward was anything but clear.

In the following weeks, both Jack and Suze expressed a range of emotions. At times they showed a tender interest in the boy and his well-being. One month after his birth, Suze told me they had decided to name their son. They had thought a great deal about his naming, offering "Sam" as a first name, Jack's last name, and two middle names, as tradition dictated in Suze's family.

In some of my meetings with Jack, he expressed his anger toward hospital personnel and other officials who he believed had falsified drug tests and lied about the drugs found in Suze's system. Jack shared with me his grief and guilt relating to his first failed marriage and relationship with his first son whom he had essentially lost when his homelessness and unemployment became long-term problems. He wanted this parenting experience to be different, but he was unable to secure stable housing or work, his age was an issue for him, and his health was compromised. As a result of these and other issues, his belief in his capacity to parent Sam waned.

Suze often expressed her frustration with me and the agency, and her fear that I was plotting to steal her child. At other times, she talked about Sam's "adoptive parents" and how happy she was that he was going to be adopted by such a loving family who wanted her to play a long-term role in his life. Given her troubled childhood and her own difficult experience with the child welfare system, Suze's reluctance to trust me or anyone in our agency was understandable, and I tried to honor her resistance and empathize with her perspective. Sometimes Jack and Suze simply withdrew altogether, failing to visit with the baby or meet with me. They always had an excuse, but clearly, this was another indication of their deep ambivalence.

After many delays and much back and forth in court regarding Jack's willingness to relinquish the child, the case moved forward. I had to write my court report making a recommendation for the **dispositional hearing**. I recommended that the court offer Jack 6 months of reunification services and that the court deny reunification services to Suze. Denying reunification services to a parent, what is called a **reunification bypass**, requires specific legal standards, but given that Suze's parental rights to her preschooler had just been terminated under very similar circumstances, the law allowed the court to deny Suze the opportunity to reunify. Suze did not contest this recommendation, nor did she appear in court for the hearing.

During the next 6 months, Jack did not fulfill any of the obligations in his reunification case plan except for occasional visits with Sam. These visits were tender and sweet, but he always referred to Sam's caregivers as the "adoptive parents" and continued to talk about relinquishing the boy. I was no longer assigned to Sam's case at the time of the **six-month status review hearing**, but his new social worker recommended to the court that Jack's reunification services be terminated. Jack contested the recommendation, arguing that he was "just not quite ready to give up" and a trial was set for the following month. During those 4 weeks, Jack made some efforts toward the goals of his case plan. He initiated contact with a nonprofit agency to try to secure housing, and he finally gave consent for the social worker to also try to secure housing on his behalf. Sadly, at this point, Jack's efforts were too little, too late. At the trial, the judge ordered Jack's reunification services terminated and set the next hearing to terminate Jack and Suze's parental rights.

Sam—regularly referred to as Joaquin—was now about a year old and had lived with Mr. and Mrs. Jaffe all of his young life. At the following hearing Jack and Suze's parental rights were terminated without their objection. The court then scheduled Joaquin's **adoption finalization hearing**. Suze had long since stopped visiting or contacting her son or the agency, but Jack stayed involved, visiting when he could, and talking with Mr. and Mrs. Jaffe about the baby's growth and development. Suze's aunt also stayed closely involved and developed an ongoing relationship with Joaquin and with Mr. and Mrs. Jaffe.

Around the time of Joaquin's adoption finalization, I too was undergoing major life changes. I was recently married and my husband and I were planning a move to southern California. At the prospect of a new job, I considered leaving the field of child welfare. Ever since high school I'd had goals of becoming a CPS worker. I'd now worked in the field over 10 years, and I still found the work passionately inspiring. Protecting children and empowering families to move from dire situations to positive change is enormously satisfying work. But the work is also hard, very hard. I was growing weary of the politics and tedium of sometimes bureaucratic work, too many nights were sleepless and filled with worry about the children and families I worked with, and the fine line I was frequently asked to balance between doing what I felt was right and doing what the rules required was taxing. After careful consideration, I decided that I would leave child welfare for less stressful work, as soon as we moved.

But then Joaquin's adoption hearing was held, almost 2 years after he entered foster care, and 1 week after I made my decision to leave the field. Mr. and Mrs. Jaffe invited me, the ongoing worker, and the adoption worker to attend. I've attended many adoption finalizations, and they are all very touching. Yet Joaquin's adoption finalization was truly memorable. The courtroom was filled with family and loved ones happy to welcome the boy into the family. Every seat in the gallery was taken and the walkways were full of people holding gifts and balloons. Extended family members were there, and they spoke English, Spanish, and Italian; little Joaquin cheerfully interacted with all of them, talking and understanding all three languages.

Before the court proceedings, the family's Rabbi gave Joaquin an additional Jewish name and offered a blessing. Mr. Jaffe performed a song that he wrote for his son and said a few words to the assembled guests, thanking them for welcoming Joaquin into their family. Mr. Jaffe then turned to me and my colleagues. He praised the quality of our case work, and he thanked us for our hearts and kindness. He then addressed his friends and family and told them that we—social workers—should be admired for the work we do every day: "It's crazy," he said of our jobs, "You can't even imagine how crazy, and they do it day after day." Then he said something that has stayed with me to this day; he said, "There are a lot of really bad things that happen in the world, bad things that we all try really hard not to think about because it's tough just to think about them. But these social workers, they pick a particularly bad one of those bad things and they try really hard to make it better. Every day, they keep at it. We should all be very thankful for what they do."

The Court made the adoption order and Joaquin's adoption was finalized to thunderous applause. We all shared our smiles and laughter, hugs, and thanks.

I walked out of the court house and called my husband right away. I told him that I was foolish to think that I was going to stop being a child welfare worker. It's the only thing I ever want to do.

Veronica Perez

We see in this case all of the principles enacted with little obvious conflict. First, when the baby was born, it was clear that he had not been and might not be cared for safely by his parents. The hospital staff and the child welfare worker assessed the situation against the first principle (*Parents who care for their children safely should be free from government intrusion in their family*) and determined that some degree of involvement was required. The child welfare worker noted Jack's fervent interest in enacting his role as a father and hoped that this important strength could form the basis for the baby's safety in this fragile family. The caseworker's goal was to enact the principle: *Children should be raised with their family of origin* (principle 3). But he also knew that *children should be safe* (principle 2). As such, his serious concerns about the baby's safety, the parents' capacities, and the baby's extreme vulnerability led him to recommend an out-of-home placement. He attempted to identify and contact extended family, enacting the principle: *When children cannot live with family, they should live with extended relatives* (principle 4), but relatives were unavailable, inappropriate, or unwilling. The child welfare worker next identified a foster family, the Jaffe's, to serve as the baby's caregivers since *children should be raised in families* (principle 5). The caregivers that he selected, committed to the baby's long-term stability either through reunification with his birth parents, or adoption, showed their devotion to the principle of permanence: *Children should have a sense of permanence—that the caregivers they live with will care for them permanently* (principle 6). The new child welfare worker and foster parents, intending to enact the principle that *families' cultural heritage should be respected* (principle 7), pursued an open adoption where the baby could have ongoing contact with his birth parents and other extended relatives throughout his childhood and beyond.[6] Throughout the case, the child welfare workers associated with this family attempted to engage the parents, to enact the principle that *parents should have a say in the decisions that affect their lives* (principle 8). The baby's birth father was encouraged to think through the implications of a relinquishment, and his wishes to pursue an open adoption were honored. Because of the baby's age, of course, the infant could not be consulted about his views.

Even in the case described herein, where many of the principles were enacted with little controversy, the decisions the child welfare workers made were neither simple nor painless. With rich, saturated services, could this family have been sufficiently strengthened to raise their baby safely? Would this baby's ultimate well-being have been enhanced if raised with his original family? Working in the field of child welfare involves a high degree of ambiguity—sometimes about the present, and often about the future. The principles help to determine a path forward in practice; they do not necessarily answer the ultimate question: Is this the right thing to do?

How might we determine what is truly "right?" Perhaps if child welfare workers had insight into the future—not just a month or a few years ahead, but the future of a lifetime, we could discern whether the decisions made in child welfare were right and just. Measuring whether a child's behavior problems increase or decrease a few months or years following placement is, of course, important, but it doesn't tell us enough about whether children were better off in life because of the choices child welfare workers made. The long-term studies that ask adults to reflect on their experiences with the child welfare system typically suggest an array of responses from greatly positive to desperately negative, depending very much on the circumstances of their original family and the circumstances of the substitute family arranged for them by the state.[7]

In part because of this uncertainty, foundational principles are needed to help guide practice. They form the basis of decision making because they reflect commonly shared values about children, families, and the standards for state engagement. Without them, all caseworkers might abide by a different compass, with significant implications for inequities across and between families.

Although the principles may be important to good child welfare practice, they may not be sufficient to guarantee just child welfare practice. The stories that make the newspaper headlines too often hint at child welfare decision making that was incorrect— children unnecessarily separated from parents, children left in the home of an unsafe parent, or kin who did not protect a child. A close look at many of these cases often reveals a complex family struggling with many challenges and a child welfare worker trying to enact principled practice at the expense of a competing principle. Journalists need to tell simple stories with limited space. It's easy to tell a story about the caseworker who ignored child safety, or disrespected culture, or disregarded the client's voice. It's a straightforward story, but it too often misses the complexity of trying to privilege all of the principles of child welfare simultaneously—something that most child welfare workers may be unlikely to accomplish.

Training for Principled Practice

As is evident from these stories, enacting principled child welfare practice is a challenge. Critical listening skills, critical thinking skills, skills associated with cultural humility, advocacy skills, self-reflection, knowledge of evidence-based services, and leadership skills are all employed in the work.[8] Graduate-level training to specialize in the field of child welfare and to develop and hone these skills is essential if we expect to see a child welfare workforce that can thoughtfully employ principled practice and know when to privilege one principle over another in the face of complexity.

Evidence from a number of studies suggests that MSW-trained social workers may produce better outcomes for families, probably the most important outcome indicator of all. Children served by an MSW-trained social worker stay in care for a shorter duration than children served by staff without an MSW degree.[9] And MSW-trained social workers more successfully perform a range of complex tasks associated with the work in child welfare than staff without a similar degree.[10] They may also be better prepared to collaborate with parents who are substance involved—a substantial proportion of the population touched by child welfare.[11]

But in many jurisdictions across the country, child welfare agencies are staffed with thoughtful, dedicated individuals who do not possess an MSW degree and/or who are not trained for this specialty area of social work practice. That needs to change.

Students should be taught how to enact core practice competencies, and these competencies should be aligned with principles of practice so that staff have a reasonable road map in the work. Students should be engaged in understanding the complexity of the families and the difficulty of the work—if the field is ever presented as simple and straightforward, we've got it wrong. Classrooms that encourage students to disagree respectfully but forcefully about how to respond to child welfare cases will allow them to reflect on the principles underlying the work and to determine why they privilege one principle over another. Child welfare workers should be keenly attuned to what will be gained and what will be lost for children and for parents when one principle wins out over another. And although child welfare decisions that focus on the losses children and parents sustain can take its emotional toll on workers, the intellectual task of selecting a principled path that can garner the most likely win should be an invigorating challenge.

The principles themselves should also be assessed critically by students and child welfare workers. Our brief review of the historical context shaping the field of child welfare suggests that the values we employ today to guide the work are socially constructed. For example, family placements are promoted today, whereas in previous eras group placements were preferred. Extended family is embraced today, whereas they were intentionally excluded in the past. Foster parents are encouraged to make permanency commitments to the children in their care, whereas this was shunned before. These transformations in our values may signal a more enlightened understanding of children, families, culture, and development, but they are also reflections of the zeitgeist of our times and are thus permeable and responsive to new, culturally constructed ideas. In other words, there is nothing sacrosanct about the principles we employ today to guide practice and policy. The principles do not reflect an absolute "right." They are, instead, widely held, context-specific notions that reflect contemporary perspectives on the relationship of the state to vulnerable children and families. Child welfare workers of the future may look back on our principles of today and note that we were in error. Therefore, in preparing students for the workforce, the principles should be tested, debated, and adjusted as needed. The child welfare of tomorrow may bear few similarities to our practice today.

Considerations for Principled Policy

Although the focus here has centered largely on child welfare practice as it embodies several fundamental principles, it should be noted that the principles we adopt in this field have enormous implications for policy and for the politics of policymaking in child welfare. For example, as described in Chapter 3, when we enact a principle that *children should be safe* (principle 2), we not only articulate a value about children's rights in a complex society, but we simultaneously limit the state's involvement in children's lives and narrow the government's responsibilities to kids. Were we to adopt a children's well-being framework, the policy implications would be vast and the state's responsibility to children would expand considerably. To play out such a notion, what would such a principle look like? Perhaps something like the following: *Children's well-being should be secured by their parents; child welfare workers will support well-being when parents are unable to fulfill their obligations.* But what are the parameters of well-being? And is child welfare the most appropriate profession to attend to children's well-being? If well-being includes educational, health, or mental health outcomes, will child welfare workers deliver those services? As described previously, the principles that currently guide child welfare have not always been with us. Perhaps a principle of child well-being will be adopted in the future. If so, the policy implications will be substantial. Children's human rights may be better secured under the umbrella of a well-being principle, but the touch of the state also will be felt by families more prominently. Given the racial overtones that have historically shaped this field, children of color might be the most likely to benefit from such an expansion, but they also might be the most likely to lose.

Our family of origin principle also has policy implications. Principle 3, *children should be raised with their family of origin,* inclines the field toward a family preservation orientation, but it leaves open the door for child protection if children's safety (principle 2) is breached. If policymakers were to establish a hierarchy of principles such that *family* always prevailed, we would reduce the state's obligation of concern for children's safety and thereby tread on children's individual rights in society. This would, of course, have significant policy implications in the sense that the justification for the child welfare system itself would diminish measurably and the policy framework that allows for children's protection would largely dissolve. Do we want to live in a society where families are free to parent their children as they choose? Where family and community are relied on to feel the tug of obligation when a child is hurt? Maybe. But if we make these choices, we must be prepared for the outcomes that may accrue to children if they are in danger and no one responds. The system we've currently devised is imperfect at best, tragic at worst. Replacing the system with nothing at all entails other social risks that would be equally consequential.

Policies that too narrowly interpret a principle can result in difficult dilemmas for child welfare workers and untenable circumstances for children. For example, policy attention has recently turned to the principle of family-based care (principle 5): *Children should be raised in families.* When policymakers privilege family-based care to the exclusion of group care (as described in Chapter 6), we enact a widely held value, but we may inadvertently limit opportunities for the therapeutic care that some children may require. Policies that too greatly incentivize family-based care or that punish state systems for the use of group care bring the benefit of values-based clarity to the work, but they may also bring the hazard of inflexibly responding to children's diverse needs. In other words, when policies are considered that overrely on these principles to narrowly interpret complicated family circumstances, the rules governing child welfare practice may limit the discretion staff require to carry out individualized services customized to the unique needs of children and families.

Just as practitioners should be principled in their work with families, policymakers, too, should recognize the complexity of principled child welfare. Their efforts to use policy as a tool for championing one principle in child welfare will ultimately result in conflict with other deeply held beliefs about children, parents, and government's responsibility to families. Policymakers' honest engagement with the competing considerations at stake in child welfare will help the public, the press, and the field to reject simplistic, unrealistic antidotes and grapple with the reality of a field that is messy, complicated, and sometimes fraught. History shows that policymakers, attracted to the simplicity of a values framework (e.g., think "life, liberty, and the pursuit of happiness"), find the details of enactment in a complex society enormously vexing.[12] Articulating the principles and the inevitable conflicts between and among each of the principles is the important challenge in the field of child welfare—a challenge that policymakers should honestly and zealously embrace.

Ultimately, the policy frames that guide this work translate into practice on the front lines by adults who care deeply for children and families. These are the individuals who embrace the task of child protection with eyes wide open about the difficulties of the work. They know that children's lives, their health and future, are at stake. Working in the field of child welfare within a framework of basic principles is likely to secure greater justice for families across diverse states and jurisdictions. But the work will never be simple. Child welfare practice requires astute professionals who weigh the benefits and hazards of enacting one principle over another. They do this work for the sake of America's vulnerable children and families.

Notes

ABOUT THE BOOK

1. Clasca, A. (July 8, 2015). Email communication.

CHAPTER 1

1. Fang, X., Brown, D. S., Florence, C. S., & Mercy, J. A. (2012). The economic burden of child maltreatment in the United States and implications for prevention [Abstract]. *Child Abuse & Neglect, 36*(2), 156–165. Retrieved March 12, 2016, from http://www.sciencedirect.com/science/article/pii/S0145213411003140
2. Danese, A., Moffitt, T. E., Harrington, H., Milne, B. J., Polanczyk, G., Pariante, C. M., & Caspi, A. (2009). Adverse childhood experiences and adult risk factors for age-related disease. *Archives of Pediatrics and Adolescent Medicine, 163*(12), 1135–1143; Felitti, V., Anda, R., Nordenberg, D., Williamson, D., Spitz, A., Edwards, V., Koss, M. P., & Marks, J. S. (1998). Relationship of childhood abuse and household dysfunction to many of the leading causes of death in adults. *American Journal of Preventive Medicine, 14*(4), 245–258; Gilbert, R., Widom, C. S., Browne, K., Fergusson, D., Webb, E., & Janson, S. (2009). Burden and consequences of child maltreatment in high income countries. *Lancet, 373,* 68–81. Recent evidence also indicates that women who experienced maltreatment in childhood are at a significantly increased risk of premature death. Chen, E., Turiano, N. A., Mroczek, D., & Miller, G. E. (2016). Association of reports of childhood abuse and all-cause mortality rates in women. *JAMA Psychiatry, 73*(9), 920–927.
3. Perry, B. D. (2001). The neurodevelopmental impact of violence in childhood. In D. Schetky & E. Benedek (Eds.), *Textbook of child and adolescent forensic psychiatry* (pp. 221–238). Washington, DC: American Psychiatric Press; Silverman, A. B., Reinherz, H. Z., & Giaconia, R. M. (1996). The long-term sequelae of child and adolescent abuse: a longitudinal community study. *Child Abuse and Neglect, 20*(8), 709–723.
4. Langsford, J. E., Miller-Johnson, S., Berlin, L. J., Dodge, K. A., Bates, J. E., & Pettit, G. S. (2007). Early physical abuse and later violent delinquency: A prospective longitudinal study. *Child Maltreatment, 12*(3), 233–245; Runyan, D., Wattam, C., Ikeda, R., Hassan, F., & Ramiro, L. (2002). Child abuse and neglect by parents and other caregivers. In E. Krug, L. L. L. Dahlberg, J. A. Mercy, A. B. Zwi, & R. Lozano (Eds.), *World report on violence and health* (pp. 59–86).

Geneva, Switzerland: World Health Organization. Available from http://www.who.int/violence_injury_prevention/violence/global_campaign/en/chap3.pdf; Widom, C., Marmorstein, N., & White, H. (2006). Childhood victimization and illicit drug use in middle adulthood. *Psychology of Addictive Behaviors, 20*(4), 394–403.

5. Berlin, L. J., Appleyard, K., & Dodge, K. A. (2011). Intergenerational continuity in child maltreatment: Mediating mechanisms and implications for prevention. *Child Development, 82*, 162–176; Putnam-Hornstein, E., Cederbaum, J., King, B., Eastman, A. L., & Trickett, P. K. (2015). A population-level and longitudinal study of adolescent mothers and intergenerational maltreatment. *American Journal of Epidemiology, 181*(7), 496–503. For a review of some of the developmental consequences of child maltreatment, see Putnam, F. (2006). The impact of trauma on child development. *Juvenile and Family Court Journal*, 1–11.
6. U.S. Department of Health & Human Services, Administration for Children and Families, Administration on Children, Youth and Families, Children's Bureau. (2016). *Child maltreatment 2014*. Available from http://www.acf.hhs.gov/programs/cb/research-data-technology/statistics-research/child-maltreatment.
7. According to the Commission to Eliminate Child Abuse and Neglect Fatalities, official reports of child maltreatment-related fatalities underestimate the scope of the problem. The commission estimates that closer to 3,000 children die each year in the United States due to maltreatment. See Commission to Eliminate Child Abuse and Neglect Fatalities. (2016). *Within our reach: A national strategy to eliminate child abuse and neglect fatalities*. Washington, DC: Government Printing Office.
8. Hussey, J., Chang, J. J., & Kotch, J. B. (2006). Child maltreatment in the United States: Prevalence, risk factors, and adolescent health consequences. *Pediatrics, 118*(3), 933–942.
9. For a review of some of the evidence, see Huston, A. C., McLoyd, V. C., & Coll, C. G. (2008). Children and poverty: Issues in contemporary research. *Child Development, 65*(2), 275–282; McLeod, J., & Shanahan, M. (1993). Poverty, parenting, and children's mental health. *American Sociological Review, 58*, 351–366; McLoyd, V. C. (1998). Socioeconomic disadvantage and child development. *The American Psychologist, 53*, 185–204.
10. Low SES was defined as an annual family income below $15,000, or an adult head of household with less than a high school diploma, or any household member participating in a government-sponsored poverty-related program.
11. Sedlak, A. J., Mettenburg, J., Basena, M., Petta, I., McPherson, K., Greene, A., and Li, S. (2010). *Fourth National Incidence Study of Child Abuse and Neglect (NIS–4): Report to Congress*. Washington, DC: U.S. Department of Health and Human Services, Administration for Children and Families.

12. Putnam-Hornstein, E., Needell, B., King, B., & Johnson-Montoyama, M. (2013). Racial and ethnic disparities: A population-based examination of risk factors for involvement with child protective services. *Child Abuse and Neglect, 37*(1), 33–46.
13. Berger, L. M. (2005). Income, family characteristics, and physical violence toward children. *Child Abuse and Neglect, 29*(2), 107–133; Coulton, C. J., Crampton, D. S., Irwin, M., Spilsbury, J. C., & Korbin, J. E. (2007). How neighborhoods influence child maltreatment: A review of the literature and alternative pathways. *Child Abuse and Neglect, 31* (11/12), 1117–1142; Drake, B., Jolley, J. M., Lanier, P., Fluke, J., Barth, R. P., & Jonson-Reid, M. (2011). Racial bias in child protection? A comparison of competing explanations using national data. *Pediatrics, 127*(3), 471–478.
14. U.S. Department of Health & Human Services, Administration for Children and Families, Administration on Children, Youth and Families, Children's Bureau. (2016). *Child maltreatment 2014*. Available from http://www.acf.hhs.gov/programs/cb/research-data-technology/statistics-research/child-maltreatment.
15. U.S. Department of Health & Human Services, Administration for Children and Families, Administration on Children, Youth and Families, Children's Bureau. (2016). *Child maltreatment 2014*. Available from http://www.acf.hhs.gov/programs/cb/research-data-technology/statistics-research/child-maltreatment.
16. I use the term "child welfare worker" or "caseworker" throughout the book. I would argue (and I do so in Chapter 10) that the complexity of child welfare work requires an MSW degree. In some jurisdictions currently, MSW-trained social workers serve as child welfare workers; in others, less specialized training is required. Specialized training programs for BSW and MSW students have been available in some Schools of Social Work for over three decades. A conservative estimate of the number of graduates from these programs each year may equal close to 2,000 (Zlotnick & Pryce, 2013). Zlotnik, J. L., & Pryce, P. (2013). The status of the use of Title IV-E funding in BSW & MSW programs. *Journal of Public Child Welfare, 7*(4), 430–446.
17. Nissly, J., Mor Barak, M., & Levin, A. (2005). Stress, social support, and workers' intentions to leave their job in public child welfare. *Administration in Social Work, 29*(1), 79–100. Recent evidence indicates that the reasons staff leave the field of child welfare largely have to do with the organizational context in which they work. When workers felt unsupported, or when they could not make their voice heard within their agency, they were more likely to leave. See Griffiths, A., & Royse, D. (2017). Unheard voices: Why former child welfare workers left their positions. *Journal of Public Child Welfare, 11*(1), 73–90.
18. See, for example, the National Child Welfare Workforce Initiative (http://www.ncwwi.org).
19. Chen, S-Y., & Scannapieco, M. (2010). The influence of job satisfaction on child welfare workers' desire to stay: An examination of the interaction effect of self-efficacy and supportive supervision. *Children and Youth Services Review, 32*(4), 482–486.

20. Aarons, G. A., & Palinkas, L. (2007). Implementation of evidence-based practice in child welfare: Service provider perspectives. *Administration and Policy in Mental Health and Mental Health Services Research, 34*, 411–419; Webb, M. B., Dowd, K., Harden, B. J., Landsverk, J., & Testa, M. (2010). *Child welfare and child well-being: New perspectives from the National Survey of Child and Adolescent Well-being.* New York, NY: Oxford University Press.
21. Glisson, C., & Green, P. (2011). Organizational climate, services, and outcomes in child welfare. *Child Abuse and Neglect, 35*, 582–591; National Council on Crime and Delinquency. (2006). The relationship between staff turnover, child welfare system functioning, and recent child abuse. Retrieved from CPS Human Resources Services website: http://www.cps.ca.gov/workforceplanning/documents/06.02_Relation_Staff.pdf.
22. Gainsborough, J. (2010). *Scandalous politics.* Washington, DC: Georgetown University Press; Parton, N. (2014). *The politics of child protection: Contemporary developments and future directions.* New York, NY: Palgrave Macmillan.
23. Ellett, A., Ellis, J. I., Westbook, T. M., & Dews, D. (2007). A qualitative study of 369 child welfare professionals' perspectives about factors contributing to employee retention and turnover. *Children and Youth Services Review, 29*, 264–281 (p. 274); Westbrook, T. M., Ellis, J., & Ellett, J. (2006). Improving retention among public child welfare workers. *Administration in Social Work, 30*(4), 37–62.
24. Gelles, R. (in press). *Out of harm's way.* New York, NY: Oxford University Press.
25. See, for example, Lowry, M. (2004). Putting teeth into ASFA: The need for statutory minimum standards. *Children and Youth Services Review, 26*, 1021–1031; Wulczyn, F., Barth, R. P., Yuan, Y. Y., Harden, B. J., & Landsverk, J. (2005). *Beyond common sense: Child welfare, child well-being, and the evidence for policy reform.* New York, NY: Aldine.
26. Michael Wald has suggested that the child welfare system should be narrowly focused on securing children's safety and that other systems (e.g., health and education) might more appropriately take on the mantle of securing children's more general well-being needs. See Wald, M. S. (2015). Beyond CPS: Developing an effective system for helping children in "neglectful" families. Policymakers have failed to address the neglect of neglect. *Child Abuse & Neglect, 41*, 49–66. doi:10.1016/j.chiabu.2015.01.010. The federal government has established through its Child and Family Service Reviews (CFSR) three indicators to assess state efforts in securing children's well-being. These include families' enhanced capacities to provide for children's needs; children receiving appropriate services to meet their educational needs; and children receiving adequate services to meet their physical and mental health needs (see Child and Family Service Reviews. U.S. Department of Health and Human Services (US DHHS), Health Resources and Services Administration, Maternal and Child Health Bureau. (n.d.). Child & Family Services Reviews. Retrieved from http://www.acf.hhs.gov/programs/cb/monitoring/child-family-services-reviews). These are rather limited indicators and according to Jonson-Reid

and Drake, they represent process-oriented measures rather than outcomes. See Jonson-Reid, M., & Drake, B. (2016). Child well-being: Where is it in our data systems? *Journal of Public Child Welfare, 10*(4), 457–465.

27. Then Commissioner Bryan Samuels distributed an Information Memorandum from the Children's Bureau in 2012 which was striking for its emphasis on child well-being. It should be noted, however, that child welfare agencies were encouraged to pursue well-being goals with children who had experienced maltreatment, and therefore was relevant following the determination of eligibility, rather than a criteria for eligibility itself. See United States Department of Health and Human Services, Administration on Children, Youth and Families. (2012). *Promoting social and emotional well-being for children and youth receiving child welfare services.* Washington, DC: Children's Bureau. http://www.acf.hhs.gov/sites/default/files/cb/im1204.pdf. When child well-being is pursued, our definitional frame for well-being is typically limited to securing children's physical and mental health or their educational pursuits—hardly the boundaries of well-being most parents would find sufficient for their own children. Efforts to establish standardized strategies for measuring children's mental health are underway and should be embraced (see Rosanbalm, K. D., Snyder, E. H., Lawrence, C. N., Coleman, K., Frey, J. J., van den Ende, J., & Dodge, K. A. [2016]. Child wellbeing assessment in child welfare: A review of four measures. *Children and Youth Services Review, 68*, 1–16). The argument set forth here is not to suggest that dimensions of well-being should be unaddressed in child welfare, but to argue that well-being is not a fundamental principle upon which our US system is currently based.
28. See Gilbert, N., Parton, N., & Skivenes, M. (2011). *Child protection systems: International trends and orientations.* New York, NY: Oxford University Press.
29. Other principles that could be considered include maintaining children in their community of origin, or in their school of origin, if foster care is required. But evidence on the challenged schools and neighborhoods from which foster children hale suggests caution on the universal application of such a principle. And as earlier, I would argue that the principle of child well-being is not fundamental to child welfare in the United States. If it were, the front end of our system that determines eligibility would be completely reshaped, and the services offered to support families would look very different than they do in most jurisdictions. Further, even for children placed in care, the United States is a long way from adopting a child well-being principle as it is, as yet, an unmeasured construct that too quickly reverts to an easy assessment of on-time medical or dental appointments—a measure of well-being distant from common conceptions of the construct.
30. California's approach to training MSW-level child welfare workers includes 44 key competencies to which child welfare workers should be trained and held accountable. See http://calswec.berkeley.edu/curriculum-competencies-public-child-welfare-california

31. A look at the names of some major federal policies speaks to the principles these policies attempt to promote. For example, there are the Safe and Stable Families Act, Families First Act, Adoption and Safe Families Act, etc.
32. Lipsky has written extensively about the strategies social workers and other public employees use to embody policy in the context of the "streets." Others (Brodkin) have examined how social workers interpret policy principles. See Brodkin, E. Z. (2012). Reflections on street-level bureaucracy: Past, present, and future. *Public Administration Review*, 72(6), 940–949; Lipsky, M. (1980). *Street level bureaucracy: Dilemmas of the individual in public services.* New York, NY: Russell Sage Foundation.
33. It should be noted that the social worker's decisions resulted in Xander experiencing 5 different placements during a relatively short period of his life. The decision was not made lightly as this worker struggled with the competing values of Principle #5: Children should be raised in families vs. placement stability. I have not included "placement stability" as one of the 8 fundamental principles, but one could argue that this too is a central tenet of the field.
34. A growing body of literature suggests that some staff who regularly work with traumatized children experience vicarious or secondary trauma themselves. Efforts to guard against secondary trauma are especially important in this field to guard against burnout and negative psychological and mental health effects. See Dombo, E. A., & Blome, W. W. (2016). Vicarious trauma in child welfare workers: A study of organizational responses. *Journal of Public Child Welfare, 10*(5), 505–523; Middleton, J. S., & Potter, C. C. (2015). Relationship between vicarious traumatization and turnover among child welfare professionals. *Journal of Public Child Welfare, 9*(2), 195–216.
35. Aldgate, J. (2009) Living in kinship care: A child-centered view. *Adoption and Fostering, 33*(3), 51–63.
36. Dumbrill, G. C. (2006). Parental experience of child protection intervention: A qualitative study. *Child Abuse and Neglect, 30*(1), 27–37; Mandell, D. (2008). Power, care and vulnerability: Considering use of self in child welfare work. *Journal of Social Work Practice, 22*(2), 235–248.

CHAPTER 2

1. For a review of this legislation, see Myers, J. E. (2006). *Child protection in America: Past, present, and future.* New York, NY: Oxford University Press.
2. Johnson, K., O'Connor, D., Berry, S., Ramelmeier, D., & Pecora, P. (2014). Structuring the decision to accept a child protection report. *Journal of Public Child Welfare, 6*(2), 191–205. doi: 10.1080/15548732.2012.667736.
3. According to the most recent statistics, an estimated 3.6 million referrals were logged in the United States in 2014. Of the 3.6 million referrals, approximately 60.7% are screened in, and 39.3 are screened out. There is dramatic variation in screened-in/out policies across the states such that in some states up to 100% of cases are screened

in. U.S. Department of Health & Human Services, Administration for Children and Families, Administration on Children, Youth and Families, Children's Bureau. (2016). *Child maltreatment 2014*. Available from http://www.acf.hhs.gov/programs/cb/research-data-technology/statistics-research/child-maltreatment

4. Children's Research Center (2015). *Structured decision making policies and procedures manual, SDM 3.0*. National Council on Crime and Delinquency, CDC.
5. U.S. Department of Health & Human Services, Administration for Children and Families, Administration on Children, Youth and Families, Children's Bureau. (2016). *Child maltreatment 2014*. Available from http://www.acf.hhs.gov/programs/cb/research-data-technology/statistics-research/child-maltreatment
6. Hamarman, S., Pope, K. H., & Czaja, S. J. (2002). Emotional abuse in children: Variations in legal definitions and rates across the United States. *Child Maltreatment, 7*(4), 303–311. doi: 10.1177/107755902237261.
7. Child Welfare Information Gateway. (2016). *Mandatory reporters of child abuse and neglect*. Washington, DC: U.S. Department of Health and Human Services, Children's Bureau.
8. Crowell, K., & Levi, B. H. (2012). Mandated reporting thresholds for community professionals. *Child Welfare, 91*(1), 35–54.
9. Feng, J-Y., Chen, Y-W., Fetzer, S., Feng, M-C., & Lin, C-L. (2012). Ethical and legal challenges of mandated child abuse reporters. *Children and Youth Services Review, 34*, 276–280. doi:10.1016/j.childyouth.2011.10.026.
10. United States Department of Health and Human Services. (2016). *Child maltreatment 2014*. Washington, DC: http://www.acf.hhs.gov/programs/cb/research-data-technology/statistics-research/child-maltreatment
11. Wells, S. J., Fluke, J., & Brown, C. H. (1995). The decision to investigate: CPS practice in twelve local agencies. *Children and Youth Services Review, 17*, 523–546. doi: 10.1016/0190-7409(95)00037-D10.1016/0190-7409(95)00037-D.
12. Wells, S. J., Lyons, P., Doueck, H., Hendricks Brown, C., & Thomas, J. (2004). Ecological factors and screening in child protective services. *Children and Youth Services Review, 26*, 981–997. doi:10.1016/j.childyouth.2004.05.002. Examining 12 sites in five states, the authors found that the number of families with children under age 18 positively influenced the screen-in decision, as did the proportion of child neglect referrals.
13. Eastman, A. L., Mitchell, M. N., & Putnam-Hornstein, E. (2016). *Child Abuse and Neglect, 55*, 22–31. There is considerable evidence also that the source of the report determines the likelihood of substantiation following an investigation with reports filed by mandated reporters much more likely to be substantiated. See King, B., Lawson, J., & Putnam-Hornstein, E. (2013). Examining the evidence: Reporter identity, allegation type, and sociodemographic characteristics as predictors of maltreatment substantiation. *Child Maltreatment, 18*(4), 232–244.
14. The literature suggests contradictory findings on the role of race in screening decisions. See Child Welfare Information Gateway (2011). Addressing racial

disproportionality in child welfare. Issue brief. Washington, DC: Children's Bureau. Retrieved July 23, 2016, from https://www.childwelfare.gov/pubPDFs/racial_disproportionality.pdf; Hill, R. B. (n.d.). Disproportionality of minorities in child welfare: Synthesis of research findings. Westat. Retrieved July 23, 2016, from http://www.cssp.org/reform/child-welfare/other-resources/Disproportionality-of-Minorities-in-Child-Welfare-Synthesis-of-Research-Findings.pdf

15. Besharov, D. (1990). Gaining control over child abuse reports. *Public Welfare, 48*(2), 34–41.
16. Magruder, J., & Shaw, T. (2008). Children ever in care: An examination of cumulative disproportionality. *Child Welfare, 87*(2), 169–188.
17. In another study, the magnitude of difference between African American and White children was similar. Emily Putnam-Hornstein and associates found the cumulative rate of referral by age 5 for African American children at about 30%. Putnam-Hornstein, E., Needell, B., King, B., & Johnson-Montoyama, M. (2013). Racial and ethnic disparities: A population-based examination of risk factors for involvement with child protective services. *Child Abuse and Neglect, 37*(1), 33–46. doi:10.1016/j.chiabu.2012.08.005.
18. Ards, S. D., Myers, S. L., Ray, P., Kim, H. E., Monroe, K., & Arteaga, I. (2012). Racialized perceptions of child neglect. *Children and Youth Services Review, 34*, 1480–1491; McDaniel, M. (2006). In the eye of the beholder: The role of reporters in bringing families to the attention of child protective services. *Children and Youth Services Review, 28*, 306–324. doi:10.1016/j.childyouth.2005.04.010.
19. McDaniel, M., & Slack, K. S. (2005). Major life events and the risk of a child maltreatment investigation. *Children and Youth Services Review, 27*, 171–195. doi:10.1016/j.childyouth.2004.08.015.
20. Lane, W., Rubin, D., Monteith, R., & Christian, C. (2002). Racial differences in the evaluation of pediatric fractures for physical abuse. *Journal of the American Medical Association, 288*(13), 1603–1609. doi:10.1001/jama.288.13.1603.
21. Kesner, J. E., Robinson, M. (2002). Teachers as mandated reporters of child maltreatment: Comparison with legal, medical, and social services reports. *Children and Schools, 24*(4), 222–231. doi: 10.1093/cs/24.4.222.
22. According to the NIS-4, the US child welfare system investigated between 32% and 43% of all children who were actually maltreated (depending on the definition used). See Sedlak, A. J., Mettenburg, J., Basena, M., Petta, I., McPherson, K., Greene, A., and Li, S. (2010). *Fourth National Incidence Study of Child Abuse and Neglect (NIS–4): Report to Congress.* Washington, DC: U.S. Department of Health and Human Services, Administration for Children and Families.
23. Needell, B., Webster, D., Armijo, M., Lee, S., Dawson, W., Magruder, J., & Exel, M. (2010). Child welfare services reports for California. Retrieved January 15, 2011, from http://cssr.berkeley.edu/ucb_childwelfare As reported in Putnam-Hornstein, E. (2011). Report of maltreatment as a risk factor for injury death: A prospective birth

cohort study. *Child Maltreatment, 16*(3), 163–174. doi: 10.1177/1077559511411179. Other studies have similar findings. See Proctor, L. J., Aarons, G. A., Dubowitz, H., English, D. J., Lewis, T., Thompson, R., et al. (2012). Trajectories of maltreatment re-reports from ages 4 to 12: Evidence for persistent risk after early exposure. *Child Maltreatment, 17*, 207–217. doi: 10.1177/1077559512448472; Putnam-Hornstein, E., Simon, J. D., Eastman, A. L., & Magruder, J. (2015). Risk of re-reporting among infants who remain at home following alleged maltreatment. *Child Maltreatment, 20*, 92–103. doi: 10.1177/1077559514558586.

24. Putnam-Hornstein, E. (2011). Report of maltreatment as a risk factor for injury death: A prospective birth cohort study. *Child Maltreatment, 16*(3), 163–174: 172. doi: 10.1177/1077559511411179.
25. I use the pronoun "she" throughout for simplicity and to reflect the fact that the majority of students graduating from Schools of Social Work with MSW degrees are women. See Council on Social Work Education (2013). *2013 Statistics on social work education in the United States.* Washington, DC: CSWE. Retrieved August 4, 2016, from http://www.cswe.org/file.aspx?id=74478
26. Lindsay, D. (2004). *The welfare of children.* New York, NY: Oxford University Press.
27. Berrick, J. D. (2015). Protecting children from maltreatment in the U.S. *Arbor,* available at http://arbor.revistas.csic.es/index.php/arbor/issue/current

CHAPTER 3

1. UNICEF. (2007). Innocenti Report Card 7: *Child poverty in perspective—An overview of child well-being in rich countries*. Retrieved from http://www.unicefirc.org/publications/pdf/rc7_eng.pdf
   UNICEF. (2010). Innocenti Report Card 9: *The Children Left Behind*. Retrieved from http://www.unicef-irc.org/files/documents/d-3796-The-Children-Left-Behind-.pdf
   UNICEF. (2013). Innocenti Report card 11: *Child well-being in rich countries—a comparative review*. Retrieved from http://www.unicef.org.uk/Images/Campaigns/FINAL_RC11-ENG-LORES-fnl2.pdf
2. *The U.S. News and World Report* conducts a "best countries ranking" every X years. In its most recent assessment, the United States was still ranked no. 1 among nations overall. See Best countries (2016). *U.S. News and World Report*. Retrieved April 28, 2016, from http://www.usnews.com/news/best-countries
3. Pösö, T. (2011). Combatting child abuse in Finland: From family to child-centered orientation. In N. Gilbert, N. Parton, & M. Skivenes. *Child protection systems: International trends and orientations* (pp. 112–130). New York, NY: Oxford University Press.
4. Dessair, K., & Adriaenssens, P. (2011). Policy toward child abuse and neglect in Belgium: Shared responsibility, differentiated response. In N. Gilbert, N. Parton, & M. Skivenes. *Child protection systems: International trends and orientations.* New York, NY: Oxford University Press.

5. Berrick, J. D., Peckover, S., Poso, T., & Skivenes, M. (2015). The formalized framework for decision making in child protection care orders: A cross-country comparison. *Journal of European Social Work, 25*(4), 366–378.
6. Gilbert, N., Parton, N., & Skivenes, M. (2011). *Child protection systems: International trends and orientations.* New York, NY: Oxford University Press.
7. Skivenes, M. (2011). Norway: Toward a child-centric perspective. In N. Gilbert, N. Parton, & M. Skivenes (Eds.), *Child protection systems: International trends and orientations.* New York, NY: Oxford University Press.
8. National Survey of Child and Adolescent Well-Being Brief (n.d.) *What is substantiation? NSCAW Brief #6.* Washington, DC: Administration for Children and Families. Retrieved May 2, 2016, from http://www.acf.hhs.gov/sites/default/files/opre/caseworker_judgments_0.pdf
9. Kim, H., Wildeman, C., Jonson-Reid, M., & Drake, B. (2017). Lifetime prevalence of investigating child maltreatment among U.S. children. *American Journal of Public Health, 107,* 274–280, doi: 10.2105/AJPH.2016.303545.
10. Lowry reviews this and several of the changes embedded in this significant policy change: Lowry, M. R. (2004). Putting teeth into ASFA: The need for statutory minimum standards. *Children and Youth Services Review, 26,* 1021–1031.
11. Richard Gelles's book portrays the consequences that can result from making unreasonable efforts to maintain children in unsafe families. (Gelles, R. [1997]. *The book of David.* New York, NY: Basic Books). Ted Stein focuses his critique of the law on the lack of uniform data supporting the sensational accounts of social workers' unreasonable efforts. (Stein, T. (2003). The Adoption and Safe Families Act: How Congress overlooks available data and ignores systematic obstacles in its pursuit of political goals. *Children and Youth Services Review, 25*(9), 669–682).
12. For a review of the practice principles and approach, see Meitner, H., & Albers, M. (2012). *Introducing safety organized practice.* Children's Research Center, National Center on Crime and Delinquency. Retrieved May 3, 2016, from http://bayareaacademy.org/wp-content/uploads/2013/05/SOP-Handout-Booklet-9-20-12.pdf
13. Family team meetings are also referred to as family group decision making or family unity meetings. Although there are unique practices associated with each approach, the core philosophy and activities are similar. Crea, T. M., & Berzin, S. C. (2009). Family involvement in child welfare decision-making: Strategies and research on inclusive practices. *Journal of Public Child Welfare, 3*(3), 305–327.
14. Juhasz, I., & Skivenes, M. (2016). The population's confidence in the child welfare system—A survey study of England, Finland, Norway, and the United States (California). *Social Policy and Administration, 50*(3), 2–18.
15. According to the Guttmacher Institute, one state allows a woman to be prosecuted for assault if she uses substances while pregnant. Eighteen states consider substance use during pregnancy to be an indicator of child abuse. For further information, see Dailard, C., & Nash, E. (2000). State responses to substance abuse among pregnant

women. Guttmacher Institute. Guttmacher report on Public Policy. Retrieved May 9, 2016, from https://www.guttmacher.org/sites/default/files/pdfs/spibs/spib_SADP.pdf

16. Waldfogel, J. (2010). *What children need: The family and public policy*. Boston, MA: Harvard University Press.
17. Bartholet, E. (2014). Differential response: A dangerous experiment in child welfare. *Florida State University Law Review, 42*, 572–644.
18. For a lively debate on the merits and demerits of differential response, see Hughes, R. C., Rycus, J. S., Saunders-Adams, S. M., Hughes, L. K., & Hughes, K. N. (2013). Issues in differential response. *Research on Social Work Practice, 23*(5).
19. Child Welfare Information Gateway. (2014). Differential response to reports of child abuse and neglect. Washington, DC: U.S. Department of Health and Human Services, Children's Bureau; Schene, P. (2005). The emergency of differential response. In American Humane Association. *Differential Response in Child Welfare, Protecting Children, 20*(2), 4–8; Waldfogel, J. (1998). *The future of child protection*. Cambridge, MA: Harvard University Press.
20. Conley, A., & Berrick, J. D. (2010). Community-based child abuse prevention: Outcomes associated with a Differential Response program in California. *Child Maltreatment*. For addition information regarding the dropout or decline rate, see Bartholet, E. (2015). Differential response: A dangerous experiment in child welfare. *Florida State University Law Review, 42*, 573–643.
21. Peterson, A., Joseph, J., & Felt, M. (2014). *New directions in child abuse and neglect research*. Committee on Child Maltreatment Research, Institute of Medicine.
22. Proposition 64 passed in November 2016 with 56% approval. The law allows adults to possess, transport, and buy up to one ounce of marijuana. This author's story takes place prior to the "recreational marijuana" bill passed.
23. Brady, E. (2013). *Humboldt: Life on America's marijuana frontier*. New York, NY: Hatchett Book Group.
24. Propostion 215, the Compassionate Care Act. Prop 215 made it legal for California residents to possess and cultivate marijuana for personal use with a valid doctor's recommendation and exempted patients and their caregivers from criminal prosecution. In November, 2016, California voters passed Proposition 64, legalizing the recreational use of marijuana for individuals age 21 and older, and other provisions relating to marijuana sales and taxes.
25. Freisthler, B., Gruenewald, P., & Wolf, J. P. (2015). Examining the relationship between marijuana use, medical marijuana dispensaries, and abusive and neglectful parenting. *Child Abuse and Neglect, 48*, 170–178.
26. Wang, G. S., Roosevelt, G., & Heard, K. (2013). Pediatric marijuana exposure in a medical marijuana state. *JAMA Pediatrics, 167*(7), 630–633.
27. Barth, R. P., Wildfire, J., & Green, R. (2006). Placement into foster care and the interplay of urbanicity, child behavior problems, and poverty. *American*

Psychological Association, 76(3), 358–366; Cunningham, S., & Finlay, K. (2013). Parental substance use and foster care: Evidence from two methamphetamine supply shocks. *Economic Inquiry, 51*(1), 764–782; Grella, C. E., Needell, B., Shi, Y., & Hser, Y. I. (2009). Do drug treatment services predict reunification outcomes of mothers and their children in child welfare? *Journal of Substance Abuse Treatment, 36*(3), 278–293; McGuinness, T. M., & Schneider, K. (2007). Poverty, child maltreatment, and foster care. *Journal of the American Psychiatric Nurses Association, 13*(5), 296–303; Testa, M. F., & Smith, B. (2009). Prevention and drug treatment. *The Future of Children, 19*(2), 147–168; Young, N. K., Boles, S. M., & Otero, C. (2007). Parental substance use disorders and child maltreatment: Overlap, gaps, and opportunities. *Child Maltreatment, 12*(2), 137–149.

CHAPTER 4

1. For a lengthy analysis of the Mary Ellen legend, see Costin, L. B., Karger, H. J., & Stoesz, D. (1996). *The politics of child abuse in America.* New York, NY: Oxford University Press.
2. Some references indicate that Mary Ellen was left with the Department of Charities as a baby, was placed in an institution, and then indentured to her caregivers. According to testimony at the trial by Ms. Connolly, Mary Ellen's "stepmother," Mary Ellen was the illegitimate offspring of her first husband, Mr. McCormack. See Watkins, S. A. (1990). The Mary Ellen myth: Correcting child welfare history. *Social Work, 35*(6), 500–503.
3. Markel, H. (2009, Dec. 15). The child who put a face on abuse. *New York Times.*
4. I refer to the Mary Ellen story as a legend in line with the views of Costin et al., who suggest that the story has, over the years, taken on a shape and importance of legendary status in our field. Accounts of the story vary along a number of dimensions. Mary Ellen is variously referred to as age 8, 9, 10, or 11, depending on the source. Her caregivers are sometimes referred to as adoptive parents, guardians, stepparents, or adults to whom Mary Ellen was indentured. Following her removal, some accounts indicate she was sent to live in an orphanage and others indicate she was sent to live with Mrs. Wheeler's mother or sister; still, others indicate that she was removed from the orphanage and ultimately came to live with Mrs. Wheeler (see Costin, Karger, & Stoesz, 1996; Markel, 2009). The story has taken on the label of "legend" because it was, of course, more complicated than this simple description might suggest.
5. Costin, L. B., Karger, H. J., & Stoesz, D. (1996). *The politics of child abuse in America.* New York, NY: Oxford University Press; Gelles, R. (1997). *The book of David: How preserving families can cost children's lives.* New York, NY: Basic Books.
6. Much has been written about the differences in approach between the New York and Massachusetts Societies. The starkest difference between the two was the New York emphasis on punishing parents and placing children in institutional care, whereas the Massachusetts model focused more on parental rehabilitation

and placement in foster or boarding homes. Costin et al. indicate that some of the later work of the Massachusetts Society focused on prevention services for families, though Linda Gordon suggests that too much has been made of these claims and that the Boston Society did not depart philosophically from New York as much in this regard. See Costin, L. B., Karger, H. J., & Stoesz, D. (1996). *The politics of child abuse in America*. New York, NY: Oxford University Press; Gordon, L. (1988). *Heroes of their own lives: The politics and history of family violence.* New York, NY: Viking Penguin.

7. The debate is especially animated in the works of Barthlet and Guggenheim. See Bartholet, E. (2000). Reply: Whose children? A response to Professor Guggenheim. *Harvard Law Review, 113*, 1999–2008; Guggenheim, M. (2000). Somebody's children: sustaining the family's place in child welfare policy. *Harvard Law Review, 113*, 1716–1750.
8. See the TedTalk by Molly McGrath Tierney, wherein the speaker frames her interest in developing additional prevention services for families by suggesting that foster care is (always?) a fully harmful intervention for children. "Rethinking foster care." Retrieved May 10, 2016, from http://tedxtalks.ted.com/video/Rethinking-Foster-Care-Molly-Mc. Also see Atwood, T. (2011, March 25). Foster care: Safety net or trap door? *Backgrounder, 2535*. Retrieved July 23, 2016, from http://thf_media.s3.amazonaws.com/2011/pdf/bg2535.pdf; Barish, N. (2010, January 7). *Using the harm of removal and placement to advocate for parents.* Youth, Rights, and Justice.
9. Storer, H. L., Barkan, S. E., Stenhouse, L. L., Eichenlaub, C., Mallillin, A., & Haggerty, K. P. (2014). In search of connection: The foster youth and caregiver relationship. *Children and Youth Services Review, 42*, 110–117; Greeson, J. K., Thompson, A. E., Ali, S., & Wenger, R. S. (2015). It's good to know that you got somebody that's not going anywhere: Attitudes and beliefs of older youth in foster care about child welfare-based natural mentoring. *Children and Youth Services Review, 48*, 140–149. doi:10.1016/j.childyouth.2014.12.015; McCormick, A., Schmidt, K., & Terrazas, S. R. (2016). Foster family acceptance: Understanding the role of foster family acceptance in the lives of LGBTQ youth. *Children and Youth Services Review, 616*, 9–74. doi:10.1016/j.childyouth.2015.12.005; Singer, E. R., Berzin, S. C., & Hokanson, K. (2013). Voices of former foster youth: Supportive relationships in the transition to adulthood. *Children and Youth Services Review, 35*, 2110–2117. doi:10.1016/j.childyouth.2013.10.019.
10. Gelles, R. (2017). *Out of harm's way.: Creating an effective child welfare system.* New York: NY: Oxford University Press.
11. Some of the studies showing positive effects include: Conn, A-M., Szilagyi, M. A., Jee, S. H., Blumkin, A. K., & Szilagyi, P. G. (2015). Mental health outcomes among child welfare investigated children: In-home versus out-of-home care. *Children and Youth Services Review, 57*, 106–111; Davidson-Arad, B. (2005). Fifteen-month follow up of children at risk: Comparison of the quality of life of children removed from home and children remaining at home. *Children and Youth Services Review,*

27, 1–20; Jonson-Reid, M., & Barth, R. (2000). From maltreatment report to juvenile incarceration: The role of child welfare services. *Child Abuse and Neglect, 24*(4), 505–520; Litronik, A. J., Newton, R., Mitchell, B. E., & Richardson, K. K. (2003). Long-term follow up of young children placed in foster care: Subsequent placements and exposure to family violence. *Journal of Family Violence, 18*(1), 19–28; Taussig, H., Clyman, R. B., & Landsverk, J. (2001). Children who return home from foster care: A 6-year prospective study of behavioral health outcomes in adolescence. *Pediatrics, 108*(1), 1–7 (The Taussig et al. study did not compare children who remained at home versus placed in care, but it compared children returned home after a study in care, compared to children remaining in care.) Wald, M. S., Carlsmith, J. M., & Leiderman, P. H. (1988). *Protecting abused and neglected children*. Stanford, CA: Stanford University Press.

12. Berger, L. M., Bruch, S. K., Johnson, E. K., James, S. & Rubin, D. (2009). Estimating the "impact" of out-of-home placement on child well-being: Approaching the problem of selection bias. *Child Development, 80*, 1856–1876; Lloyd, C., & Barth, R. P. (2011). Developmental outcomes after five years for foster children returned home, remaining in care, or adopted. *Children and Youth Services Review, 33*, 1383–1391. Lawrence, C. R., Carlson, E. A., & Eglemand, B. (2006). The impact of foster care on development. *Development and Psychopathology, 18*, 57–76.
13. Outcomes addressed in the Doyle 2007 study included juvenile delinquency, female adolescent parenting, and adolescent employment. Outcomes assessed in the 2008 study included crime in adolescence. See Doyle, J. J. Jr. (2007). Child protection and child outcomes: Measuring the effects of foster care. *American Economic Review, 97*(5), 1583–1610; Doyle, J. J. (2008). Child protection and adult crime: Using investigator assignment to estimate causal effects of foster care. *Journal of Political Economy, 116*, 746–770.
14. Forsythe, P. (1992). Homebuilders and family preservation. *Children and Youth Services Review, 14*, 37–47.
15. See Schuerman, J., Rzepnicki, T. L., & Littell, J. (1994). *Putting families first: An experiment in family preservation.* New York, NY: Aldine.
16. The law requiring caseworkers to make "reasonable efforts" to avoid placing a child in care was first articulated in the Adoption Assistance and Child Welfare Act of 1980 (P.L. 96–272). The original support for family preservation services has been reauthorized in a series of bills. These include Promoting Safe and Stable Families (authorized under the Adoption and Safe Families Act (P.L. 105-89)). The bill was reauthorized again in 2001 and the Child and Family Services Improvement Act (P.L. 109–288) offered reauthorization through 2011. The Child and Family Services Improvement and Innovation Act (P.L. 112-34) extends the bill through 2016.
17. Stein, T. (2000). The Adoption and Safe Families Act: Creating a false dichotomy between parents' and children's rights. *Families in Society, 81*(6), 586–590.
18. Al, C. M. W., Stams, G. J. J. M., Bek, M. S., Damen, E. M., Asscher, J. J., & van der Laan, P. H. (2012). A meta-analysis of intensive family preservation programs: Placement

prevention and improvement of family functioning. *Children and Youth Services Review, 34*, 1472–1479.

19. Information available for the National Survey of Child and Adolescent Well-being (NSCAW), a national study of children and families touched by the child welfare system, suggests that the caregivers of children involved in child welfare have multiple needs. Between 30% and 60% of caregivers reportedly need mental health services, between 24% and 64% need substance abuse–related services, 43%–50% need financial supports, about one quarter to one third need domestic violence-related services, one fifth to two fifths need housing assistance, and one fifth to one half need employment assistance. See Dolan, M., Smith, K., Casanueva, C., & Ringeisen, H. (2012). *NSCAW II Wave 2 Report: Child and caregiver need and receipt of child welfare services post-baseline.* OPRE Report #2013- 08. Washington, DC: Office of Planning, Research and Evaluation, Administration for Children and Families, U.S. Department of Health and Human Services.
20. U.S. Department of Health and Human Services. (2015). *The AFCARS report #22.* Retrieved April 15, 2016, from http://www.acf.hhs.gov/sites/default/files/cb/afcarsreport22.pdf
21. U.S. Department of Health and Human Services. (2015). *The AFCARS report #22.* Retrieved August 5, 2016, from http://www.acf.hhs.gov/sites/default/files/cb/afcarsreport22.pdf
22. Putnam-Hornstein, E., Needell, B., King, B., & Johnson-Montoya, M. (2013). Racial and ethnic disparities: A population-based examination of risk factors for involvement with child protective services. *Child Abuse and Neglect, 37*, 33–46.
23. Depending on the year of analysis, the risk of entering care before age 18 for Native American children falls somewhere between 12% and 15%. The risk of spending time in care varies by race/ethnicity: African American: 9%–12%, Hispanic/Latino: 5%, White: 4%, Asian: 2%. See Wildeman, C., & Emanuel N. (2014). Cumulative risks of foster care placement by age 18 for U.S. children, 2000–2011. *PLoS ONE, 9*, e92785
24. Casey Family Programs has an ongoing campaign to "safely reduce the number of children in foster care across the country by 50% by the year 2020." Casey Family Programs (2010). *2020 strategy: A vision for America's children.* Seattle, WA: Casey Family Programs.
25. For information on various state responses to declines in foster care caseloads, see *Child Welfare in the News*. Child Welfare Information Gateway Library. https://www.childwelfare.gov/. Recent evidence indicates that the significant declines in foster care entries have now reversed. Since 2013, entries to foster care across the nation have started to rise. U.S. Department of Health and Human Services. (2015). *The AFCARS Report.* Washington, DC: Children's Bureau. Retrieved August 5, 2016, from https://www.acf.hhs.gov/sites/default/files/cb/afcarsreport22.pdf
26. U.S. Department of Health and Human Services. 2012. *Trends in foster care and adoption—FY 2002–FY 2011.* Washington, DC: USDHHS. http://www.acf.hhs.gov/sites/default/files/cb/trends_fostercare_adoption.pdf. Caseloads have been on the rise again in recent years. In 2014, caseloads rose to about 415,000 children

in care. U.S. Department of Health and Human Services (2015). *The AFCARS Report #22*. Washington, DC: The Children's Bureau. https://www.acf.hhs.gov/sites/default/files/cb/afcarsreport22.pdf

27. Wulczyn, F., Chen, L., & Hislop, K. B. (2007) *Foster care dynamics 2000–2005: A report from the Multistate Foster Care Data Archive.* Chicago, IL: Chapin Hall Center for Children at the University of Chicago
28. According to the U.S. Department of Health and Human Services, in 2014, 6.6 million children were referred for maltreatment. 3.2 million children received an investigation or assessment; 410,448 "victims" received a postresponse service and 890,889 "nonvictims" received a postresponse service. The total of 1,301,337 children served is approximately 19.7% of all children referred. See United States Department of Health and Human Services. (2016). *Child maltreatment 2014.* Washington, DC: http://www.acf.hhs.gov/programs/cb/research-data-technology/statistics-research/child-maltreatment
29. Eastman, A. L., Mitchell, M. N., & Putnam-Hornstein, E. (2016). Risk of re-report: A latent-class analysis of infants reported for maltreatment. *Child Abuse and Neglect, 55,* 22–31. These authors further found that some infants were at greater risk than others, depending on certain characteristics of their families. Those at the highest risk of re-referral (over 75%) had birth records that showed late or no pre-natal care, and no father was noted on the birth certificate.
30. Child Welfare Information Gateway (2011). *Family reunification: What the evidence shows.* Washington, DC: Children's Bureau. Retrieved August 5, 2016, from https://www.childwelfare.gov/pubPDFs/family_reunification.pdf
31. In the Northwest alumni study, over four fifths of adults reported that they "felt loved" by their caregiver. Pecora, P. J., Kessler, R. C., Williams, J., O'Brien, K., Downs, A. C., English, D., . . . Holmes, K. (2005). *Improving family foster care: Findings from the Northwest Family foster care alumni study.* Seattle, WA: Casey Family Programs. http://www.tandfonline.com/doi/abs/10.1080/02650533.2014.933405. Some evidence also suggests that when the relationship between the child and caregiver is positive, children's internalizing and externalizing behaviors trend positive. See Cooley, M., Wojciak, A. S., Farineau, H., & Mullis, A. (2015). The association between perception of relationship with caregivers and behaviours of youth in foster care: A child and caregiver perspective. *Journal of Social Work Practice, 29*(2), 205–221. doi:10.1080/02650533.2014.933405
32. The median across states in 2012 was 0.32%. See U.S. Department of Health and Human Services. (2013). *Child welfare outcomes 2009 to 2012: Report to Congress.* Washington, DC: Administration for Children and Families, Administration on Children, Youth, and Families. Retrieved from http://www.acf.hhs.gov/sites/default/files/cb/cw009 12.pdf#page=7
33. These estimates are derived from different sources: Courtney, M. E., Piliavin, I., Grogan-Kaylor, A., & Nesmith, A. (2001). Foster youth transitions to

adulthood: A longitudinal view of youth leaving care. *Child Welfare, 80*(6), 685–718; Pecora, P. J., Kessler, R., Williams, J., O'Brien, K., Downs, C., White, D., . . . Holmes, K. (2005). *Improving family foster care: Findings from the northwest foster care alumni study*. Seattle, WA: Casey Family Programs.

34. Havlicek, J., & Courtney, M. (2016). Maltreatment histories of aging out foster youth: A comparison of official investigated reports and self-reports of maltreatment prior to and during out-of-home care. *Child Abuse and Neglect, 52*, 110–122.

CHAPTER 5

1. Hrdy, S. B. (2009). *Mothers and others: the evolutionary origins of mutual understanding*. Cambridge, MA: Belknap Press.
2. Gutman, H. G. (1976). *The black family in slavery and freedom,1750–1925*. New York, NY: Vintage Books.
3. Federal Interagency Forum on Child and Family Statistics. (2011). *America's children: Key national indicators of well-being.* Washington, DC: U.S. Government Printing Office; Pew Research Center. (2013). *At grandmother's house we stay. One-in-ten children are living with a grandparent.* Washington, DC: Pew Research Center. Retrieved from http://www.pewsocialtrends.org/files/2013/09/grandparents_report_final_2013.pdf
4. Myers, J. E. B. (2006). *Child protection in America: Past, present, and future.* New York, NY: Oxford University Press.
5. Ingram, C. (1996). Kinship care: From last resort to first choice. *Child Welfare, 73*, 550–566.
6. Gordon, L. (2001). *The great Arizona orphan abduction.* Cambridge, MA: Harvard University Press; O'Connor, S. (2001). *Orphan trains: The story of Charles Loring Brace and the children he saved and failed.* Boston, MA: Houghton Mifflin.
7. Mizrahi, T., Lopez Humphreys, M., & Torres, D. (2009). The social construction of client participation: The evolution and transformation of the role of service recipients in child welfare and mental disabilities. *Journal of Sociology & Social Welfare, 36*(2), 35–61.
8. Daly, M., & Perry, G. (2011). Has the child welfare profession discovered nepotistic bias? *Human Nature, 22*, 350–369.
9. Proch, K. & Hess, P. M. (1987). Parent-child visiting policies of voluntary agencies. *Children and Youth Services Review, 9*, 17–28; Rowe, J., Cain, H., Hundleby, M., & Keane, A. (1984). Long-term foster care. London, UK: Batsford.
10. Baker, A. J., Creegan, A., Quinones, A., & Rozelle, L. (2016). Foster children's views of their birth parents: A review of the literature. *Children and Youth Services Review, 67*, 177–183. doi:10.1016/j.childyouth.2016.06.004; Timms, J., & Thoburn,

J. (2003). Your shout! A survey of the views of 706 children and young people in public care. London, UK: NSPCC.

11. Geenen, S. & Powers, L. E. (2007). "Tomorrow is another problem": The experiences of youth in foster care during their transition to adulthood. *Children and Youth Services Review, 29*(8), 1085–1101; McCoy, H., McMillen, J., & Spitznagel, E. (2008). Older youth leaving the foster care system: Who, what, when, where, and why? *Child Youth Services Review, 30*(7), 735–745. doi: 10.1016/j.childyouth.2007.12.003.
12. Herring, D. J. (2008). Kinship foster care: Implications of behavioral biology research. *Legal Studies Research Paper Series,* Working Paper No. 2008-01. file:///C:/Users/dberrick/Downloads/SSRN-id1083743.pdf; Hrdy, S. B. (2009). *Mothers and others: The evolutionary origins of mutual understanding*. Cambridge, MA: Belknap Press; Silk, J. B. (1990). Human adoption in evolutionary perspectives. *Human Nature, 1*, 25–52.
13. *Youakim v. Miller* decision (44 U.S. 125, 99 S. Ct. 957 (1979)).
14. Specifically, funding is available when the child in care has been removed from a home that is "Title IV-E eligible," which means that the birth parent's income at the time of removal was an amount equal to what would have made her eligible for AFDC (when AFDC still existed) in 1996.
15. Personal Responsibility and Work Opportunity Reconciliation Act of 1996, 42 U.S.C. § 671(a)(19) (2006).
16. Casey, A. E. (2013). *The kinship diversion debate.* Baltimore, MD: Author.
17. Barbell, K., & Freundlich, M. (2001). *Foster care today.* Washington, DC: Casey Family Programs.
18. National Commission on Family Foster Care (1991). *A blueprint for fostering infants, children and youth.* Washington, DC: Child Welfare League of America.
19. Juhn, C., & Potter, S. (2006). Changes in labor force participation in the United States. *The Journal of Economic Perspectives, 20*(3), 27–46.
20. Mallon, G. (2014). *Lesbian, gay, bisexual and trans foster and adoptive parents: Recruiting, assessing, and supporting an untapped resource for children and youth* (2nd ed.). Washington, DC: Child Welfare League of America.
21. Geen, R. (2003). Kinship foster care: An ongoing, yet largely uninformed debate. In R. Geen (Ed.), *Kinship care: Making the most of a valuable resource* (pp. 1–23). Washington, DC: The Urban Institute Press.
22. Bernstein, N. (2002). *The lost children of Wilder: The epic struggle to change foster care.* New York, NY: Vintage Books.
23. NABSW: National Association of Black Social Workers. (1972). *Position statement on transracial adoptions.* Retrieved March 30, 2016, from http://c.ymcdn.com/sites/nabsw.org/resource/collection/E1582D77-E4CD-4104-996A-D42D08F9CA7D/NABSW_Trans-Racial_Adoption_1972_Position_(b).pdf
24. See, for example, Hayes, P. (1993). Transracial adoption: Politics and ideology. *Child Welfare, 72*(3), 301–310; Hollingsworth, L. D. (1997). The effect of

transracial/ transethnic adoption on children's racial and ethnic identity and self-esteem: A meta-analytic review. *Marriage and Family Review, 25*(1-2), 99–130;

25. Curtis, C., & Alexander, R. (1996). The multi-ethnic placement act: Implications for social work practice. *Child and Adolescent Social Work Journal, 13*(5), 401–410.
26. U.S. Department of Health and Human Services (2015). *The AFCARS Report #22*. U.S. Department of Health and Human Services, Administration for Children and Families, Administration on Children, Youth, and Families, Children's Bureau. Retrieved March 14, 2016, from http://www.acf.hhs.gov/sites/default/files/cb/afcarsreport22.pdf
27. Perry, G., Daly, M., & Macfarlan, S. (2014). Maternal foster families provide more stable placements than paternal families. *Children and Youth Services Review, 46*, 155–159.
28. Chamberlain, P., Price, J., Reid, J., Landverk, J., Fisher, P., & Stoolmiller, M. (2006). Who disrupts from placement in foster and kinship care? *Child Abuse and Neglect, 30*, 409–424; Winokur, M., Holtan, A., & Valentine, D. (2009). Kinship care for the safety, permanency, and well-being of children removed from the home for maltreatment. *Cochrane Database of Systematic Reviews*, Issue 1. Art. No. CD006546.
29. Newton, R., Litrownik, A. & Landsverk, J. (2000). Children and youth in foster care: Disentangling the relationships between problem behaviors and number of placements. *Child Abuse and Neglect, 24*(10), 1363–1374.
30. See Berrick, 2000, for a review, and Connell et al. 2009; Koh & Testa, 2011: Berrick, J. D. (2000). The benefits of kinship care. In Kluger, M., Alexander, G., & Curtis, P. (Eds.), *What works in child welfare?* Washington, DC: Child Welfare League of America; Connell, C., Vanderploeg, J. J., Katz, K. H., Caron, C., Saunders, L., & Tebes, J. (2009). Maltreatment following reunification: Predictors of subsequent child protective services contact after children return home. *Child Abuse and Neglect: The International Journal, 33*(4), 218–228; Koh, E., & Testa, M. (2011). Children discharged from kin and non-kin foster homes: Do the risks of foster care re-entry differ? *Children and Youth Services Review, 33*(9), 1497–1505.
31. Berrick, J. D. (2000). The benefits of kinship care. In Kluger, M., Alexander, G., & Curtis, P. (Eds.), *What works in child welfare?* Washington, DC: Child Welfare League of America.
32. Crumbley, J., & Little, R. L. (1997). *Relatives raising children: An overview of kinship care*. Washington, DC: Child Welfare League of America.
33. Zinn, A. (2012). Kinship foster family type and placement discharge outcomes. *Children and Youth Services Review, 34*(4), 602–614.
34. Sakai, C., Lin, H., & Flores, G. (2011). Health outcomes and family services in kinship care: Analysis of a national sample of children in the child welfare system. *Archives of Pediatrics & Adolescent Medicine, 165*(2), 159–165.
35. Grogan-Kaylor, A. (2001). The effect of initial placement into kinship foster care on reunification from foster care: A bivariate probit analysis. *Social Service Review*,

27(4), 1–27; Rubin, D., Downes, K., O'Reilly, A., Mckonnen, R., Luan, X. & Localio, R. (2008). Impact of kinship care on behavioral well-being for children in out-of-home care. *Archives of Pediatric Adolescent Medicine, 162*(6), 350–356; Winokur, M., Holtan, A., & Valentine, D. (2009). Kinship care for the safety, permanency, and well-being of children removed from the home for maltreatment. *Cochrane Database of Systematic Reviews,* Issue 1. Art. No. CD006546

36. Berrick, J. D. (1998). When children cannot remain home: Foster family care and kinship care. *The Future of Children, 8,* 72–87; Berrick, J. D., & Needell, B. (1999). Recent trends in kinship care: Public policy, payments, and outcomes for children. In Curtis, P.A. & Dale, G. (Eds.), *The foster care crisis: Translating research into practice and policy.* Lincoln: University of Nebraska Press; Winokur, M., Holtan, A., & Valentine, D. (2009). Kinship care for the safety, permanency, and well-being of children removed from the home for maltreatment. *Cochrane Database of Systematic Reviews,* Issue 1, Art. No. CD006546
37. Courtney, M. E., & Needell, B. (1997). Outcomes of kinship care: Lessons from California. In J. D. Berrick, R. Barth, & N. Gilbert (Eds.), *Child welfare research review, Vol. II.* New York, NY: Columbia University Press.
38. Thornton, J. L. (1991). Permanency planning for children in foster homes. *Child Welfare, 70*(5), 593–601.
39. Testa, M. F. (2004). When children cannot return home: Adoption and guardianship. *The Future of Children, 14*(1), 115–129.
40. Magruder, J., Webster, D., & Shlonsky, A. (2015). *Relative guardianships: Increased options for sustained permanency.* New Orleans, LA: Society for Social Work Research National Conference.
41. ChildFocus. (2010). *Kinship adoption: Meeting the unique needs of a growing population.* Retrieved August 13, 2015, from http://childfocuspartners.com/wp-content/uploads/CF_Kinship_Adoption_Report_v5.pdf
42. Dolan, M., Smith, K., Casanueva, C., & Ringeisen, H. (2011). *NSCAW II Baseline report: Introduction to NSCAW II.* OPRE Report #2011-27a, Washington, DC: Office of Planning, Research and Evaluation, Administration for Children and Families, U.S. Department of Health and Human Services.
43. Cuddeback, G. (2004). Kinship family foster care: a methodological and substantive synthesis of research. *Children and Youth Services Review, 26,* 623–639; Ehrle, J., & Geen, R. (2002). Kin and non-kin foster care—findings from a national survey. *Children and Youth Services Review, 24,* 15–35; Gleeson, J. P., O'Donnell, J., & Bonecutter, F. J. (1997). Understanding the complexity of practice in kinship foster care. *Child Welfare, 76,* 801–826.
44. Grant, R. (2000). The special needs of children in kinship care. *Journal of Gerontological Social Work, 33,* 17–33.
45. Barth, R. P., Green, R., Webb, M. B., Wall, A., Gibbons, C., & Craig, C. (2008). Characteristics of out-of-home caregiving environments provided under child welfare services. *Child Welfare, 87,* 5–39; Berrick, J. D., Barth, R. P., & Needell, B. (1994). A comparison of kinship foster homes and foster family homes: Implications for

kinship foster care as family preservation. *Children and Youth Services Review, 16*(1-2), 33–64.

Fox, A., Berrick, J. D., & Frasch, K. (2000). Safety, family, permanency, and child well-being: What we can learn from children. *Child Welfare, 87*(1), 63–90; U.S. Census Bureau (2011). As cited in: Casey, A. E. (2012). *Stepping up for kids.* Washington, DC.: Annie E. Casey Foundation.

46. Brisebois, K., Kernsmith, P. D., & Carcone, A. I. (2013). The relationship between caseworker attitudes about kinship care and removal decisions. *Journal of Family Social Work, 16*(5), 403–417.
47. Widom, C. S., Czaja, S. J., & DuMont, K. A. (2015). Intergenerational transmission of child abuse and neglect: Real or detection bias? *Science, 347*(6229), 1480–1485. The authors indicate that some transmission may be related to detection bias; however, sexual abuse and neglect appear to have effects beyond surveillance bias.
48. Bailey, J. A., Hill, K. G., Oesterle, S., & Hawkins, J. D. (2009). Parenting practices and problem behavior across three generations: monitoring, harsh discipline, and drug use in the intergenerational transmission of externalizing behavior. *Developmental Psychology, 45*, 1214–1226.
49. See http://www.familyfinding.org.
50. Studies on the effects of family finding show mixed results. Some studies show increases in children's legal permanency as a result of family finding; effects on placement stability and case plan goals were not evident. See Vandivere, S. & Malm, K. (2015). *Family finding evaluations: A summary of recent findings.* Washington, DC: Child Trends. Retrieved May 11, 2016, from http://www.childtrends.org/wp-content/uploads/2015/01/2015-01Family_Finding_Eval_Summary.pdf
51. Monahan, D. J., Smith, C. J., & Greene, V. L. (2013). Kinship caregivers: Health and burden. *Journal of Family Social Work, 16*, 392–402.
52. U.S Social Security Act, sec. 475. [42 U.S.C. 675] 5(A).
53. Although Shannon knew her social worker from previous meetings, she was not closely connected to her as she was to her foster parents. Practice changes in child welfare since the time of this story would suggest a trauma-informed approach—a strategy to make Shannon's experience of change predictable and comforting. In current child welfare practice, a worker would probably ask the foster parent to transport the child to the birth mother's home. The child would thus be spared the frightening prospect of being taken from her foster parent in a stranger's car, and the foster parents and birth parent could settle the child in her new surroundings together.

CHAPTER 6

1. See Ramey, J. B. (2013). *Child care in black and white: Working parents and the history of orphanages.* Urbana, IL: University of Illinois Press.
2. Bernstein, N. (2004). *The lost children of Wilder.* New York, NY: Pantheon Books.

3. For more information on the origins of orphanages for African American children, see Billingsley, A., & Giovannoni, J. M. (1972). *Children of the storm: Black children and American child welfare.* New York, NY: Harcourt, Brace, Jovanovich.
4. For an extensive review of this history in New York, see Bernstein, N. (2002). *The lost children of Wilder.* New York, NY: Vintage.
5. See Gordon, L. (1999). *The great Arizona orphan abduction.* Cambridge, MA: Harvard University Press; Holt, M. (1992). *The orphan trains: Placing out in America.* Lincoln, NE: University of Nebraska Press; Ramey, J. (1992). *Child care in black and white: Working parents and the history of orphanages.* Urbana, IL: University of Illinois Press.
6. Birk, M. (2015). *Fostering on the farm: Child placement in the rural Midwest.* Champaign, IL: University of Illinois Press.
7. *Proceedings of the Conference on the Care of Dependent Children*, 1909 (reprint, New York, NY: Arno, 1971).
8. As cited in Billingsley, A., & Giovannoni, J. (1972). *Children of the storm: Black children and American child welfare.* New York, NY: Harcourt, Brace, Jovanovich citing statistics from *Children under institutional care* (1927) and *Child welfare statistics* (1969). Marshall Jones also indicates that at the height of the depression in the 1930s there were over 144,000 children living in orphanages in the United States. By 1951, that number had declined to about 95,000, and by 1970 there were further reductions to about 63,000. Jones, M. (1989). The crisis of the American orphanage, 1931–1940. *Social Service Review, 63*(4), 613–629.
9. Dishion, T. J., McCord, J., & Poulin, F. (1999). When interventions harm: Peer groups and problem behavior. *American Psychologist, 54*(9), 755–764; Mahoney, J. L., Stattin, H., & Lord, H. (2004). Unstructured youth recreation center participation and antisocial behavior development: Selection influences and the moderating role of antisocial peers. *International Journal of Behavioral Development, 28,* 553–560.
10. Knorth, E. J., Harder, A. T., Zandberg, T., & Kendrick, A. J. (2008). Under one roof: A review and selective meta-analysis on the outcomes of residential child and youth care. *Children and Youth Services Review, 30,* 123–140.
11. See Dozier, M., Kaufman, J., Kobak, R., O'Connor, T. G., Sagi-Schwartz, A., Scott, S., Shauffer, C., Smetana, J., van IJzendoorn, M. H., & Zeanah, H. (2014). Consensus statement on group care for children and adolescents: A statement of policy of the American Orthopsychiatric Association. *American Journal of Orthopsychiatry, 84*(3), 219–225. doi.org/10.1037/ort0000005; Berrick, J. D., Barth, R. P., Needell, B., & Jonson-Reid, M. (1998). *The tender years: Toward developmentally-sensitive child welfare services for very young children.* New York, NY: Oxford University Press.
12. Breland-Noble, A. M., Elbogen, E. B., Farmer, E. M. Z., Dubs, M. S., Wagner, H. R., & Burns, B. J. (2004). Use of psychotropic medications by youths in therapeutic foster are and group homes. *Psychiatric Services, 55*(6), 706–708; Breland-Noble,

A. M., Farmer, E. M. Z., Dubs, M. S., Potter, E., & Burns, B. J. (2005). Mental health and other service use by youth in therapeutic foster care and group homes. *Journal of Child and Family Studies, 14*(2), 167–180.

13. Barth, R. P., Greeson, J. K. P., Guo, S., Green, R. L., & Hurley, S. (2007). Outcomes for youth receiving intensive in-home therapy or residential care: A comparison using propensity scores. *American Journal of Orthopsychiatry, 77*(4), 497–505; James, S., Roesch, S., & Zhang, J. (2012). Characteristics and behavioral outcomes for youth in group care and family-based care—a propensity score matching approach using national data. *Journal of Emotional and Behavioral Disorders, 20*(3), 144–156.
14. Lee, B. R., & Thompson, R. (2008). Comparing outcomes for youth in treatment foster care and family-style group care. *Children and Youth Services Review, 30*(7), 746–757.
15. DeSwart, J. J. W., Van den Broek, H., Stams, G. J. J. M., Asscher, J. J., Van der Laan, P. H., Holsbrink-Engels, G. A., & Van der Helm, G. H. P. (2012). *Children and Youth Services Review, 34*, 1818–1824; French, K. M., & Cameron, G. (2002). Treatment of choice or a last resort? A review of institutional mental health placements for children and youth. *Child and Youth Care Forum, 32*, 307–339.
16. The terms *residential care* and *group care* are used interchangeably in this chapter to denote congregate care environments. Residential care is typically considered a "higher" or more restrictive level of care, reserved for children with more serious mental health needs. "Treatment foster care" is usually distinguished from foster care in that the caregivers are usually better trained and supported and are prepared to care for more behaviorally or emotionally challenging children. For a review of some of the evidence comparing treatment foster care to group care, see McCurdy, B. L. & McIntyre, E. K. (2004). And what about residential . . .? Reconceptualizing residential treatment as a stop-gap service for youth with emotional and behavioral disorders. *Behavioral Interventions, 19*, 137–158; Henggeler, S. W., Rowland, M. D., Halliday-Boykins, C., Sheidow, A. J., Ward, D. M., & Randall, J. (2003). One-year follow-up of multisystemic therapy as an alternative to the hospitalization of youths in psychiatric crisis. *Journal of the American Academy of Child and Adolescent Psychiatry, 42*(5), 543–551; Barth, R. P., Greeson, J. K. P., Guo, S., Green, R.L., Hurley, S., & Sisson, J. (2007). Outcomes for youth receiving intensive in-home therapy or residential care: A comparison using propensity scores. *American Journal of Orthopsychiatry, 77*(4), 497–505.
17. Wulczyn, F., Alpert, L., Martinez, Z., & Weiss, A. (2015). Within and between state variation in the use of congregate care. Chicago, IL: Chapin Hall Center for Children.
18. James, S., Leslie, L. K., Hurlburt, M. S., Slymen, D. J., Landsverk, J., Davis, I., Mathiesen, S. G., & Zhang, J. (2006). Children in out-of-home care: Entry into intensive or restrictive mental health and residential care placements. *Journal of Emotional and Behavioral Disorders, 14*(4), 196–208; Trout, A. L., Hagaman, J. L.,

Chemelka, M. B., Gehringer, R., Epstein, M. H., & Reid, R. (2008). The academic, behavioral, and mental health status of children and youth at entry to residential care. *Residential Treatment for Children and Youth, 25*(4), 359–374.

19. U.S. Department of Health and Human Services (May 15, 2015). *A national look at the use of congregate care in child welfare.* Washington, DC: U.S. Department of Health and Human Services, Administration for Children and Families, Children's Bureau. Retrieved May 27, 2016, from http://www.acf.hhs.gov/programs/cb/resource/congregate-care-brief.
20. Barber, J. G., Delfabbro, P. H., & Cooper, L. L. (2001). The predictors of unsuccessful transition to foster care. *Journal of Child Psychology and Psychiatry, and Allied Disciplines, 42,* 785–790.
21. James, S., Landsverk, J., & Slymen, D. J. (2004). Placement movement in out-of-home care: Patterns and predictors. *Children and Youth Services Review, 26*(2), 185–206; Wulczyn, F., Kogan, J., & Harden, B. J. (2003). Placement stability and movement trajectories. *The Social Service Review, 76,* 212–236.
22. Farmer, E. M. Z., Wagner, H. R., Burns, B. J., & Richards, J. T. (2003). Treatment foster care in a system of care: Sequences and correlates of residential placements. *Journal of Child and Family Studies, 12,* 11–25; James, S., Landsverk, J., & Slymen, D. J. (2004). Placement movement in out-of-home care: Patterns and predictors. *Children and Youth Services Review, 26*(2), 185–206.
23. James, S., Leslie, L. K., Hurlburt, M. S., Slymen, D. J., Landsverk, J., Davis, I., Mathiesen, S. G., & Zhang, J. (2006). Children in out-of-home care: Entry into intensive or restrictive mental health and residential care placements. *Journal of Emotional and Behavioral Disorders, 14*(4), 196–208.
24. James, S., Landsverk, J., Leslie, L. K., Slymen, D. J., & Zhang, J. (2008). Entry into restrictive care placements: Placements of last resort? *Families in Society, 89*(3), 348–359.
25. A recent national study suggests that about two fifths of children placed in congregate care settings have "no clinical indicators." See U.S. Department of Health and Human Services (May 15, 2015). *A national look at the use of congregate care in child welfare.* Washington, DC: U.S. Department of Health and Human Services, Administration for Children and Families, Children's Bureau. Retrieved May 27, 2016 from http://www.acf.hhs.gov/programs/cb/resource/congregate-care-brief. See also Barth, R. P. (2005). Residential care: From here to eternity. *International Journal of Social Welfare, 14,* 158–162; Lyons, J. S., Libman-Mintzer, L. N., Kisiel, C. L., & Shallcross, H. (1998). Understanding the mental health needs of children and adolescents in residential treatment. *Professional Psychology, Research and Practice, 29*(6), 582–587.
26. Barth, R. P., Wildfire, J., Green, R., & NSCAW Research Group. (2006). Placement into foster care: What are the contributions of poverty, geography, and children's behavior problems? *American Journal of Orthopsychiatry, 76*(3), 358–366; James, S.,

Landsverk, J., Leslie, L., Slymen, D., & Zhang, J. (2008). Entry into restrictive care settings—placement of last resort? *Families in Society, 89*(3), 348–359.

27. Therolf, G. (June 22, 2015). L.A. County's foster center should be closed immediately, panel says. *Los Angeles Times.*
28. See *Child welfare in the news* at http//www.childwelfare.gov
29. James, S., Landsverk, J., Leslie, L. K., Slymen, D. A., & Zhang, J. (2008). Entry into restrictive care settings—placements of last resort? *Families In Society-The Journal Of Contemporary Social Services, 89*(3), 348–359.
30. U.S. Department of Health and Human Services (2015). *AFCARS Report #22.* Washington, DC: Administration for Children and Families, Administration on Children, Youth, and Families, Children's Bureau. Retrieved May 27, 2016 from http://www.acf.hhs.gov/sites/default/files/cb/afcarsreport22.pdf
31. U.S. Department of Health and Human Services (May 15, 2015). *A national look at the use of congregate care in child welfare.* Washington, DC: U.S. Department of Health and Human Services, Administration for Children and Families, Children's Bureau. Retrieved May 27, 2016, from http://www.acf.hhs.gov/programs/cb/resource/congregate-care-brief
32. Other states with low utilization of congregate care (5% or less) include Kansas, Maine, and Washington. States with high utilization rates (over 20%) include Connecticut, Minnesota, New Hampshire, North Dakota, Pennsylvania, Rhode Island, South Carolina, South Dakota, Vermont, West Virginia, and Wyoming. Findings are based on an analysis of AFCARS data by Child Trends, shown in Annie E. Casey Foundation. (2015). *Every kid needs a family: Policy Report.* Baltimore, MD: Annie E. Casey Foundation.
33. U.S. Department of Health and Human Services. (May 15, 2015). *A national look at the use of congregate care in child welfare.* Washington, DC: U.S. Department of Health and Human Services, Administration for Children and Families, Children's Bureau. Retrieved May 27, 2016 from http://www.acf.hhs.gov/programs/cb/resource/congregate-care-brief
34. McMillen, J. C., Scott, L. D., Zima, B. T., Ollie, M. T., Munson, M. R., & Spitznagel, E. (2004). Use of mental health services among older youths in foster care. *Psychiatric Services (Washington, DC), 55*(7), 811–817.
35. U.S. Department of Health and Human Services (May 15, 2015). *A national look at the use of congregate care in child welfare.* Washington, DC: U.S. Department of Health and Human Services, Administration for Children and Families, Children's Bureau. Retrieved May 27, 2016, from http://www.acf.hhs.gov/programs/cb/resource/congregate-care-brief
36. Sigrid James has conducted extensive study of group care models. For a review of the evidence on the effectiveness of various models see: James, S. (2011). What works in group care? A structured review of treatment models for group homes and residential care. *Children and Youth Services Review, 33*, 308–321.

37. Chamberlain, P., & Reid, J. B. (1991). Using a specialized foster care treatment model for children and adolescents leaving the state mental hospital. *Journal of Community Psychology, 19*, 266–276; Chamberlain, P., & Reid, J. B. (1998). Comparison of two community alternatives to incarceration for chronic juvenile offenders. *Journal of Consulting and Clinical Psychology, 66*(4), 624–633; Eddy, J. M., & Chamberlain, P. (2000). Family management and deviant peer association as mediators of the impact of treatment condition on youth antisocial behavior. *Journal of Consulting and Clinical Psychology, 5*(68), 857–863.
38. U.S. Department of Health and Human Services (May 15, 2015). *A national look at the use of congregate care in child welfare.* Washington, DC: U.S. Department of Health and Human Services, Administration for Children and Families, Children's Bureau. Retrieved May 27, 2016 from http://www.acf.hhs.gov/programs/cb/resource/congregate-care-brief
39. The distribution of psychotropic medications to children and youth in foster care has become a national issue requiring an urgent response. We see from this story that some children are prescribed psychotropic medications to help manage their mental health and behavior. Estimates from California suggest that approximately 11% of foster youth are taking psychotropic medications, though there is significant variation in the likelihood of medication use depending on placement type and placing agency. Over 30% of children served by the probation department (juvenile delinquency) are prescribed medications. See Webster, D., Armijo, M., Lee, S., Dawson, W., Magruder, J., Exel, M., . . . Kai, C. (2016). *CCWIP reports*. Retrieved July 23, 2016, from University of California at Berkeley California Child Welfare Indicators Project website. Available at http://cssr.berkeley.edu/ucb_childwelfare. According to the National Survey of Child and Adolescent Well-being (NSCAW), almost 30% of children living in nonrelative foster care, and about one third of children in group/residential care take psychotropic medications. These are not limited to adolescents. The group of children most likely to be taking psychotropic medications was comprised of children ages 6–11. In some cases (about 13%), children were taking up to three medications simultaneously. See Stambaugh, L., Leslie, L., Ringeisen, H. Smith, K., & Hodgkin, D. (2012). Psychotropic medication use by children in child welfare. OPRE Report #2012-33. Washington, DC: Office of Planning, Research and Evaluation, Administration for Children and Families, U.S. Department of Health and Human Services.
40. Casanueva, Wilson, E., Smith, M., Dolan, M., Ringeisen, H., & Horne, B. (2012). *NSCAW II wave 2 report: Child well-being,* OPRE report #2012-38, Washington, DC: Office of planning, research and evaluation, administration for children and families, U.S. Department of Health and Human Services.
41. James, S. (2011). What works in group care? A structured review of treatment models for group homes and residential care. *Children and Youth Services Review, 33*, 308–321.

CHAPTER 7

1. Carlson, M. J., & Meyer, D. R. (2014). Family complexity: Setting the context. *Annals of the American Academy of Political and Social Science, 654*.
2. For a discussion, see: Cook, K. (2014) The family: What is it, how do we study it and why?. *Journal of Family Studies, 20*(1), 2–4. http://www.tandfonline.com/doi/pdf/10.5172/jfs.2014.20.1.2
3. Galvin, K. M., Brommel, B. J., & Bylund, C. L. (2004). *Family communication: Cohesion and change.* New York, NY: Pearson, p. 6.
4. Cancian, M., Meyer, D.R., & Reed, D. (2010). Promising anti-poverty strategies for families. Madison, WI: Institute for Research on Poverty, University of Wisconsin, Madison. Retrieved July 24, 2016, from http://www.irp.wisc.edu/publications/fastfocus/pdfs/FF6-2010.pdf
5. According to the Census Bureau, in 2012, 10% of US children live with a grandparent, increasing from 7% in 1992. Of these households, about one third have no parent present. See Ellis, R. R., & Simmons, T. (2012). *Coresident grandparents and their grandchildren: 2012*. Washington, DC: U.S. Department of Commerce, Census Bureau. Retrieved July 24, 2016, from http://www.census.gov/content/dam/Census/library/publications/2014/demo/p20-576.pdf
6. Gates, G. J. (2013). *LGBT parenting in the United States.* Los Angeles, CA: The Williams Institute, University of California at Los Angeles. Retrieved July 24, 2016, from http://williamsinstitute.law.ucla.edu/wp-content/uploads/LGBT-Parenting.pdf
7. Edin, K., & Nelson, T. J. (2013). *Doing the best I can: Fatherhood in the inner city.* Berkeley: University of California Press.
8. Child Welfare Information Gateway (n.d.) *Concept and history of permanency in U.S. child welfare.* Washington, DC: Children's Bureau. Retrieved July 24, 2016, from https://www.childwelfare.gov/topics/permanency/overview/history/
9. For a discussion about the importation of permanency concepts to Europe, see Selwyn, J., & Sturgess, W. (2002). Achieving permanency through adoption: Following in U.S. footsteps? *Adoption and Fostering, 28,* 6–15.
10. Testa, M. (2005). The quality of permanence: Lasting or binding? Subsidized guardianship and kinship foster care as alternatives to adoption. *Virginia Journal of Social Policy and Law, 12*(3), 499–534.
11. Wulczyn, F. (2004). Family reunification. *The Future of Children, 14*(1), 95–113. Infants and adolescents are less likely to reunify compared to children of other ages and African American children are also less likely to reunify compared to other racial/ethnic groups. Although reunification is the most likely exit from the foster care system, it is not necessarily durable. About 30% of children re-enter care following a reunification. See also Child Welfare Information Gateway. (2011). *Family reunification: What the evidence shows.* Washington, DC: Children's Bureau.

Retrieved August 4, 2016, from https://www.childwelfare.gov/pubPDFs/family_reunification.pdf

12. Legal guardianship is used increasingly by relatives as a strategy to secure children's permanency without terminating the parental rights of the birth parent. For more information regarding guardianship, see Testa, M. (2008). New permanency strategies for children in foster care. In Lindsey, D., & Shlonsky, A. (Eds.), *Child Welfare Research: Advances in practice and policy.* New York, NY: Oxford University Press.
13. Pertman, A. (2011). *Adoption nation: How the adoption revolution is transforming our families –and America.* Cambridge, MA: Harvard Common Press.
14. Children's Bureau. (n.d.). Child welfare outcomes report data. Washington, DC: Children's Bureau. Retrieved July 24, 2016, from http://cwoutcomes.acf.hhs.gov/data/tables/adopted_overview?http://cwoutcomes.acf.hhs.gov/data/overview
15. According to Child Trends, almost 1.8 million children in the United States are adopted. Of these, 37% were adopted from foster care, 38% were adopted privately, and about one quarter were adopted internationally. See Vandivere, S., Malm, K., and Radel, L. (2009). *Adoption USA: A chartbook based on the 2007 National Survey of Adoptive Parents.* U.S. Department of Health and Human Services, Office of the Assistant Secretary for Planning and Evaluation. Available at http://aspe.hhs.gov/hsp/09/NSAP/chartbook/. According to one source, about 136,000 children were adopted in 2008, a 6% increase from 2000. Although the number of adoptions rose, the rate per 100,000 adults declined by about 5% from 61.5 per 100,000 to 58.3 per 100,000. See Child Welfare Information Gateway (2011). *How many children were adopted in 2007 and 2008?* Washington, DC: Children's Bureau. Retrieved July 24, 2016, from https://www.childwelfare.gov/pubs/adopted0708/
16. Christiansen, Ö., Havik, T., & Anderssen, N. (2010). Arranging stability for children in long term out-of-home care. *Children and Youth Services Review, 32*, 913–921.
17. Vinnerljung, B., & Hjern, A. (2011). Cognitive, educational, and self-support outcomes of long-term foster care versus adoption: A Swedish national cohort study. *Children and Youth Services Review, 33*, 1902–1910.
18. For reviews, see Brodzinsky, D. M., Smith, D. W., & Brodzinsky, A. B. (1998). *Children's adjustment to adoption: Developmental and clinical issues.* Thousand Oaks, CA: Sage; Triseliotis, J. (2002). Long-term foster care or adoption? The evidence examined," *Child and Family Social Work, 7*(31), 23–33; van den Dries, L., Juffer, F., van IJzendoorn, M. H., & Bakermans-Kranenburg, M. J. (2009). Fostering security? A meta-analysis of attachment in adopted children, *Children and Youth Services Review, 31*(3), 410–421.
19. See Testa, 2005; Testa & Miller, 2014. Testa, M. (2005). The quality of permanence: Lasting or binding? Subsidized guardianship and kinship foster care as

alternatives to adoption. *Virginia Journal of Social Policy and Law, 12*(3), 499–534.; Testa, M., & Miller, J. (2014). Evolution of legal guardianship as a child welfare resource. In G. P. Mallon & P. M. Hess (Eds.), *Child welfare for the 21st century, 2nd ed.* (pp. 355–372). New York, NY: Columbia University Press.

20. Patten, E. (2004). Subordination of subsidized guardianship in child welfare proceedings. *The NYU Review of Law and Social change, 29*, 237–276.
21. Fostering Connections to Success and Increasing Adoptions Act of 2008. P.L. 110–351 §42 U.S.C. 1305 (2008).
22. Testa, M. (2005). The quality of permanence: Lasting or binding? Subsidized guardianship and kinship foster care as alternatives to adoption. *Virginia Journal of Social Policy and Law, 12*(3), 499–534v
23. Perez suggests that relational permanence—enduring relationships that last a lifetime—is more important than legal permanence. See Perez, A. (2014). *Are we putting the cart before the horse? Understanding legal and relational permanence among young adults with foster care histories.* Retrieved from ProQuest.
24. Leathers, S. (2005). Separation from siblings: Associations with placement adaptation and outcomes among adolescents in long-term foster care. *Children and Youth Services Review, 28*(7), 793–819.
25. Gustavsson, N., & MacEachron, A. (2010). Sibling connections and reasonable efforts in public child welfare. *Families in Society: The Journal of Contemporary Social Services, 91*(1), 39–44.
26. According to California data, as of January, 2016, about half of children in foster care with two or more siblings were living together with all of their siblings. Almost three quarters were living with at least some of their siblings. The larger the sibling group, the less likely children were all placed together. For children with six or more siblings, for example, only about 15% enjoy an out-of-home care placement together. These are point-in-time data. We do not have data on how or whether these placement patterns vary over time. See Webster, D., Armijo, M., Lee, S., Dawson, W., Magruder, J., Exel, M., . . . Romero, R. (2016) *CCWIP reports.* Retrieved May 16, 2016, from University of California at Berkeley California Child Welfare Indicators Project website. Available at http://cssr.berkeley.edu/ucb_childwelfare/
27. Herrick, M. A., & Piccus, W. (2005). Sibling connections: The importance of nurturing sibling bonds in the foster care system. *Chldren and Youth Services Review, 28*(7), 845–861.
28. Hegar, R. L., & Rosenthal, J. A. (2011). Foster children placed with or separated from siblings: Outcomes based on a national sample. *Children and Youth Services Review, 33*(7), 1245–1253.
29. Linares, L. O., Li, M., Shrout, P. E., Brody, G. H., & Pettit, G. S. (2007). Placement shift, sibling relationship quality, and child outcomes in foster care: A controlled study. *Journal of Family Psychology, 21*(4), 736–743.

CHAPTER 8

1. An excellent review of the Mary Ellen story is provided by Costin, L. A., Karger, H. J., & Stoesz, D. (1996). *The politics of child abuse in America.* New York, NY: Oxford University Press.
2. O'Connor, S. (2004). *Orphan trains: The story of Charles Loring Brace and the children he saved and failed.* Chicago, IL: University of Chicago Press.
3. For more information about the role of the state in coercing or supporting assimilation through social or moral reform, see Gusfield, J. R. (1966). *Symbolic crusade: Status politics and the American temperance movement.* Urbana: University of Illinois Press.
4. Linda Gordon's superb description of the process of becoming unethnic depending on the child's value to the receiving community is worth reading: Gordon, L. (2001). *The great Arizona orphan abduction.* Boston, MA: Harvard University Press.
5. Billingsley, A., & Giovannoni, J. (1972). *Children of the storm: Black children and American child welfare.* New York, NY: Harcourt, Brace and Jovanovich; Ramey, J. B. (2013). *Child care in black and white: Working parents and the history of orphanages.* Chicago: University of Illinois Press. Some evidence also suggests that a number of African American orphanages were established by White churches in the North—most notably the Quakers.
6. Racial and religious separation is discussed in detail in Bernstein, N. (2002). *The lost children of Wilder: The epic struggle to change foster care.* New York, NY: Pantheon Books; Billingsley and Giovannoni also report on the segregated orphanages established in California that served Japanese-only or Chinese-only children, or children of other national origins.
7. Roberts, D. (2002). *Shattered bonds: The color of child welfare.* New York, NY: Basic Civitas Books. For additional information on informal child sharing in the African American community, see Stack, C. (1983). *All our kin.* New York, NY: Basic books.
8. McRoy, R. (1990). A historical overview of black families. In S. M. Logan, E. M. Freeman, and R. McRoy, *Social work practice with black families: A culturally specific perspective.* New York, NY: Longman.
9. Mintz, S. (2004). *Huck's raft: A history of American childhood.* Cambridge, MA: Belknap Harvard University Press.
10. Trattner, W. I. (1999). The civil war and after. In W. I. Trattner, *From poor law to welfare state* (6th ed.) (pp. 77–107). New York, NY: Free Press.
11. As cited in Billingsley, A., & Giovannoni, J. (1972). *Children of the storm: Black children and American child welfare.* New York, NY: Harcourt, Brace, Jovanovich. Nina Bernstein also recounts the practices among private child-serving agencies to select children based upon hair texture and/or skin color. Bernstein, N. (2001). *The lost children of Wilder: The epic struggle to change foster care.* New York, NY: Pantheon Books.
12. Hegar, R. L., & Scannapieco, M. (1995). From family duty to family policy: The evolution of kinship care. *Child Welfare, 74*, 200–216.

13. Billingsley, A., & Giovannoni, J. (1972). *Children of the storm: Black children and American child welfare.* New York, NY: Harcourt, Brace, Jovanovich. We also see the state's evolving role vis-à-vis African American children and the child welfare system as we examine adoption practice. Legal adoption of African American children was a rare event in the history of child welfare. In many states, African American children were simply excluded from state efforts to adopt. In the late 1940s, the U.S. Children's Bureau began to include African American children in their list of "special needs children" and early efforts to recruit African American families for African American children began (for more information, see http://pages.uoregon.edu/adoption/topics/AfricanAmerican.htm). In the 1960s, adoption recruitment efforts intensified and attention turned to the potential for transracial adoptive placements for African American children. The number of children adopted across racial lines was small (about 2,500 at the peak), but it was controversial. As detailed in Chapter 5, the National Association of Black Social Workers called for a ban on transracial placements in 1972 and the practice dropped off sharply for a time thereafter. For more information on the history of services to African American children, see Jiminez, J. (2006). The history of child protection in the African American community: Implications for current child welfare policies. *Children and Youth Services Review, 28*, 888–905; Smith, C. J., & Devore, W. (2004). African American children in the child welfare and kinship system: From exclusion to over inclusion. *Children and Youth Services Review, 26*, 427–446.
14. See Frame, L. (1999). Suitable homes revisited. *Children and Youth Services Review;* Quadagno, J. (1996). *The color of welfare.* New York, NY: Oxford University Press.
15. Swann, C. A., & Sylvester, M. S. (2006). The foster care crisis: What caused caseloads to grow? *Demography, 43*, 309–335.
16. Wulczyn, F., & Goerge, R. (1992). Foster care in New York and Illinois: The challenge of rapid change. *Social Service Review, 66*(2), 278–294; Berrick, J. D., Needell, B., Barth, R. P., & Jonson-Reid, M. (1998). *The tender years: Toward developmentally-sensitive child welfare services for very young children.* New York, NY: Oxford University Press.
17. U.S. Department of Health and Human Services (2014). *The AFCARS report.* Washington, DC: U.S. Department of Health and Human Services, Administration for Children and Families, Children's Bureau. Retrieved June 24, 2016, from https://www.acf.hhs.gov/sites/default/files/cb/afcarsreport21.pdf
18. U.S. Census Bureau. (2015). *America's children: Key national indicators of well-being.* Washington, DC: ChildStats.gov. Retrieved June 24, 2016, from http://www.childstats.gov/americaschildren/demo1.asp
19. It is important to acknowledge the difference in the meaning of terms often used in debates about racial/ethnic representation in child welfare. Disproportionality refers to a population that is "out of proportion with respect to an appropriate reference population" (Wulczyn & Lery, 2007, p. 5). Disparity refers to a lack of

equality (Wuldzyn & Lery, 2007)—or a between-groups comparison (Boyd, 2014). Boyd, R. (2014). African American disproportionality and disparity in child welfare: Toward a comprehensive conceptual framework. *Children and Youth Services Review, 37,* 15–27; Wulczyn, F., & Lery, B. (2007). Racial disparity in foster care admissions, Chapin Hall Center for Children. Chicago, IL: University of Chicago Press. Also see Putnam-Hornstein, E., Needell, B., King, B., & Johnson-Montoya, M. (2013). Racial and ethnic disparities: A population-based examination of risk factors for involvement with child protective services. *Child Abuse and Neglect, 37,* 33–46.

20. The exact figure is 11.5%. Wildeman, C., & Emanuel, N. (March, 2014). Cumulative risk of foster care placement by age 18 for U.S. children. *PlosOne, 9*(3).
21. For a thoughtful review of the state's relationship to many tribal communities, see Zinn, A. (1998). *A people's history of the United States.* New York, NY: Harper Perennial.
22. Dunbar-Ortiz, R. (2015). *An indigenous people's history of the United States.* New York, NY: Beacon Press.
23. Lomawaima, J. T. (1999). The unnatural history of American Indian Education. In K. C. Swisher & J. W. Tippeconnic III (Eds.), *Next steps: Research and practice to advance Indian education* (pp. 3–31). Charleston, WV: ERIC Clearinghouse on Rural Education and Small Schools; Adams, D. W. (1995). *Education for extinction: American Indians and the boarding school experience 1875–1928* (pp. 1–391). Lawrence: University Press of Kansas.
24. Indian Child Welfare Program, Hearings Before the Subcommittee on Interior and Insular Affairs, United States Senate, 93rd Congress, Second Session on Problems That American Indian Families Face in Raising Their Children and How These Problems Are Affected by Federal Action or Inaction, April 8 and 9, 1974. Washington, DC: U.S. Government Printing Office, 1975.
25. Byler, W. (1977) in S. Unger (Ed.), *The destruction of American Indian families.* New York, NY: Association on American Indian Affairs. As cited in: O'Sullivan, M. D. (2016). "More destruction to these family ties": Native American women, child welfare, and the solution of sovereignty. *Journal of Family History, 41*(1), 19–38.
26. Limb, G. E., Chance, T., & Brown, E. F. (2004). An empirical examination of the Indian Child Welfare Act and its impact on cultural and familial preservation for American Indian children. *Child Abuse and Neglect, 28,* 1279–1289.
27. National Indian Child Welfare Association. (2007). *Time for reform: A matter of justice for American Indian and Alaskan Native children.* Portland, OR: NICWA. Retrieved June 25, 2016, from http://www.pewtrusts.org/~/media/legacy/uploadedfiles/wwwpewtrustsorg/reports/foster_care_reform/nicwareportpdf.pdf
28. Wildeman, C., & Emanuel, N. (March, 2014). Cumulative risk of foster care placement by age 18 for U.S. children. *PlosOne, 9*(3).
29. See Everett, J., & Chipungu, S. P., & Leashore, B. (Eds.) (2004). *Child welfare revisited: An Africentric perspective.* New Brunswick, NJ: Rutgers University Press;

Robert, D. (2002). *Shattered bonds: The color of child welfare.* New York, NY: Basic Civitas Books.

30. Derezotes, D., Poertner, J., & Testa, M. (2004). *Race matters in child welfare.* Washington DC: Child Welfare League of America; Foster, E. M., Hillemeier, M. M., & Bai, Y. (2011). Explaining the disparity in placement instability among African American and white children in child welfare: A Blinder– Oaxaca decomposition. *Children and Youth Services Review, 33*(1), 118–125; Magruder, J., & Shaw, T. V. (2008). Children ever in care: An examination of cumulative disproportionality. *Child Welfare, 87*(2), 169–188.
31. Some proponents of this theory include Bartholet, E., Wulczyn, F., Barth, R., & Lederman, C. (2011). *Race and child welfare.* Chicago, IL: Chapin Hall Center for Children; Drake, B., Jolley, J.M., Lanier, P., Fluke, J., Barth, R.P., & Jonson-Reid, M. (2011). Racial bias in child protection? *Pediatrics,* 127, 471–478; Font, S., Berger, L., & Slack, K. (2012). Examining racial disparity in child protective services case decisions. *Children and Youth Services Review, 34*, 2188–2200; Lanier, P., Maguire-Jack, K., Walsh, T., Drake, B., & Hubel, G. (2014). Race and ethnic differences in early childhood maltreatment in the United State. *Journal of Developmental behavioral Pediatrics, 35*, 419–426.
32. This theoretical line of argument is offered by these authors (and others): Chand, A. (2000). The over-representation of black children in the child protection system: Possible causes, consequences and solutions. *Child and Family Social Work, 5*(1), 67–78; Webb, E., Maddocks, A., & Bongilli, J. (2002). Effectively protecting black and minority ethnic children from harm: Overcoming barriers to the child protection process. *Child Abuse Review, 11*(6), 394–410.
33. For a detailed review of many of these issues, see Derezotes, D. M., Poertner, J., & Testa, M. (2004). *Race matters in child welfare.* Washington, DC: Child Welfare League of America. And for a review of the role of implicit bias in US society, see Staats, C., Capatosto, K., Wright, R. A., & Jackson, V. W. (2016). *Implicit bias review.* Columbus, OH: Kirwan Institute, The Ohio State University.
34. See Sedlak, A. (1987). *Study of National Incidence and Prevalence of Child Abuse and Neglect.* Washington, DC: United States Department of Health and Human Services. Available online at http://library.childwelfare.gov/cwig/ws/library/docs/gateway/Blob/12686.pdf?w=+NATIVE%28%27IPDET+PH+IS+%27%27NIS-1%27%27%27%29&upp=0&rpp=-10&order=+NATIVE%28%27year%2Fdescend%27%29&r=1&m=2"; Sedlak, A. (1991). *National Incidence and Prevalence of Child Abuse and Neglect 1988: Revised Report.* Washington, DC: United States Department of Health and Human Services. Available online at http://library.childwelfare.gov/cwig/ws/library/docs/gateway/Blob/7415.pdf?w=+NATIVE%28%27IPDET+PH+IS+%27%27NIS-2%27%27%27%29&upp=0&rpp=-10&order=+NATIVE%28%27year%2Fdescend%27%29&r=1&m=3; Sedlak, A., & Broadhurst, D. (1996). *Third National Incidence Study on Child Abuse and Neglect, Final Report.* Washington, DC: United States Department of

Health and Human Services. Available online at http://library.childwelfare.gov/cwig/ws/library/docs/gateway/Blob/13635.pdf?w=+NATIVE%28%27IPDE-T+PH+IS+%27%27NIS-3%27%27%27%29&upp=0&rpp=-10&order=+NA-TIVE%28%27year%2Fdescend%27%29&r=1&m=6

35. Chibnall, S., Dutch, N., Jones-Harden, B., Brown, A., & Gourdine, R. (2010). *Children of color in the child welfare system: Perspectives from the child welfare community*. Washington, DC: United States Department of Health and Human Services, Children's Bureau. Available at http://www.childwelfare.- gov/pubs/otherpubs/children/litreview.cfm
36. Sedlak, A., McPherson, K., & Das, B. (2010). *Supplementary analyses of race differences in child maltreatment rates in the NIS-4*. Washington, DC: United States Department of Health and Human Services, Administration on Children, Youth and Families. Available online at http://www.acf.hhs.gov/programs/opre/abuse_neglect/natl_incid/nis4_supp_analysis_race_diff_mar2010.pdf
37. Drake, B., & Jonson-Reid, M. (2011). NIS interpretations: Race and the National Incidence studies of child abuse and neglect. *Children and Youth Services Review, 33*, 16–20.
38. Dorothy Roberts has written powerfully about whether "community rights" are breached when a disproportionate share of a community's members have been served unjustly by the state. See Roberts, D. (2002). *Shattered bonds: The color of child welfare*. New York, NY: Basic Civitas.
39. Fontes, L. A. (2002). Child discipline and physical abuse in immigrant Latino families: Reducing violence and misunderstandings. *Journal of Counseling and Development, 80*, 31–40; Leon, A. M., & Ziegielewski, S. F. (1999). The psychological impact of migration: Practice considerations in working with Hispanic women. *Journal of Social Work Practice, 13*(1), 69–82.
40. Pison, G. (2010). The number and proportion of immigrants in the population: International comparisons. *Population and Societies*. As cited in Earner I., & Kriz, K. (2015). Child protection in the context of competing policy mandates. In M. Skivenes, R. Barn, K. Kriz, & T. Poso (Eds.), *Child welfare systems and migrant children*. New York, NY: Oxford University Press.
41. Dettlaff, A. J., & Rycraft, J. R. (2006). The impact of migration and acculturation on Latino children and families: Implications for child welfare practice. *Protecting Children, 21*(2), 6–21.
42. Dettlaff, A., & Finno-Velasquez, M. (2013). Child maltreatment and immigration enforcement: Considerations for child welfare and legal systems working with immigrant children. *Children's Legal Rights Journal, 33*(1), 37–63.
43. Larsen, L. J. (2004). The foreign-born population in the United States: 2003. Current Population Reports, P20-551. Washington, DC: United States Census Bureau.
44. Johnson-Motoyama, M., Putnam-Hornstein, E., Dettlaff, A., Zhao, K., Finno-Velasquez, M., & Needell, B. (2014). Disparities in reported and substantiated

infant maltreatment by maternal Hispanic origin and nativity: A birth cohort study. *Maternal and Child Health Journal, 19*(5), 958–968.

45. See Cifuentes, M., Clemmons, M. P., & Gomez, I. (2006). Migration: A critical issue for child welfare. *Protecting Children, Special issue, 21*(2).
46. Partida, J. (1996). The effects of immigration on children in the Mexican-American community. *Child and Adolescent Social Work Journal, 13*(3), 241–254.
47. Solis, J. (2003). Re-thinking illegality as a violence against, not by Mexican immigrants, children, and youth. *Journal of Social Issues, 59*, 15–31.
48. Smart, J. F., & Smart, D. W. (1995). Acculturative stress of Hispanics: Loss and challenge. *Journal of Counseling and Development, 73*, 390–396.
49. Simoni, J. M. (1993). Latina mothers' help seeking at a school-based mutual support group. *Journal of Community Psychology, 21*, 188–199.
50. United States Department of Health and Human Services (US DHHS). (1997). Child Maltreatment 1995. Washington, DC: US Government Printing Office; US DHHS. (2007). *Child maltreatment 2005*. Washington, DC: US Government Printing Office.
51. US DHHS. (2014). *Child maltreatment 2014*. Washington, DC: US Government Printing Office.
52. Dettlaff, A., Earner, I., & Phillips, S. D. (2009). Latino children of immigrants in the child welfare system: Prevalence, characteristics, and risk. *Children and Youth Services Review, 31*, 775–783; Putnam-Hornstein, E., & Needell, B. (2011). Predictors of child protective service contact between birth and age five: An examination of California's 2002 birth cohort. *Children and Youth Services Review, 33*(11), 2400–2407. http://dx.doi.org/10.1016/j.childyouth.2011.07.010; Shaw, T. V., Putnam-Hornstein, E., Magruder, J., & Needell, B. (2008). Measuring racial disparity in child welfare. *Child Welfare, 87*(2), 23–36.
53. Putnam-Hornstein, E., Needell, B., King, B., & Johnson-Montoya, M. (2013). Racial and ethnic disparities: A population-based examination of risk factors for involvement with child protective services. *Child Abuse and Neglect, 37*, 33–46.
54. Dettlaff, A., Earner, I., & Phillips, S. D. (2009). Latino children of immigrants in the child welfare system: Prevalence, characteristics, and risk. *Children and Youth Services Review, 31*, 775–783.
55. Maguire-Jack, K., Lanier, P., Johnson-Motoyama, M., Welch, H., & Dineen, M. (2015). Geographic variation in racial disparities in child maltreatment: The influence of county poverty and population density. *Child Abuse and Neglect, 47*, 1–13.
56. For example, in Putnam-Hornstein and associates' study, non-native-born Latino families who were categorized as low-income were more likely to share other characteristics of protection such as an older maternal age, the presence of a father at birth, and healthy birth outcomes. See Putnam-Hornstein, E., Needell, B., King, B., & Johnson-Motoyama, M. (2013). Racial and ethnic disparities: A population based examination of risk factors for involvement with child protective services. *Child Abuse and Neglect, 37*, 33–46.

57. At least three authors have put forth conceptual frames to explain racial / ethnic disproportionalities and disparities in child welfare. Their frames have much in common but are also somewhat dissimilar. Barth offers four main contributing factors: (1) risk, incidence, and benefits; (2) child welfare services decision making; (3) placement dynamics; and (4) the multiplicative model. Fluke and associates propose a three-part explanatory model, including (1) disproportionate and disparate need; (2) racial bias and discrimination in the child welfare system and other ecologies; (3) child welfare system processes and resources. And Boyd proposes a five-part model. These include (1) human decision making (bias); (2) agency-system factors; (3) placement dynamics; (4) policy impact; and (5) disproportionate need. See Boyd, R. (2014). African American disproportionality and disparity in child welfare: Toward a comprehensive conceptual framework. *Children and Youth Services Review, 37*, 15–27; Barth, R. P. (2005). Child welfare and race: Models of disproportionality. In D. M. Derezotes, J. Poertner, & M. F. Testa (Eds.), *Race matters in child welfare: The overrepresentation of African American children in the system* (pp. 25–46). Washington, DC: Child Welfare League of America; Fluke, J., Harden, B., Jenkins, M., & Ruehrdanz, A. (2010). Research synthesis on child welfare disproportionality and disparities. American Humane Association, 1–80. Retrieved from http://www.cssp.org/publications/child-welfare/alliance/Disparities-and-Disproportionality-in-Child-Welfare_An-Analysis-of-the-Research-December-2011.
58. Macartney, S. (2011). *Child poverty in the United States 2009 and 2010: Selected race groups and Hispanic origin.* Washington, DC: US Census Bureau. Retrieved June 28, 2016, from https://www.census.gov/prod/2011pubs/acsbr10-05.pdf
59. Drake, B., & Rank, M. (2009). The racial divide among American children in poverty: Reassessing the importance of neighborhood. *Children and Youth Services Review, 31*, 1264–1271.
60. See Ernst, J. S. (2001). Community-level factors and child maltreatment in suburban county. *Social Work Research, 25*(3), 133–142; Fryer, G. E., & Miyshi, T. (1995). A cluster analysis of detected and substantiated child maltreatment incidents in rural Colorado. *Child Abuse and Neglect, 19*(3), 363–369; Paulsen, D. (2003). No safe place: Assessing spatial patterns of child maltreatment victimization. *Journal of Aggression, Maltreatment and Trauma, 8*(102), 477–478; Zielinski, D. S., & Bradshaw, C. P. (2006). Ecological influences on the sequelae of child maltreatment: A review of the literature. *Child Maltreatment, 11*(1), 49–62. Notably, new research indicates that White children living in poor neighborhoods are at higher risk of a child maltreatment referral than African American children. This theory of "differential assortment" suggests that White families remaining in disproportionately poor neighborhoods may be living there in part due to a number of other factors that would place their children at risk of maltreatment (e.g., substance abuse, mental health concerns). See Drake, B., & Rank, M. (2009). The racial divide among American children in poverty: Reassessing the importance of neighborhood. *Children and Youth Services Review, 31*, 1264–1271.

61. Jonson-Reid, M., Drake, B., & Kohl, P. L. (2009). Is the overrepresentation of the poor in child welfare caseloads due to bias or need? *Children and Youth Services Review, 31*, 422–427.
62. Drake, B., Lee, S. M., & Jonson-Reid, M. (2009). Race and child maltreatment reporting: Are blacks overrepresented? *Children and Youth Services Review, 31*, 309–316.
63. Anderson, K. (1998). A Canadian child welfare agency for urban natives: The clients speak. *Child Welfare, 77*(4), 441–460; Corby, B., Millar, M., & Young, L. (1996). Parental participation in child protection work: Rethinking the rhetoric. *British Journal of Social Work, 26*(4), 475–790.
64. Diorio, W. D. (1992). Parental perceptions of the authority of public child welfare caseworkers. *Families in Society, 73*(4), 222–235; Dumbrill, G. C. (2006). Parental experience of child protection intervention: A qualitative study. *Child Abuse and Neglect, 30*(1), 27–37; Mandell, D. (2008). Power, care and vulnerability: Considering use of self in child welfare work. *Journal of Social Work Practice, 22*(2), 235–248.
65. See Colby, S. L., & Ortman, J. M. (2015). Projections of the size and composition of the US population: 2014 to 2060. *Current Population Reports*. https://www.census.gov/content/dam/Census/library/publications/2015/demo/p25-1143.pdf; Perez, A. D., & Hirschman, C. (2009). The changing racial and ethnic composition of the US population: Emerging American identities. *Population Development Review, 35*(1), 1–51. http://www.ncbi.nlm.nih.gov/pmc/articles/PMC2882688/pdf/nihms-102416.pdf

CHAPTER 9

1. Alpert discusses the punitive nature of child welfare services. See Alpert, L. T. (2005). Research review: Parents' service experience—a missing element in research on foster care outcomes. *Child and Family Social Work, 10*(4), 361–366.
2. Sykes, J. (2011). Negotiating stigma: Understanding mothers' responses to accusations of child neglect. *Children and Youth Services Review, 33*, 448–456.
3. Habermas, J. (1996). *Between facts and norms*. Cambridge, MA: The MIT Press.
4. Dumbrill has written extensively about the power imbalance between child welfare workers and parents. Dumbrill, G. C. (2006). Parental experience of child protection intervention: A qualitative study. *Child Abuse and Neglect, 30*(1), 27–37.
5. Child Welfare Information Gateway. (n.d.). *Philosophy and key elements of family-centered practice*. Washington, DC: Children's Bureau. https://www.childwelfare.gov/topics/famcentered/philosophy/. The following key element is listed on the same website: "Developing a relationship between parents and service providers characterized by mutual trust, respect, honesty, and open communication." The reader might note that the first element noted in the text refers to the family, but the second element refers only to the parent. Why parents should be offered mutual trust, respect, honesty, and open communication, and not children, is not clear.

6. Smith, B., & Donovan, S. (2003). Child welfare practice in organizational and institutional contexts. *The Social Service Review, 77*(4), 541–563. doi: 10.1086/378328
7. Corby, B., Millar, M., & Young, L. (1996) Parental participation in child protection work: rethinking the rhetoric. *British Journal of Social Work, 26*, 475–492.
8. Smith, B., & Donovan, S. (2003). Child welfare practice in organizational and institutional contexts. *The Social Service Review, 77*(4), 541–563. doi: 10.1086/378328
9. Gladstone, J., Dumbrill, G., Leslie, B., Koster, A., Young, M., & Ismaila, A. (2014). Understanding worker–parent engagement in child protection casework. *Children and Youth Services Review, 44*, 56–64.
10. Berrick, J. D., Dickens, J., Poso, T., & Skivenes, M. (2016). Parents' involvement in care order decisions: A cross-country study of front-line practice. *Child and Family Social Work, 22*(2), 626–637.
11. Hojer, I. (2011). Parents with children in foster care—How do they perceive their contact with social workers? *Social Work in Action, 23*(2), 111–123; Kapp and Propp (2002). Client satisfaction methods: Input from parents with children in foster care. *Child and Adolescent Social Work Journal, 19*, 227–245; Lietz, C. (2011). Theoretical adherence to family centered practice: Are strengths-based principles illustrated in families' descriptions of child welfare services? *Children and Youth Services Review, 33*(6), 888–893. doi: 10.1016/j.childyouth.2010.12.012.
12. Schofield, G., Moldestad, B., Hojer, I., Ward, E., Skilbred, D., Young, J., & Havik, T. (2011). Managing loss and a threatened identity: Experiences of parents of children growing up in foster care, the perspectives of their social workers and implications for practice. *British Journal of Social Work, 41*, 71–92, doi:10.1093/bjsw/bcq073
13. Marcenko, M. O., Brown, R., DeVoy, P. R., & Conway, D. (2010). Engaging parents: Innovative approaches in child welfare. *Protecting Chidlren, 25*(1), 23–35; Shemmings, D., & Shemmings, Y. (1996). Building trust with families when making enquiries. In D. Platt & D. Shemmings (Eds.), *Making enquiries into alleged child abuse and neglect: Partnership with families.* Chichester, England: John Wiley & Sons.
14. Skramstad, H., & Skivenes, M. (2015) Child welfare workers' views of fathers in risk assessment and planned interventions, a comparison between English and Norwegian workers. *Child and Family Social Work*, doi: 10.1111/cfs.12220
15. Dawson, K., & Berry, M. (2002). Engaging families in child welfare services: An evidence-based approach to best practice. *Child Welfare, 81*(2), 293–317; Farrell, A., Luján, M. L., Britner, P. A., Randall, K. G., & Goodrich, S. A. (2012). "I am part of every decision": Client perceptions of engagement within a supportive housing child welfare programme. *Child and Family Social Work, 17*(2), 254–264; Littell, J. H. (2001). Client participation and outcomes of intensive family preservation services. *Social Work Research, 25*, 103–114; McLendon, T. McLendon, D., Dickerson, P. S., Lyons, J. K., & Tapp, K. (2012). Engaging families in the child

welfare process utilizing the Family-directed Structural Assessment Tool. *Child Welfare, 91*(6), 43–58.

16. Hojer, I. (2011). Parents with children in foster care—How do they perceive their contact with social workers? *Social Work in Action, 23*(2); Schofield, G., & Ward, E. (2011). *Understanding and working with parents of children in long-term foster care*. London, UK and Philadelphia, PA: Jessica Kingsley Publishers.
17. Kemp, S. et al. (2009). Engaging parents in child welfare services: Bridging family needs and child welfare mandates. *Child Welfare, 88*(1), 101–126.
18. Dumbrill, G. (2006). Parental experience of child protection intervention: a qualitative study. *Child Abuse and Neglect, 30*, 27–37; Crea, T., & Berzin, S. (2009). Family involvement in child welfare decision-making: strategies and research on inclusive practices. *Journal of Public Child Welfare, 3*, 305–327; Klease, C. (2008). Silenced stakeholders: responding to mothers' experiences in the child protection system. *Children Australia, 33*, 21–28; Hall, C., & Slembrouck, S. (2011). Interviewing parents of children in care: perspectives, discourses and accountability. *Children and Youth Services Review, 33*, 457–465; Virokannas, E. (2011) Identity categorisation of motherhood in the context of drug abuse and child welfare services. *Qualitative Social Work, 10*, 329–345.
19. The United States has signed the Convention, but it has not ratified it—a process that involves the President and the US Senate. The United States was instrumental in drafting portions of the treaty under the Reagan administration, three of the articles of the convention were adapted directly from the US Constitution. The convention was adopted by the United Nations in 1989 and signed in 1995 by the US Ambassador to the UN thereafter; however, the Convention has not been submitted to the Senate by any sitting US president. In 2015, Somalia ratified the convention, leaving the United States as the only member of the United Nations that has yet to sign the treaty. See http://www.un.org/apps/news/story.asp?NewsID=52129#.V5VOx_krLIU; http://www.unicef.org/crc/index_30229.html
20. Mason, M. (2005). The U.S. and the international children's rights crusade: Laggard or leader? *Journal of Social History, 38*, 955–963.
21. Fass, P., & Mason, M. (2000). *Childhood in America*. New York, NY: New York University Press; Mintz, S. (2004). *Huck's raft: A history of American childhood*. Cambridge, MA: Harvard University Press.
22. Archard, D. (2004). *Children: Rights and childhood*. New York, NY: Routledge.
23. Committee on the rights of the child. (2009). Fifty-first session Geneva, 25. http://www2.ohchr.org/english/bodies/crc/docs/AdvanceVersions/CRC-C-GC-12.pdf (p. 3).
24. Archard, D., & Skivenes, M. (2009a). Hearing the child. *Child & Family Social Work, 14*, 391–399.
25. Council of Europe. (2011). *Guidelines of the Committee of Ministers of the Council of Europe on Child-Friendly Justice*. Strasbourg: Council of Europe. Retrieved July 22, 2016, from http://www.coe.int/t/dghl/standardsetting/childjustice/.

26. Warshak, R. (2003). Payoffs and pitfalls of listening to children. *Family Relations, 52*(4), 373–384. Retrieved from http://www.jstor.org/stable/3700318; Hearing a child's voice in divorce: A judge's experience. https://etd.ohiolink.edu/!etd.send_file?accession=antioch1457977765&disposition=inline
27. Berrick, J. D., Dickens, J., Poso, T., & Skivenes, M. (2015). Children's involvement in care order decision making: A cross-country comparison. *Child Abuse and Neglect, 49*, 128–141.
28. Hart, R. (1992). *Children's participation: From tokenism to citizenship*. Florence, Italy: UNICEF.
29. Abrioux, E. (1998). Degrees of participation: A spherical model—the possibilities for girls in Kabul, Afghanistan. In V. Johnson, E., Ivan-Smith, G. Gordon, P. Pridmore, & P. Scott (Eds.), *Stepping forward: Children and young people's involvement in the development process.* London: Intermediate Technology Publications as cited in Dickens, J. (2016). *Social work and social policy*. London, UK: Routledge.
30. Thomas, N. (2000). *Children, family and the state. Decision-making and child participation*. Bristol, UK: The Policy Press; Thomas, N. (2007). Towards a theory of children's participation. *International Journal of Children's Rights, 15*, 199–218.
31. Representation of Children in Child Abuse and Neglect Proceedings (2014). Available at https://www.childwelfare.gov/pubPDFs/represent.pdf
32. Roesch-Marsh, A., Gillies, A., & Green, D. (2016). Nurturing the virtuous circle: Looked after children's participation in reviews, a cyclical and relational process. *Child and Family Social Work, 22*(2), 904–913.
33. McMahon, J. (2004). What do children look for in social workers? *Fostering Perspectives, 9*(1), 1–3.
34. Baker, A. J., Creegan, A., Quinones, A., & Rozelle, L. (2016). Foster children's views of their birth parents: A review of the literature. *Children and Youth Services Review*, 67, 177–183. doi:10.1016/j.childyouth.2016.06.004

CHAPTER 10

1. The origins of the Hippocratic oath are Greek, though the principles have been adjusted for contemporary practitioners. Today, many medical professionals swear to an oath that may embody a "first do no harm" provision. Medical professionals are also guided by an elaborate Code of Ethics. See American Medical Association Code of Medical Ethics. Retrieved July 15, 2016, from http://www.ama-assn.org/ama/pub/physician-resources/medical-ethics/code-medical-ethics.page

2. National Society of Professional Engineers (2007). *Code of ethics for engineers*. Retrieved July 15, 2016, from https://www.nspe.org/sites/default/files/resources/pdfs/Ethics/CodeofEthics/Code-2007-July.pdf
3. National Education Association. *Code of ethics.* Retrieved July 15, 2016, from http://www.nea.org/home/30442.htm

4. National Association of Social Workers (2008). *Code of ethics.* Retrieved July 15, 2016, from https://www.socialworkers.org/pubs/code/default.asp
5. I do not claim that the eight principles articulated here are exhaustive. Others may be identified, though I would caution that too numerous a set of principles will create confusion for practitioners and policymakers who may be tempted to pick and choose those most expedient rather than attending to those that are foundational.
6. Another step the foster parents could have taken to further their respect for the family's cultural heritage would have been to maintain the child's given name (he was ultimately named "Sam" by his birth parents and was also given two middle names—a cultural tradition in the birth mother's family).
7. See, for example, work that characterizes the experiences of children who participated in the orphan trains a century ago and studies of foster care alumni who experienced care several decades ago. O'Connor, S. (2004). *Orphan trains: The story of Charles Loring Brace and the children he saved and failed.* Chicago, IL: University of Chicago Press; Pecora, P. J., Kessler, R. C., Williams, J., O'Brien, K., Downs, A. C., English, D., . . . Holmes, K. (2005). *Improving family foster care: Findings from the Northwest Family foster care alumni study.* Seattle, WA: Casey Family Programs.
8. This list is derived from the list of "core competencies" required of MSW-level child welfare workers in California, though the list of competencies goes well beyond these. See California Social Work Education Center (2011). *Integrated foundation and advanced competencies for public child welfare in California.* Berkeley, CA: California Social Work Education Center.
9. Ryan, J. P., Garnier, P., Zyphur, M., & Zhai, F. (2006). Investigating the effects of caseworker characteristics in child welfare. *Children and Youth Services Review, 28,* 993–1006.
10. Albers, E., Reilly, T., & Rittner, B. (1993). Children in foster care: Possible factors affecting permanency planning. *Child and Adolescent Social Work Journal, 10*(4), 329–341.
11. Littell, J. H., & Tajima, E. A. (2000). A multilevel model of client participation in intensive family preservation services. *Social Service Review, 74*(3), 405–435.
12. See Wilson, J. O. (2015). *The idea of America: Our values, our legacy, our future.* Williamsburg, W.V.: The Colonial Williamsburg Foundation.

Glossary

30-day services plan A written plan developed by the child welfare worker in collaboration with the parent to include the services the parent may need to help her or him parent the child safely. The services are put in place for 30 days while the child welfare worker continues to assess the needs of the family and the safety of the child. See http://ccrwf.org/publications/child-welfare-primer/

adoption finalization hearing Adoption is a legal determination of parent/child status; the most permanent of the "permanent plans" a court can make for children in the child welfare system after their birth parents' parental rights are terminated by a formal judicial process. The adoption finalization hearing is typically scheduled for at least 120 days after termination of parental rights to give parents and counsel ample time to file an appeal, if desired. See http://adoptionlawgroup.com/fost-adopt/

concurrent planning An approach to case planning designed to speed the process that will result in a permanent plan for the child and minimize placement changes. It is accomplished by selecting a foster home for a child that first serves as a temporary placement while reunification efforts proceed, but which is intended to become permanent (especially via adoption) if/when reunification is ruled out at the permanency hearing. See https://www.childwelfare.gov/pubPDFs/concurrent_evidence.pdf

continuance When the court, for good cause, continues the hearing to a later date in order to collect additional information (e.g., evidence, reports, assessments) required to make informed decisions. See http://www.courts.ca.gov/documents/Dogbook_2Ed_online.pdf

continuing worker (unit) The title given to a child welfare worker in some California counties and other jurisdictions who is assigned to the case after the disposition hearing. This worker serves the family during voluntary or court-mandated in-home services, or during voluntary or court-mandated out-of-home services. The worker typically follows the child until the case is dismissed, reunified, transferred to the Adoption unit, or the child emancipates. In some jurisdictions this might be called an ongoing or permanent placement worker. See http://ccrwf.org/publications/child-welfare-primer/

Core Practice Model A term used in California that refers to a framework for practice based upon common values about children and families. Some of these values include, for example, using prevention services to keep children safe; work with families built on partnership and mutual respect; giving families access to effective services, etc. For more information, see http://calswec.berkeley.edu/california-child-welfare-core-practice-model-0

County Counsel The child welfare agency's attorney. See http://www.chhs.ca.gov/Child%20Welfare/InsightsVolXI-Fall2016.pdf

Court Family Maintenance case *See* Family Maintenance.

Court Family Reunification case *See* Family Reunification.

Court unit The name of a unit in some public child welfare agencies that provides services and prepares cases for presentation to the court prior to the dispositional hearing. The Court unit is frequently paired with the Emergency Response (ER) unit to provide intake services to families (some counties may call this the Court Dependency Unit [CDU] or Dependency Investigations [DI]). See http://ccrwf.org/publications/child-welfare-primer/

Dependency Investigations (DI) worker (or unit) The name of a unit in some public child welfare agencies in which child welfare workers (DI workers) conduct investigations of child maltreatment allegations after a child has been preliminarily removed from his or her home, either by an Emergency Response child welfare worker or by law enforcement. The child welfare worker recommends that the Court make findings regarding whether the child was a victim of abuse and/or neglect, and if so, whether the child should be returned home with services or remain out of home; if neither, the DI worker will recommend that the Court dismiss the case. See http://ccrwf.org/publications/child-welfare-primer/

detention The act of "detaining" the child, or temporarily separating a child from his or her parent(s). See http://ccrwf.org/publications/child-welfare-primer/

detention hearing A court hearing to determine whether the child will be "detained" (or placed out of home) pending resolution of the conditions alleged in the petition to have created serious harm or risk of abuse and/or neglect. See https://www.childwelfare.gov/pubPDFs/planning.pdf

Differential Response (Alternative Response) A child welfare system reform that enables child welfare agencies to differentiate its initial response to reports of child abuse and neglect based on several factors. Families selected into Differential Response would typically present with fewer safety risks than children selected into the traditional child welfare system. See https://www.childwelfare.gov/topics/responding/alternative/

disposition hearing A court hearing that determines who will have custody of a child. See https://www.childwelfare.gov/pubPDFs/planning.pdf

emergency foster home A licensed foster home prepared to serve children on an "emergency" basis, usually for a temporary period while a longer, more stable relative home or foster home is secured for the child. See https://www.childwelfare.gov/pubPDFs/homestudyreqs.pdf

Emergency Response (ER) The name of a unit in many public child welfare agencies in California that is responsible for contacting children and families following a child maltreatment referral to the hotline. The ER worker is tasked with completing an investigation of the maltreatment allegation. If the investigation finds that the parents do not pose an immediate and high risk of maltreating their child or there is inconclusive evidence to substantiate abuse, the emergency response social worker can decide to leave the child at home and may offer caregivers up to 30 days of emergency response services or up to 6 months of voluntary Family Maintenance services. If the emergency response social worker (or a police officer) determines that the child cannot remain safely at home, immediate steps are taken to remove and place the child in a safe environment, such as an emergency foster home. See http://ccrwf.org/publications/child-welfare-primer/

Emergency Response social worker *See* Emergency Response.

Emergency Response supervisor The supervisor for staff serving in the Emergency Response unit. See http://ccrwf.org/publications/child-welfare-primer/

emergency shelter Similar to an emergency foster home, the shelter is licensed to care for children on a temporary basis until a longer lasting, more permanent relative caregiver or foster home can be identified for the child. See http://ccrwf.org/publications/child-welfare-primer/

family book Also called a profile book, this "book" includes pictures and stories about a prospective adoptive family, designed to initially introduce and familiarize a child with the family that he or she may come to live with. See http://www.adoptionstar.com/creating-your-adoption-family-profile-book/

family finding A series of strategies to identify, locate, and engage relative family members when children are living in out-of-home care. For more information, see http://www.familyfinding.org/

Family Maintenance The name of an approach or unit in California that can be either court ordered or voluntary, where children who are at a relatively lower risk of maltreatment recurrence can remain in their homes with monitoring and services provided under the supervision of child welfare workers. See http://ccrwf.org/publications/child-welfare-primer/

Family Maintenance Plan *See* Family Maintenance. For families participating in Family Maintenance, the plan is a written document that clarifies the services the agency will provide to the family, and the steps the family must take to keep the child safe. See http://ccrwf.org/publications/child-welfare-primer/

Family Reunification The name of an approach or unit in many California counties designed for families whose children have been removed from the home with court oversight. "FR" provides children and their parents with services to accelerate the children's safe return home. See http://ccrwf.org/publications/child-welfare-primer/

Family Reunification Review (hearing) When children are involuntarily separated from their families and placed in foster care, the court is involved in regularly reviewing the circumstances of the case and the conditions that initially brought the child into care. These hearings, which may occur every 6 months or more frequently, may result in a child returned home, or may result in an extension of a stay in foster care. See http://www.chhs.ca.gov/Child%20Welfare/InsightsVolXI-Fall2016.pdf

Family Reunification Services *See* Family Reunification.

family team meeting A meeting that brings together a family and other interested parties such as friends, neighbors, and community members, with staff from the child welfare agency and other helping agencies (e.g., mental health, schools, etc). Working together, the members learn what the family hopes to accomplish, set realistic goals, identify the family's strengths and needs, and make a plan for who will do what to keep children safe. See http://www.aecf.org/resources/four-approaches-to-family-team-meetings/

fost-adopt A foster care placement where the foster parents agree to adopt the child if/when parental rights are terminated. See https://adoption.com/wiki/Foster-Adoption_(Glossary)

Foster Family Agency (FFA) A private, nonprofit agency that is state licensed, inspected, and approved to certify that foster homes meet the state regulations pertaining to care of children placed away from their families. The FFA acts as a contractor to the state or county, receiving foster care funds to provide supervision, training, and support services, and providing a stipend to its foster families to provide for children placed in their homes. See http://www.cdss.ca.gov/cdssweb/entres/forms/English/LIC9128.PDF

full disclosure meeting A meeting with a prospective adoptive family. All of the pertinent details of a child's family history, physical health, mental health, and behaviors are shared. See http://www.nrcpfc.org/cpt/component-two.htm

guardianship (typically called "legal guardianship") A permanency option for a child. Guardianship is court ordered and confers a legal relationship between a child and an adult. The guardian is appointed to provide supervision and care until the child reaches maturity. Under guardianship, the birth parent retains parental rights to the child. See https://www.childwelfare.gov/topics/permanency/guardianship/

hold Based upon concerns about the infant's safety, a hospital can put a "protective hold" on the child's discharge for an unspecified period of time until the child welfare agency or police clear the baby for release. See http://studylib.net/doc/7744010/dss-policy-and-procedure-guide

hotline screener The hotline screener receives phone calls from mandated and non-mandated reporters. Based on information received during the call, the screener will either deploy a child welfare worker to the child to gather additional information, or he or she may close the case and offer referrals to local services. See https://www.childwelfare.gov/topics/responding/iia/screening/

ice-breaker meeting A meeting that typically includes the foster parent(s), the birth parent(s), and the child welfare worker. The focus of the conversation is on the child and the child's needs in the new foster home. The meeting also allows the foster parent and birth parent to begin to know one another so that they can work together to attend to the child's well-being. See http://www.nrcpfc.org/fewpt/partnerships.htm

immediate response Following a call to the hotline, if the nature of the call suggests imminent danger, a child welfare worker will be deployed to investigate the child's needs right away. In some states, an immediate response occurs within 24 hours; in California, an immediate response usually occurs within 2 hours. See http://ccrwf.org/publications/child-welfare-primer/

interstate compact for the placement of children (ICPC) A series of procedures that allow for a child to be placed in a foster or adoptive home across state boundaries. See http://www.aphsa.org/content/AAICPC/en/resources/ICPCFAQ.html

jurisdiction hearing A judicial hearing that determines whether the allegations in the petition are true. See http://www.courts.ca.gov/1205.htm

Ongoing unit *See* continuing worker (unit).

permanency A safe, stable, and permanent living situation for children. The first permanency goal is reunification. If or when reunification cannot be achieved, adoption is the next best permanency option, followed by legal guardianship. See https://www.childwelfare.gov/topics/permanency/

pos tox *See* "tox positive."

Placement unit A specialized unit in some public child welfare agencies charged with identifying appropriate homes for children placed in out-of-home care. See https://www.bsa.ca.gov/pdfs/reports/2011-101.1.pdf

planned permanent living arrangements (PPLA) Formerly referred to as long-term foster care, the term was changed with the development of the Adoption and Safe Families Act as a further means of limiting the number of children whose planned long-term arrangements included foster care. Children with a PPLA plan typically continue to live in foster care following a permanency planning hearing with annual permanency reviews until they "age out" of the child welfare system. See https://www.childwelfare.gov/topics/outofhome/foster-care/oppla-appla/

"pre-dispo" case Typically, this will refer to the period of time between the detention hearing and the dispositional hearing. See http://www.childsworld.ca.gov/res/SIPs/2015/KernSIP_ProgressReport.pdf

prenatal substance abuse In some states, prenatal substance use can be considered a form of child maltreatment. In California, the law stipulates that prenatal substance use can be considered physical abuse under the following conditions: There is a positive toxicology finding for a newborn infant or his or her mother *or* other credible information that there was prenatal substance abuse by the mother *and* there is indication that the mother will continue to use substances rendering her unable to fulfill the basic needs of the infant upon discharge from the hospital. Indicators may include but are not limited to the type of drug (the more addictive the drug the more likely there will be continued use), pattern of past use, behavior during hospitalization, statements by the mother or others regarding use, *and* willingness/ability to care for infant, etc. See http://aia.berkeley.edu/media/pdf/AIAFactSheet_PrenatalSubExposure_2012.pdf

pumping and dumping Refers to expressing (pumping) breast milk that might be tainted with drugs and throwing out (dumping) the milk. This continues until the breast milk is free of traces of drugs and can be offered to the baby safely. See http://www.thebump.com/a/what-does-pump-and-dump-mean

reasonable efforts Those efforts required of child welfare agencies to help preserve or reunify families. See https://www.childwelfare.gov/topics/systemwide/laws-policies/statutes/reunify/

reunification bypass An order not to offer reunification services to the parent based on any one of several serious child maltreatment conditions. See http://leginfo.legislature.ca.gov/faces/codes_displaySection.xhtml?lawCode=WIC§ionNum=361.5.

Risk Profile A form used in some public child welfare agencies that identifies the child's main strengths and vulnerabilities, including any significant health or mental health concerns. The form is provided to the foster caregivers prior to placement. See http://www.ccrwf.org/wp-content/uploads/2009/03/final_web_pdf.pdf

safety plan "A safety plan ensures the child's safety while simultaneously working with the family. The plan focuses on the actions and tasks required to controls threats of danger" (p. 21). See http://nrccps.org/wp-content/uploads/2010/11/The_Guide.pdf.

screener narrative The text written by a hotline screener to capture as much relevant information about the child maltreatment referral as possible. See https://www.auditor.ca.gov/pdfs/reports/2013-110.pdf

secondary trauma Secondary traumatic stress (STS), also known as vicarious trauma or compassion fatigue, refers to the experience of people—usually professionals—who are exposed to others' traumatic stories and as a result can develop their own traumatic symptoms and reactions. Child welfare staff have to deal with both direct and secondary exposure to dangerous situations—this combination can result in occupational stress. See ACS-NYU Children's Trauma Institute. (2012). *Addressing secondary traumatic stress among child welfare staff: A practice brief*. New York, NY: NYU Langone Medical Center.

seven-day notice In many child welfare jurisdictions, foster parents are given the option to notify the agency if they can no longer keep the child in their care. The foster parents are typically required to give the agency at least seven days' notice of the pending move. See http://www.advokids.org/legal-tools/information-for-caregivers/7-days-notice-of-placement-change/

shake Shake consists of small pieces of cannabis flower that break off of larger buds, generally as the result of regular handling. See https://www.leafly.com/news/cannabis-101/what-is-shake

six-month status review hearing See *family reunification review hearing.*

social work court officer The social worker representing the county in the courtroom. See http://www.chhs.ca.gov/Child%20Welfare/InsightsVolXI-Fall2016.pdf

"Structured Decision Making" hotline tool Used in some public child welfare agencies as a screening form to help determine how quickly a response must be made. See http://www.childsworld.ca.gov/pg1332.htm

Structured Decision Making (SDM) tool This research-based system of tools identifies the key points in the life of a child welfare case and uses structured assessments to improve the consistency and validity of each decision. The SDM model additionally includes clearly defined service standards, mechanisms for timely reassessments, methods for measuring workload, and mechanisms for ensuring accountability and quality controls.

See http://www.nccdglobal.org/assessment/sdm-structured-decision-making-systems/child-welfare

sustained the allegation An allegation is an assertion made in court. The child welfare worker is required to prove with supporting evidence that the allegation is true and, if so, the court will sustain the allegation. See https://www.childwelfare.gov/pubpdfs/cpswork.pdf

team decision meeting See *family team meeting.*

tox positive Otherwise known as a toxicology screen for illegal substances, the screen detects, usually through a urine sample, drug use prior to delivery. See http://www.healthline.com/health/toxicology-screen#Overview1

voluntary family maintenance case Refers to families who voluntarily accept services from the child welfare agency without court oversight. See http://ccrwf.org/publications/child-welfare-primer/

WIC 300 The juvenile dependency and delinquency courts are separate in California. The dependency courts typically attend to issues identified in the California Welfare and Institutions Code (WIC) 300-series, the laws that frame child maltreatment-related issues. For more information on the WIC, see http://www.leginfo.ca.gov/cgi-bin/calawquery?codesection=wic

WIC 600 The juvenile delinquency and dependency courts are separate in California. The delinquency courts typically attend to issues identified in the California Welfare and Institutions Code (WIC) 600-series, the laws that frame delinquency infractions. For information on the WIC, see http://www.leginfo.ca.gov/cgi-bin/calawquery?codesection=wic

wraparound services According to the California Department of Social Services, wraparound is a planning process as much as it is a service delivery model. Wraparound "values the engagement of the child and his/her family in a manner that shifts from a problem focused view of issues to building on individual strengths to improve family and child well being. The process is used to engage the family as they identify their own needs and create methods and a plan to meet those needs. The goal is to provide intensive, individualized services and supports to families that will allow children to live and grow up in a safe, stable, permanent family environment." See http://www.childsworld.ca.gov/pg1320.htm

wraparound team The informal and formal support person engaged in enacting a wraparound services plan. See *wraparound services*.

About the Authors

Jill Duerr Berrick, MSW, PhD, is the Zellerbach Family Foundation Chair at the School of Social Welfare, UC Berkeley. She also serves as codirector (with Neil Gilbert) of the Center for Child and Youth Policy on the Berkeley campus.

Erika Altobelli, MSW, LCSW, came to UC Berkeley with an interest in helping families succeed. Although she never intended to stay in the field of child welfare when she took her first job in 1995, she has never left the field. She currently serves as a social worker in Northern California.

Alyssa Barkley, MSW, LCSW, had experience working with foster youth before she joined UC Berkeley's MSW program and wanted to help improve outcomes for children following care. She graduated in 2013 and took a job in a local county. She now works in a nonprofit child welfare agency on the central coast.

Traci Bernal, MSW, worked with children for 12 years, and 2 years as a CASA prior to joining UC Berkeley's MSW program. She graduated in 2012, got a job in a local county child welfare agency, and has worked in the Adoption unit ever since. Traci currently serves as a social worker in a Bay Area county.

Maria Burch, MSW, LCSW, joined Berkeley's graduate program with an interest in working with Latino families interacting with the child welfare system. She graduated in 2009 and works at the front end of the child welfare system as a hotline screener. She currently serves as a social worker in a Bay Area county.

Viviana Colosimo-Blair, MSW, worked with children and families in various fields, including domestic violence, teaching, and outdoor adventure, before she came to Berkeley for her graduate degree. Her prior jobs involved families touched by maltreatment, so it was a natural fit to pursue child welfare. After obtaining her MSW from Berkeley in 2011, she took a job in child welfare in a rural California county. She has remained in the field, continuing to work in various rural communities in the state.

Freny Dessai, MSW, was an eligibility worker for welfare and Medicaid benefits before she came to UC Berkeley. Following graduation in 2008, she took a position as a child welfare worker in a local county and was later selected as a US Congressional Fellow, working for the Senate Finance Committee. She currently works in the field of child development in Europe.

Trudi Frazel, MSW, knew long ago that she wanted to help families in the child welfare system. She received her MSW degree in 2008 and thereafter worked in various counties in several positions, including as a child welfare supervisor. She now serves as a trainer for new social workers and provides consultation regarding program development in emerging areas in the field.

Leslie Laughlin, MSW, ACSW, worked for 10 years in the Emergency Response unit investigating child maltreatment and assessing families' needs following her 2002 MSW degree from Berkeley. She left public child welfare to work in a private nonprofit child welfare agency for a few years, and recently joined the first ever mental health crisis center in a rural Northern California county, providing rapid access to professional help for people who are overwhelmed by emotional distress and trauma.

Sasha McGowan, MSW, worked in group homes for 3 years before she came to UC Berkeley. She graduated in 2014 and currently serves as a social worker in a Bay Area county. In addition to her work in child welfare, she also provides foster parent support to a youth from a county elsewhere in the Bay Area.

Monica Montury, MSW, LCSW, worked in a high-level group home before graduate studies. She received her MSW in 2010 and was hired as a public child welfare worker in a central California county thereafter. Today, she serves as a supervisor in the same county where she began her career.

Veronica Perez, MSW, graduated from UC Berkeley's School of Social Welfare in 2007. Since then, she has worked with child welfare agencies in the San Francisco Bay Area and Southern California. Ms. Perez' childhood experiences inspired her to dedicate herself to promoting the well-being of children and she continues to enjoy immense satisfaction from her career as a child welfare worker.

Hanna Rashkovsky, MSW, PPSC, was a middle school teacher in the Washington, DC, area when she realized she wanted to help those at-risk youth from within their homes. She received her MSW in 2011 from UC Berkeley and worked in public child welfare in a rural Northern California county. In 2016, she started working for Seneca Family of Agencies as an Assistant Director in the Seneca Institute for Advanced Practice.

Socorro Reynoso, MSW, LCSW, spent time in the care of her grandparents during adolescence due to child welfare issues and knew she wanted to help youth get through the system successfully. She graduated with her MSW degree in 2010 and moved to Southern California. She recently left public child welfare to serve as an administrator of a group home for adolescent females.

Martha Angelica Rodriguez, MSW, grew up in low socioeconomic communities around other immigrant families, where many were unfamiliar with US laws and how they apply to families. These communities had some community resources, but very few knew how to access them. After graduating from UC Berkeley in 2010, she took a job in a bilingual unit of a local child welfare agency. She now serves as a pediatric medical social worker.

Wendy Wiegmann, MSW, PhD, experienced foster care as a child and came to the field to make a positive difference in this complex system. She graduated with her MSW from UC Berkeley in 2007 and worked for two counties before returning to Berkeley for her PhD. She currently serves as the Project Director for the California Child Welfare Indicators Project at UC Berkeley.

Index